IMAGES
of Rail

SUMPTER VALLEY RAILWAY

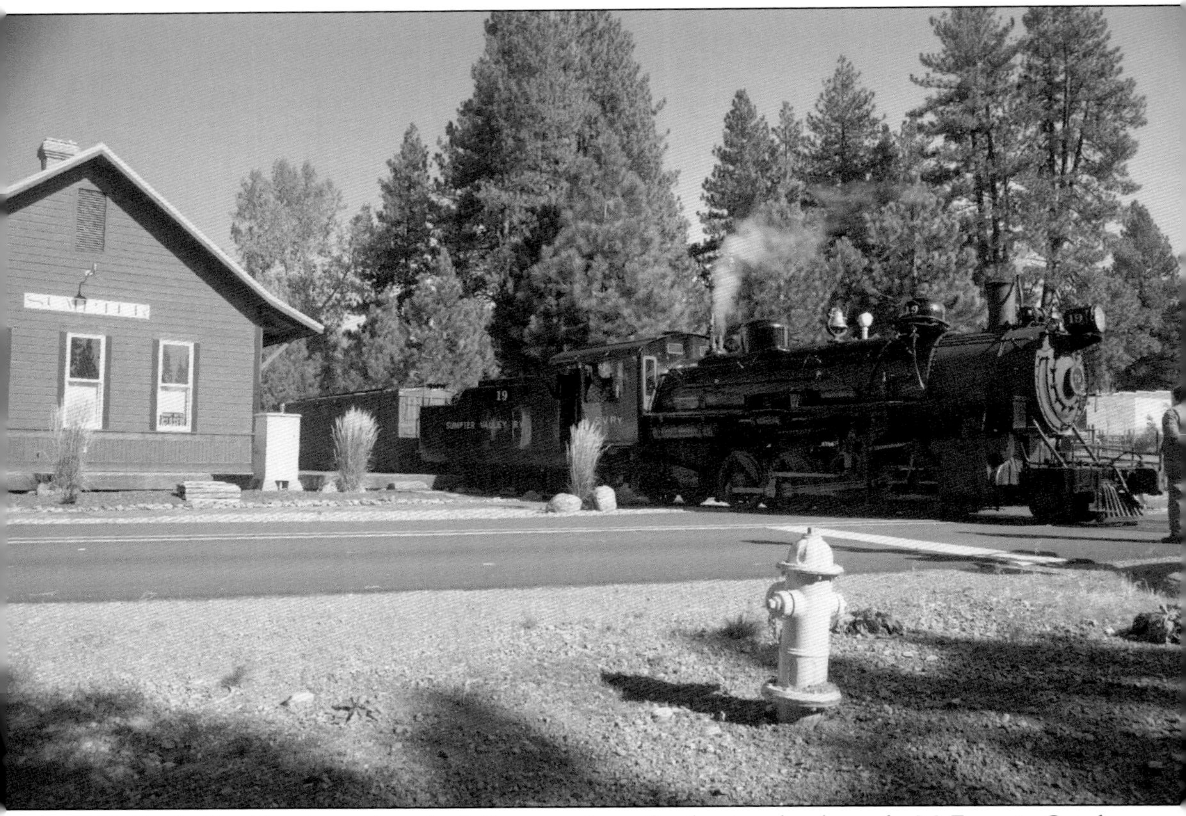

Mikado No. 19 waits at the rebuilt Sumpter depot for the signal to leave for McEwen in October 2008. (Mike Greenwood Collection.)

ON THE COVER: Former Utah and Northern Railway Mogul (2-6-0) No. 11 pauses with an Austin-bound passenger train at the newly completed Tipton depot around 1904. Standing from left to right are Jim Hunt (fireman) and F. M. Shurtliff (engineer). (H. R. Griffiths Collection; National Rail Historical Society, Pacific Northwest Chapter.)

IMAGES
of Rail

SUMPTER VALLEY RAILWAY

Alfred Mullett and Leonard Merritt

ARCADIA
PUBLISHING

ISBN 978-0-7385-7125-6

Published by Arcadia Publishing
Charleston, South Carolina

Printed in the United States of America

Library of Congress Control Number: 2008938760

For all general information contact Arcadia Publishing at:
Telephone 843-853-2070
Fax 843-853-0044
E-mail sales@arcadiapublishing.com
For customer service and orders:
Toll-Free 1-888-313-2665

Visit us on the Internet at www.arcadiapublishing.com

To Ron Harr for a lifetime of dedication in preserving the history of the Sumpter Valley Railway.

Contents

ACKNOWLEDGMENTS

Ron Harr has been instrumental in the creation of this book. He has spent the last 40 years gathering and organizing information on the Sumpter Valley Railway. Without his efforts, this book would still be an idea.

Special thanks go to my coauthor, Leonard Merritt, for untold hours of digging, finding photographs and history, and giving me the time to focus on the writing.

Thanks to Mallory Hope Farrell for writing *Rails, Sagebrush and Pine*. This book helped keep memories of this railroad alive.

Thanks to Ron Bacon for introducing Leonard to the railroad.

Special thanks go to the following people and organizations: Diana Pearson of the Baker County Library, Baker City, Oregon, for going well beyond the call of duty to help find photographs and opening up the library collections; Karen Clay and Shirley Roberts of the Eastern Oregon University Pierce Library Collection; Taylor Rush of Sumpter Valley Railroad Restoration, Inc., for allowing the use of their vast archives; Jayne Primrose at the Grant County Historical Museum; LaRue Pryse at the Prairie City DeWitt Museum; Glen Comstock of the Portland branch of the National Railway Historical Society; Coi Drummond-Gehrig at the Denver Public Library Western History/Genealogy Collection; and the Oregon Historical Society.

Of course, there were many individuals who generously opened their collections, including Ron Harr, Martin Hanson, Gary Tuford, Bret Bane, Matt Mattioda, Casey Carlson, Taylor Rush, J. E. Lewis, Mike Greenwood, and any others we may have missed in the list—many thanks to you.

Thanks to the friends who helped edit and review the book: Beth, Mike, Cheryl, Casey, Ron, and Taylor.

Grateful appreciation goes to Barb and Jay Phillips of the Sumpter Bed and Breakfast.

Many thanks go to our editor at Arcadia Publishing, Sarah Higginbotham, for being a source of encouragement and constructive correction.

Last but not least, thanks to our families and friends who have had to put up with us going Sumpter Valley crazy for the last seven months and just nodded with understanding.

The authors have made every effort to identify the primary source for all photographs used in the book. If that was not available, the secondary source is listed.

—Alfred Mullett
Portland, Oregon
December 2008

Introduction

Northeast Oregon is traditionally thought of as being largely flat with rolling hills. In reality, it is a mix of dry semi-arid plains, punctuated by the folds and twists of layer upon layer of mountain ranges. These ranges carry names such as the Blue Mountains, Wallowas, Elkhorns, Strawberrys, Malheurs, and the Little Alps. To the first settlers coming west to Oregon, the tree-covered mountain ranges that served as gate keepers were little more than obstacles to them arriving at the fertile John Day Basin and, farther west, the Willamette Valley.

In the early 1860s, David Eccles's family and some of their fellow Mormons traveled the Oregon Trail and spent a short time living in the Willamette Valley. While crossing the Wallowas, Eccles saw range after range covered thickly with pine and fir trees.

A few years later, the Eccles family returned to Salt Lake City, Utah. Starting with nothing but ambition, Eccles built an empire based on timber, rails, and banking. During this time, he became a large shareholder in the then struggling Union Pacific Railway (UPRy).

In 1889, David Eccles, his brother, W. H. Eccles, Charles Nibley, Joseph West, and F. M. Shurtliff incorporated the Oregon Lumber Company (OLC) in Baker, Oregon. They soon began building a sawmill and planing mill in South Baker.

The next order of business was to get the logs to the mills. David Eccles first secured a contract with the Oregon Railway and Navigation Company (OR&N) to be a primary provider of railroad ties. Next he bent the ear of the UPRy management, which was rapidly closing down or converting to standard gauge all of its narrow-gauge holdings, to get first pick on their equipment sales.

In August 1890, a Union Pacific train dropped off carloads of rail, tie-plates, spikes, and other accoutrements of a railroad. Soon South Baker had a dual-gauge yard and narrow-gauge tracks wending along the banks of the Powder River. A narrow-gauge 4-4-0 (American) locomotive, labeled 285, was also dropped off, and the slow march into the Elkhorn Mountains began.

The winter of 1890 was especially harsh, so line building was delayed, but by October 1891, the railroad had reached McEwen (milepost 22.379). The former sleepy stage stop blossomed into a town complete with mercantile enterprises, taverns, a fraternity hall, a church, and a Chinatown.

John Stoddard, a close friend and father-in-law of David Eccles, formed the Stoddard Lumber Company (SLC) and began building a mill of his own next to the OLC site in South Baker. At McEwen, the SLC went north and south from the Sumpter Valley Railway (SVRy) mainline and began lacing the hills with steel. Not long after, the Baker White Pine Lumber Company (BWP) was organized and also built a mill in South Baker, and its lines ran south from Curry.

At this time, both the OLC and SLC shipped full logs to their South Baker mills. Later the OLC would adopt the practice of rough cutting the lumber at the mills located near the logging areas, then shipping the rough-cut timber to South Baker for finishing. Railroad ties provided the core income for the sawmills. These were used to build the SVRy, UPRy, and OR&N.

Though the mining camp of Sumpter was only 8 miles away, the railroad took four years to get there. It has been said that there was some sort of gentleman's agreement between David Eccles and Thomas McEwen, a very successful stage and freight hauler, which postponed the arrival of the rails until 1896. The other factor in the slow growth of the railway was Eccles's vision of the line being primarily a logging railroad that paid its own way, and thus he tended to follow the timber grants.

The hard rock gold rush at Sumpter finally spurred the SVRy on. Eccles saw a ready customer for goods and services. At Sawmill Gulch, just outside Sumpter (milepost 29.750), the SVRy put in a wye (a three-way turning point that resembles a "Y"). This has been referred to as S-Wye since that time. After some issues with the U.S. Forest Service, who owned the land between S-Wye and Sumpter, the first trains pulled into the booming city.

Joseph Barton, the first superintendent of the SVRy (in function, though not title) and a friend of David Eccles from Salt Lake City, stated the following when describing the first trains into Sumpter: "[The] contract was let to construct the roadbed, and the work of grading and track laying was pushed ahead. And on October 31-1896 the extension to Sumpter was formally opened for traffic. An excursion was run from Baker. Flat cars, boxcars, any and every kind of car was in demand to carry the passenger from and back to Baker." Barton continues, "I really do not know how many passengers were handled on that day, but it seemed that almost the entire population of Baker were in Sumpter."

In short order, there were multiple passenger, freight, and logging trains running daily over the 28 miles between South Baker and Sumpter.

The railroad then pushed up Huckleberry Mountain to Larch Summit (elevation 5,094 feet). Old roadbed suggests that several different approaches to the pass were tried before the one that served the railroad the duration of its life was completed. At Larch Summit (milepost 34.580), a turning wye and station shed were built, allowing for the popular tourist trains to view the surrounding mountains from the summit.

Five miles to the west of Larch Summit, the railroad crossed Alder Springs (milepost 36.640). A long, 60-foot-high trestle spanned the gulch and became a favorite photographic backdrop.

From Alder Springs, the railway followed the North Fork of the Burnt River until it reached Whitney (milepost 43.076). In 1901, the town of Whitney was incorporated. It served as a logging community without a sawmill until 1911, when Charles Nibley built a mill that later burned and was replaced by a mill owned by the OLC. The shell of the later mill still exists, with some of the town and a few railroad buildings remaining.

In 1904, the railway crossed Tipton Summit (elevation 5,097 feet), and a siding and station were erected. A town was never established, since the primary reason for Tipton's existence was to water and fuel locomotives and act as a station for goods and services for the stage link to nearby Greenhorn City.

At White Pine (milepost 54.625), the BWP went east and south toward Curry following the timber grants. These all fed into a mill near White Pine. Though not part of the OLC, the BWP was financed by John Stoddard and used the SVRy to carry its finished product to South Baker for shipment.

The railroad dropped into Austin using a large "S" curve that crossed the valley to what was to become the town site. The famous Austin House and stage stop served as an anchor for the new town that was to become the western division point of the railroad.

An engine house and other facilities were built, as well as a short-lived sawmill. The sawmill was later moved up the mountain to Batesville. Like most of the towns that were railroad related, Austin has become little more than a pile of semi-ruined buildings.

At Batesville, later known as Bates, the OLC drove westward toward Susanville and spawned untold miles of logging feeders in every direction along its path.

Prairie City and Susanville were soon in a bidding war regarding who would get the next leg of the SVRy. By all rights, the line should have followed the easier route toward Susanville. The grades are generally gentle and downhill, and there are rich timber resources all along the route. For reasons still unknown, Eccles decided to go up Bridge Creek and over Dixie Summit (elevation 5,277 feet), then switchback down the hill into the John Day Basin and Prairie City (milepost 80.001).

On July 4, 1910, with much fanfare and celebration, the SVRy's first passenger train arrived in Prairie City. The connection through the SVRy gave Prairie City and the other farming communities of the John Day Basin a much-needed outlet for their farming resources. It also brought an influx of goods from the outside world that previously had been either difficult or impossible to get.

David Eccles Sr. died in 1912, leaving the rail and timber ventures to his son David Jr. Joseph Barton left behind notes in his diary about what Eccles Sr. was planning had time not caught up with him. There are surveys on the books done by Barton that track the SVRy mainline from Prairie City westward to John Day. It then turned south through Canyon City and then to Lakeview. If this had been completed, the SVRy could have been a shortcut across southeast Oregon to California.

Eccles Sr.'s brother, W. H. Eccles, was about to announce those plans when Eccles Jr. removed W. H. from the board of directors and silenced all plans for expansion. Soon after, W. H. moved his mill and railroad to Idaho, and through a succession of owners, it is still operating today.

On an August evening in 1917, a blow to the growth of the SVRy came when Sumpter's business district burned completely to the ground. Unfortunately, the mining industry had played out at the time and most residents opted to move elsewhere rather than rebuild.

For the next decade, the railroad continued to grow its logging operations and serve the communities that depended on it for supplies. However, the automobile began making an impact on passenger service as roads were slowly improved. By the early 1930s, the passenger service was covered either by railcar or a single combination mail/baggage/passenger car.

In 1933, the line was abandoned from Bates to Prairie City. Within a year, the Great Depression had also caused the BWP to go bankrupt, and it was taken over by Stoddard.

As World War II began, the SVRy had become little more than a lumber conveyor between the sawmill at Bates and the planing mill at South Baker. By 1947, the Eccles family made the decision to shut down the rail operations and use trucks to haul the lumber between Bates and South Baker, leaving only mill switching operations in South Baker until the mill was closed in 1961.

As with other railroads that shut down, much of the roadbed that had served the railroad went on to become the base for the burgeoning highway system. The current Elkhorn Scenic Highway that runs from Baker City to the Bridge Creek Valley owes its gentle grades and scenic views to the work of Joseph Barton. As one drives it, it isn't hard to imagine a pair of gutsy Mikados or a high-stepping, spit-and-polish Mogul leading the way through the mountains.

All was quiet along the Sumpter Valley, with many of the old structures still standing through the early 1970s. At that time, the U.S. Forest Service decided to burn or dismantle most of the remaining structures for liability reasons.

Ironically, as the last of the accessible structures were disappearing, a history-minded local named Nils Christensen was raising support for the reconstruction of the historic railway.

In 1971, the SVRy was reborn. With the support of many of the local people and several of the Eccles family members, the Sumpter Valley Railroad Restoration, Inc. (SVRR) was formed. Once again, the Union Pacific stepped in to help and donated the rail and hardware to start laying track.

Year after year, starting from McEwen and heading across the dredge tailings of what was once Pleasant Valley, the line has grown until it now runs approximately 6 miles on the original roadbed. It has two depots, one in McEwen, the other in Sumpter, and there are plans to continue growing as funds and volunteers allow.

What of all the locomotives and cars? The young SVRR has found and brought back home four of the original locomotives that served the original railroad.

No. 3, the W. H. Eccles Heisler, was located in 1971 in a mill shed in Idaho still with W. H. Eccles lettering. After an overhaul, she became the workhorse for the railroad's next 20 seasons. She is now in semi-retirement, though operational. She currently awaits routine maintenance to her driveline.

Mikados Nos. 19 and 20 were found on a scrap line in Skagway, Alaska, and were purchased for $1 from the White Pass and Yukon Railway (WP&Y). After a sea voyage to Portland, Oregon, and a barge and rail trip to McEwen, Oregon, they were cosmetically preserved. In 1992, the funds were raised and No. 19 was sent back to Portland, Oregon, with her recently recovered tender from Guatemala; four years later, she emerged fully restored. She has since become the star of the show.

No. 20 still resides behind the engine house, and as soon as funds are available, it is planned that she will be restored to what she looked like the day she arrived on the SVRy in 1920.

No. 100, the gas mechanical switcher, was restored in the Sumpter Valley shops and now serves the line doing maintenance and moving cars.

Other known remaining SVRy locomotives are Shay No. 7, which currently resides in a railroad museum in Indiana, and diesel switcher No. 101, now under restoration by the Colorado Railroad Museum in Golden, Colorado.

Many cars have been recovered. The best-known car is No. 20, one of the original Utah and Northern passenger cars acquired in 1890. She was restored, but as with any centenarian, she is showing her age and is in need of further work to ensure her long-term future.

Four of the original six Turtleback passenger cars are still in Skagway, Alaska, working daily as passenger stock on the WP&Y.

Historically, SVRy can hold the ranking of being one of the prime narrow-gauge railroads of the West.

To the day the SVRy rail was removed, it never once failed to turn a profit and, with that, never was subjected to either bankruptcy or receivership.

If one counts all the related properties together—the SVRy, OLC, SLC, BWP, and others—the SVRy total track mileage far exceeds any other narrow-gauge logging line in the United States.

Perhaps the most distinctive trait is that they were the longest running common carrier line to use wood-burning locomotives in the United States. The mainline power used wood until the arrival of the Uintah Mallets in 1941. The logging lines were using wood as late as 1946, when the rails were pulled up.

From the rail fan's perspective, another trait that puts them at the top is variety. They had the greatest mix of motive power of any narrow-gauge railroad, except perhaps the Uintah Railway. They ran everything from Brooks Moguls (2-6-0s) and Americans (4-4-0s) to lanky 10-wheelers (4-6-0s). There were the brutish Baldwin and elegant American Locomotive Company (ALCO) Mikados (2-8-2s). At the top of the list were the giant Uintah Mallets (2-6-6-2s), plus the gas/mechanical switchers. They also ran all three varieties of geared locomotives: Shays, Climaxes, and Heislers.

This book covers the Sumpter Valley mainline from its inception in 1890 through the resurrection in 1971 and current restoration. The authors hope you will enjoy reading the captions and looking at the pictures as much as we did researching, organizing, and creating this book.

So please, sit back and enjoy the book, whether through pictures, words, or both. Next time you are near Baker City on a summer or holiday weekend, turn off I-84, follow the Elkhorn Highway 20 miles to McEwen, turn left at the Sumpter Valley Railroad, and take an afternoon to get to know some of the locomotives, cars, and history you will see in this book.

One

Baker City to McEwen (1889–1897)

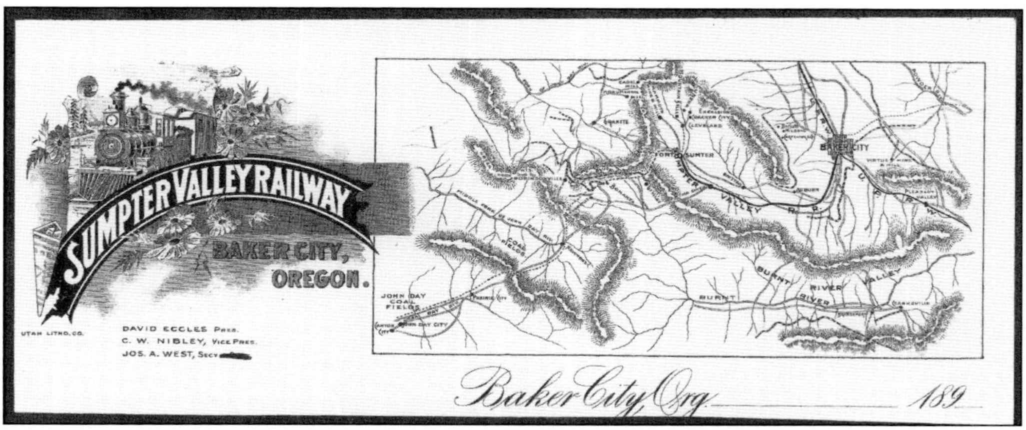

Above is the first letterhead used by the Sumpter Valley Railway. Look closely at the map and see that Sumpter is still labelled as Fort Sumter, and the route is quite different than the actual route followed by the railroad. (Emlaw Collection; National Railway Historical Society, Pacific Northwest Chapter.)

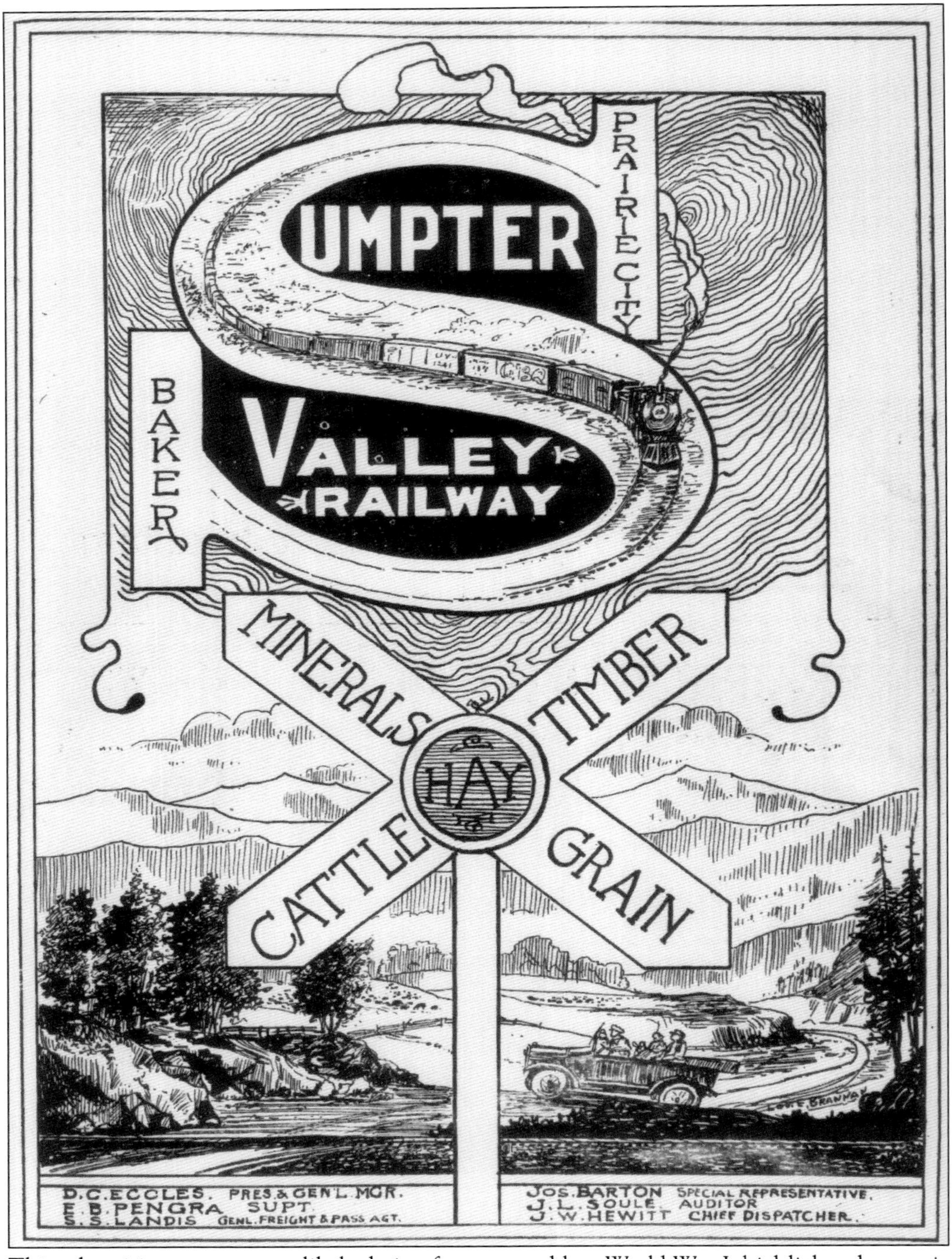

This advertising poster, most likely dating from around late World War I, highlights the scenic marvels, products, and terminals of the railroad. (Ron Harr Collection; Sumpter Valley Railroad Restoration, Inc.)

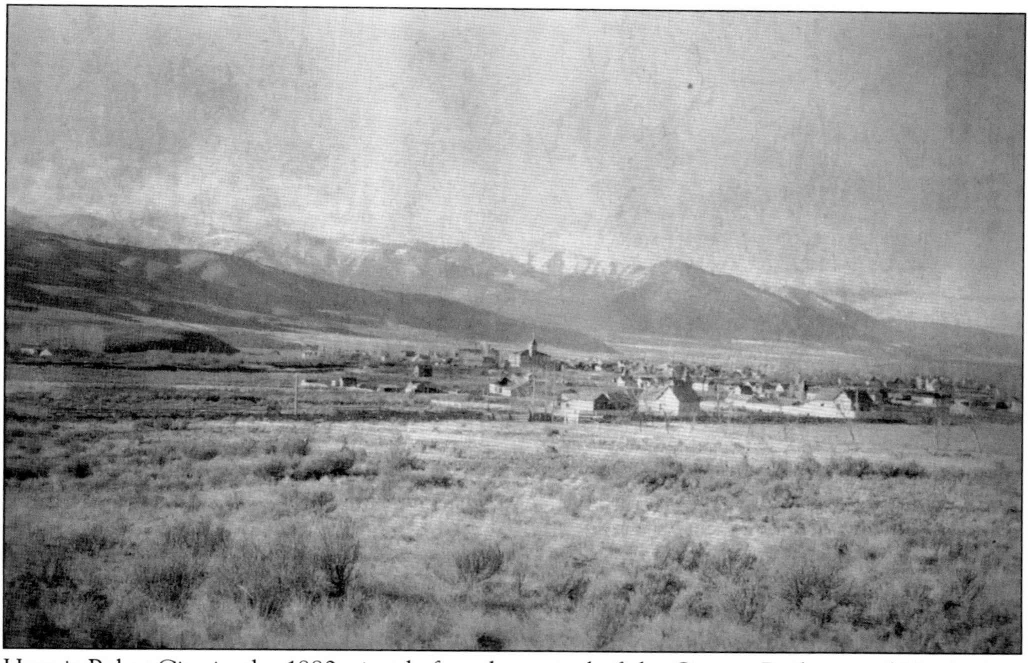

Here is Baker City in the 1880s, just before the arrival of the Oregon Railway and Navigation Company, looking from South Baker toward the Elkhorns and Little Alps. (McCord Collection; Baker County Library, Baker City, Oregon, Image No. B19.)

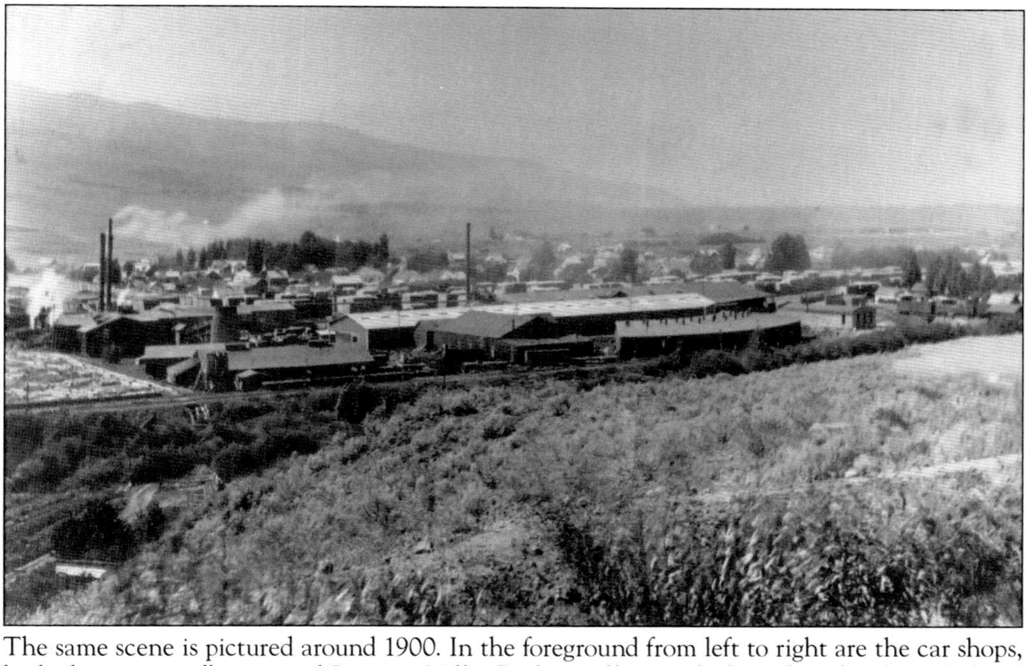

The same scene is pictured around 1900. In the foreground from left to right are the car shops, boiler house, roundhouse, and Sumpter Valley Railway offices with the rail yard in front. Behind are the Oregon Lumber Company mill and South Baker. (McCord Collection; Baker County Library, Baker City, Oregon, Image No. L-1.)

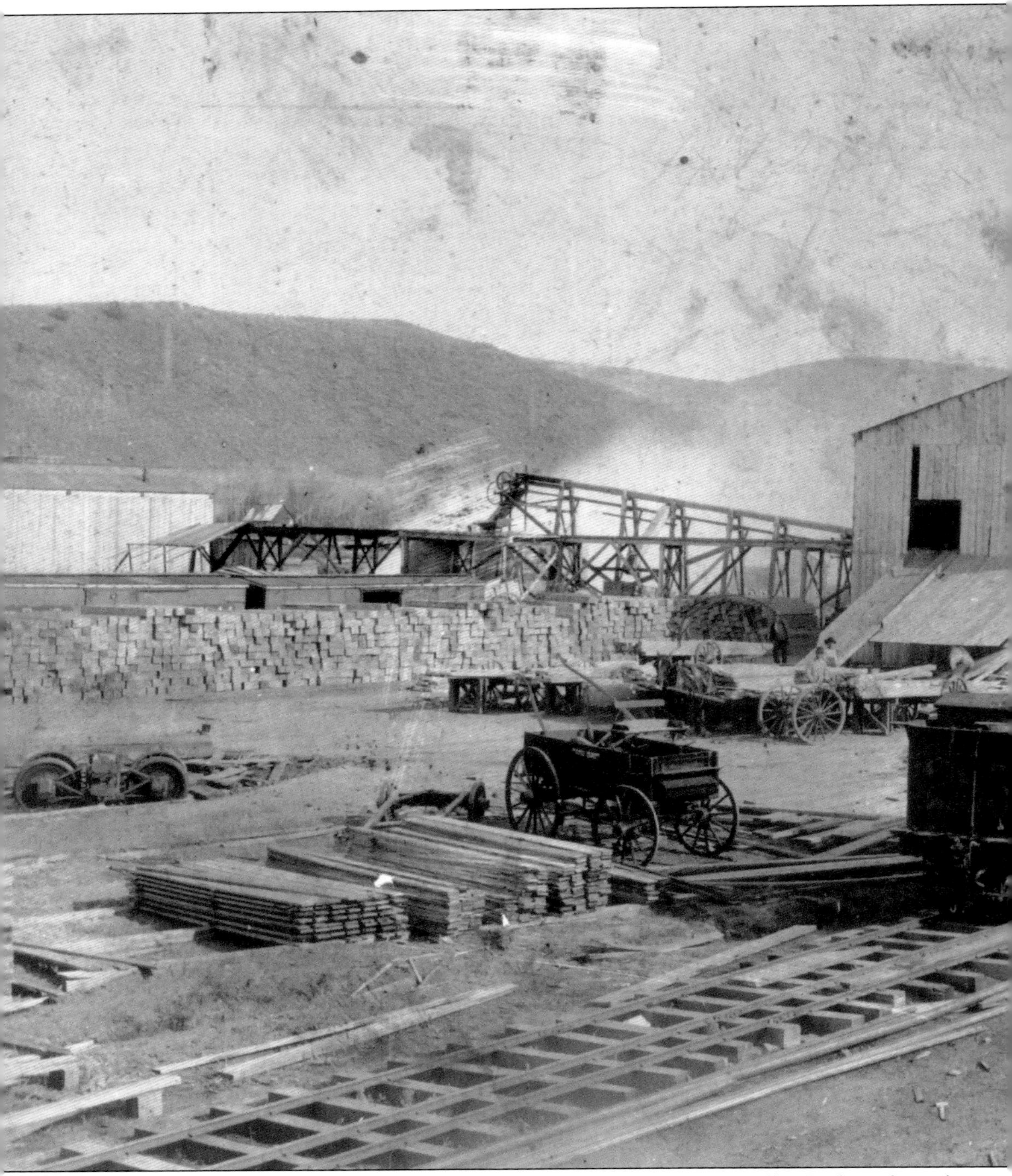

Locomotive No. 285 was the first engine purchased by the Sumpter Valley Railway from the Utah and Northern Railway. Later it became No. 15 in the 1906 general renumbering of all the locomotives. It was scrapped in the 1920s. This photograph was taken in the South Baker yard near the original Oregon Lumber Company mill in the early 1890s. In the cab is F. M. Shurtliff, who was both an engineer and a board member of the Sumpter Valley Railway. Note the dual-

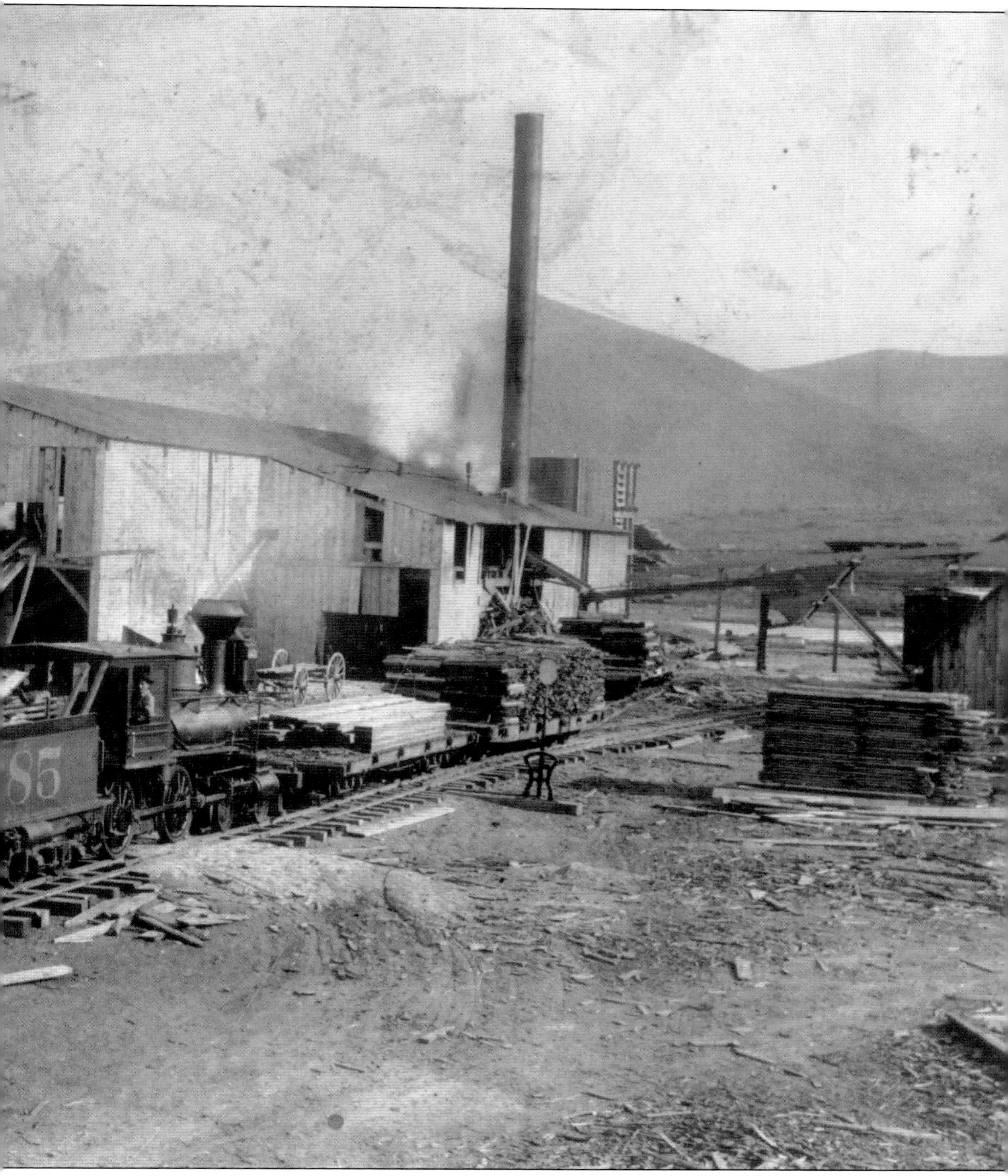

gauge track on the left with long tie spacing and standard-gauge ties. The Sumpter Valley Railway narrow gauge was 3 feet between the rails, and standard gauge is 4 feet, 8½ inches, which is the current national standard. Narrow gauge was used because of lower equipment and right-of-way costs. (F. M. Shurtliff Collection; Oregon Historical Society, OrHi72970.)

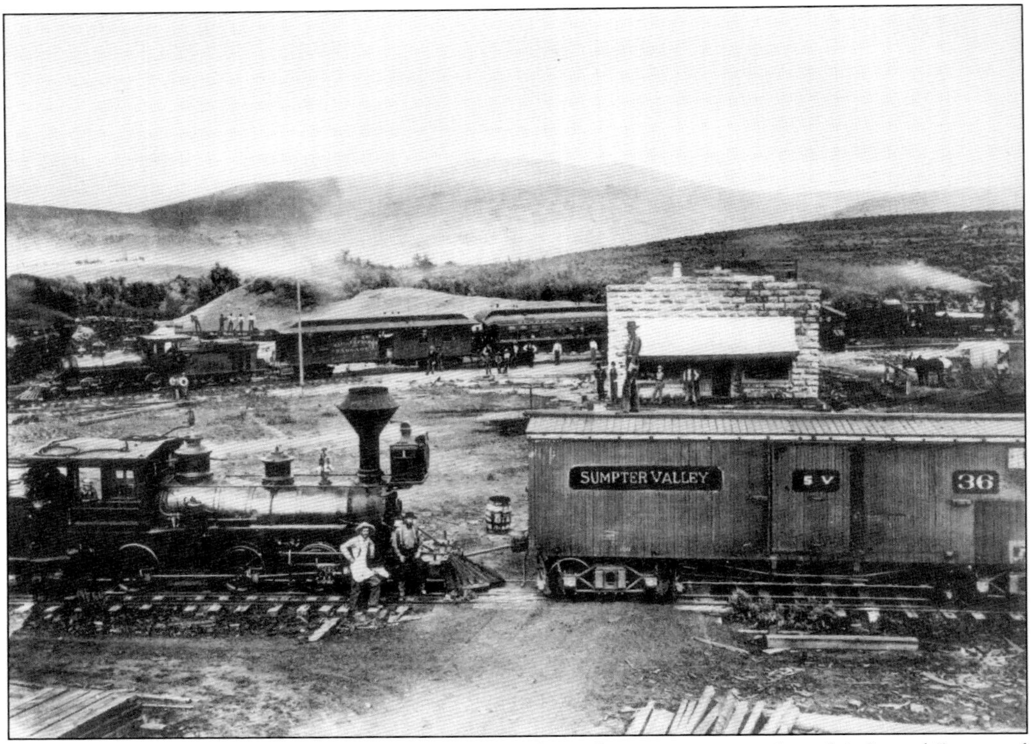

This classic publicity photograph from early 1897 shows locomotives numbered 1, 2, and 5 around the Sumpter Valley Railway's stone office building in South Baker. Note again the dual-gauge track. Also of note is the photographer's remarking of the lettering and numbering of the standard-gauge boxcar. (Photograph by L. J. Hicks; Baker County Library, Baker City, Oregon.)

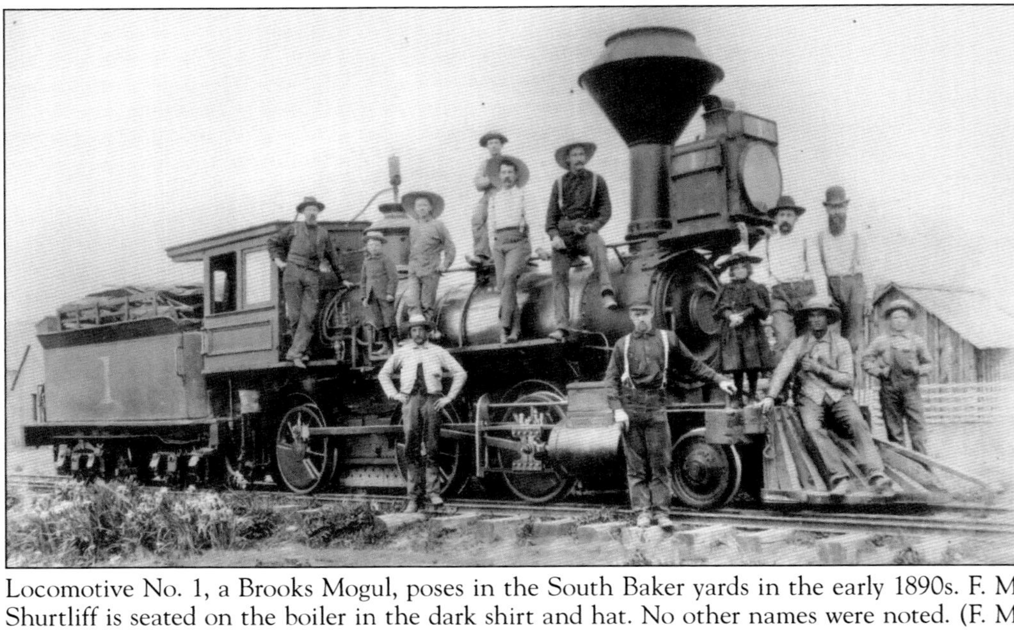

Locomotive No. 1, a Brooks Mogul, poses in the South Baker yards in the early 1890s. F. M. Shurtliff is seated on the boiler in the dark shirt and hat. No other names were noted. (F. M. Shurtliff Collection; Grant County Historical Museum, Canyon City, Oregon.)

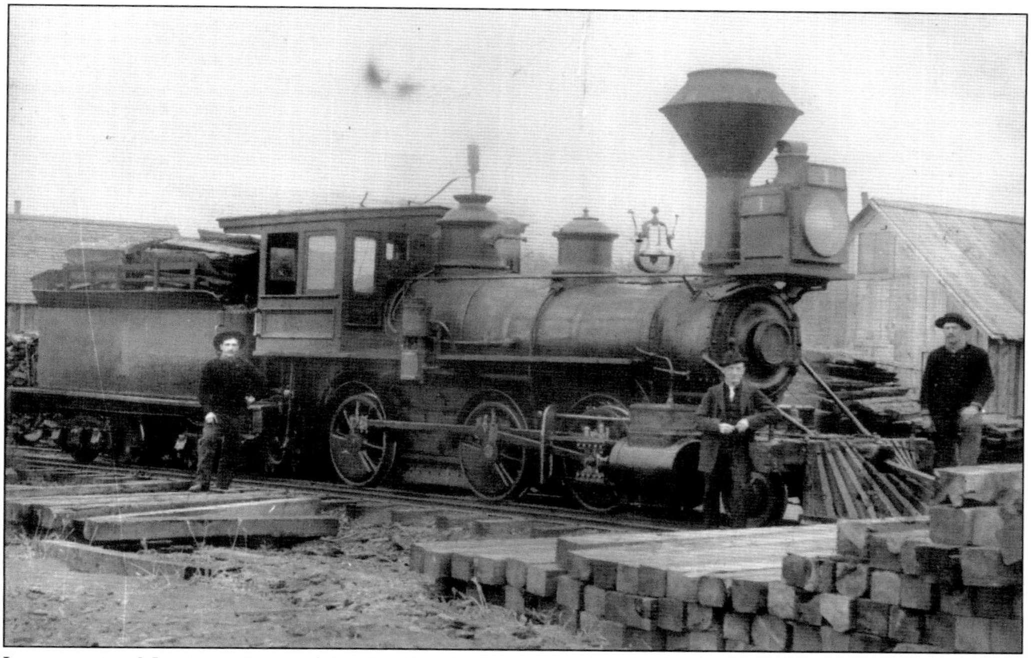

Locomotive No. 1 is pictured in the South Baker yard with F. M. Shurtliff (engineer) and Jim Hunt (fireman) standing behind a pile of railroad ties destined for the mainline to complete the route to McEwen. (F. M. Shurtliff Collection; Oregon Historical Society, Negative No. 52647.)

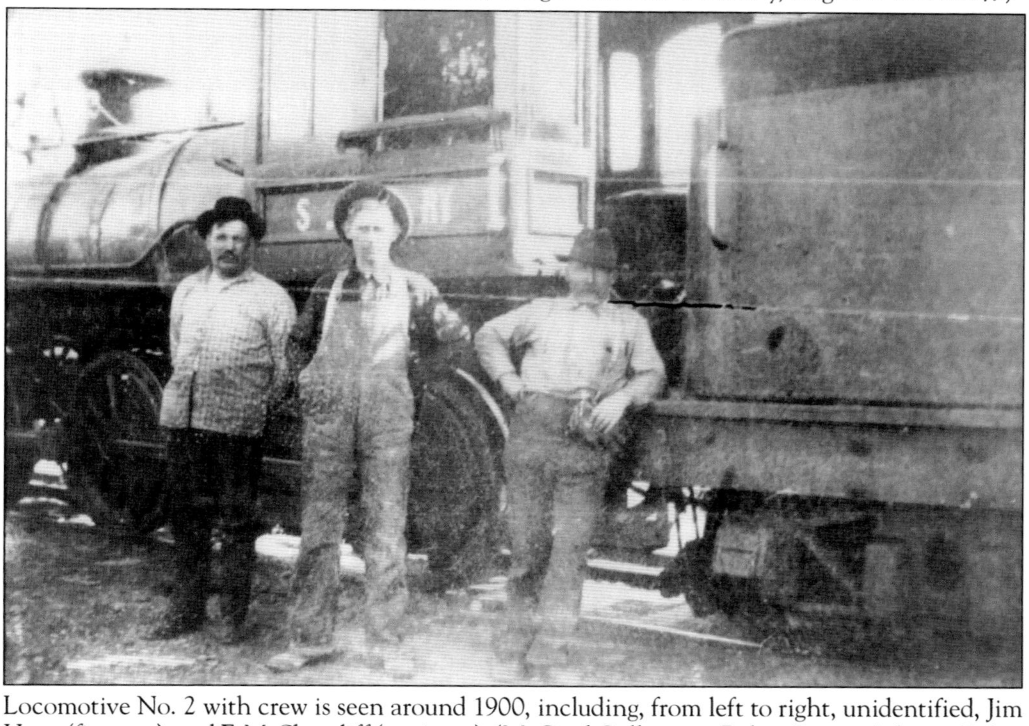

Locomotive No. 2 with crew is seen around 1900, including, from left to right, unidentified, Jim Hunt (fireman), and F. M. Shurtliff (engineer). (McCord Collection; Baker County Library, Baker City, Oregon, Image No. TR-7.)

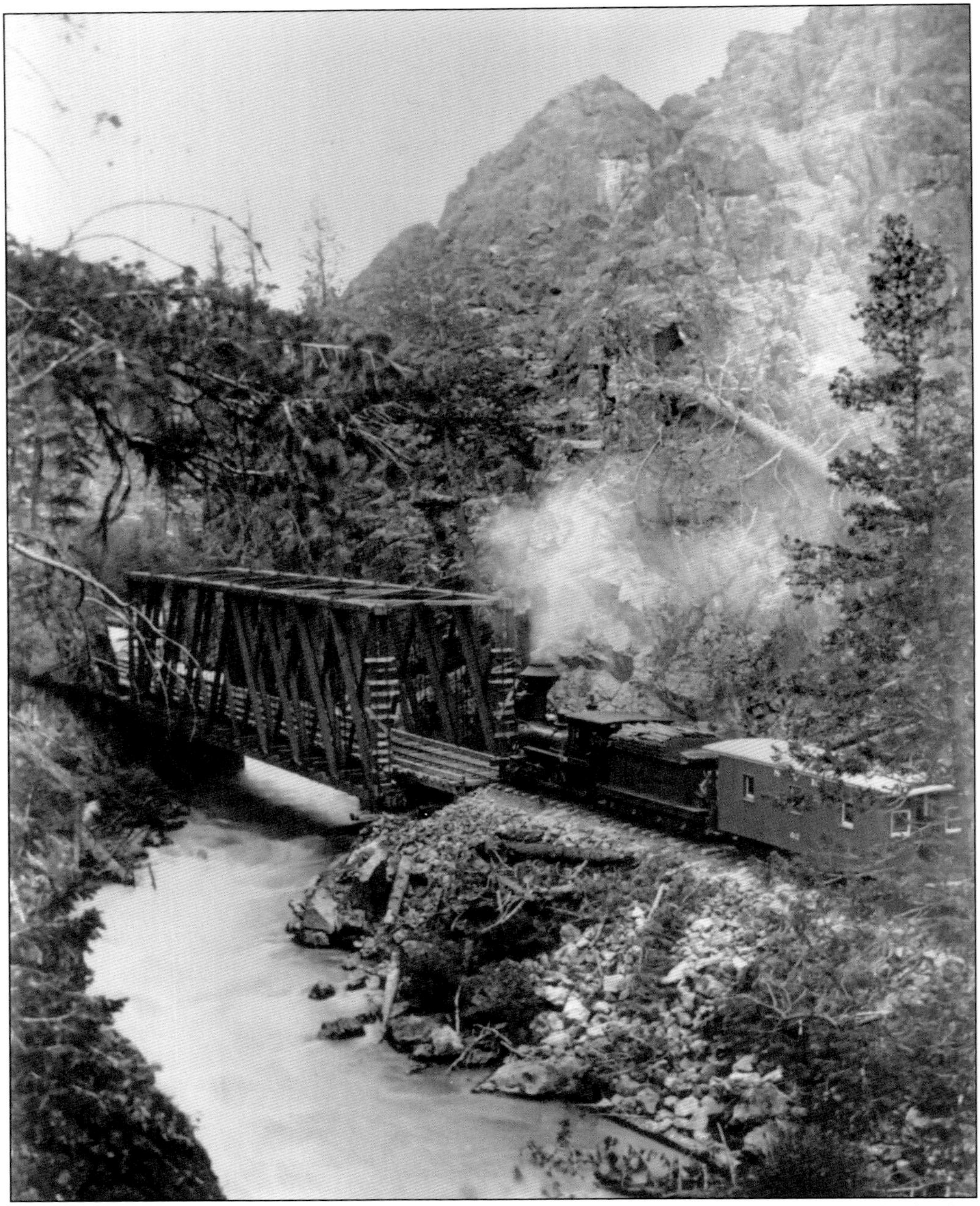

Locomotive No. 2 waits with caboose No. 02 at Devils Gate, later called Red Bridge. This bridge crossed the Powder River in Boulder Gorge. The train is en route from Baker to McEwen in the early 1890s. This location in Boulder Gorge was a popular photographic spot along the Sumpter Valley Railway. (Hazeltine Collection; Oregon Historical Society Negative No. 3832, and 21233.)

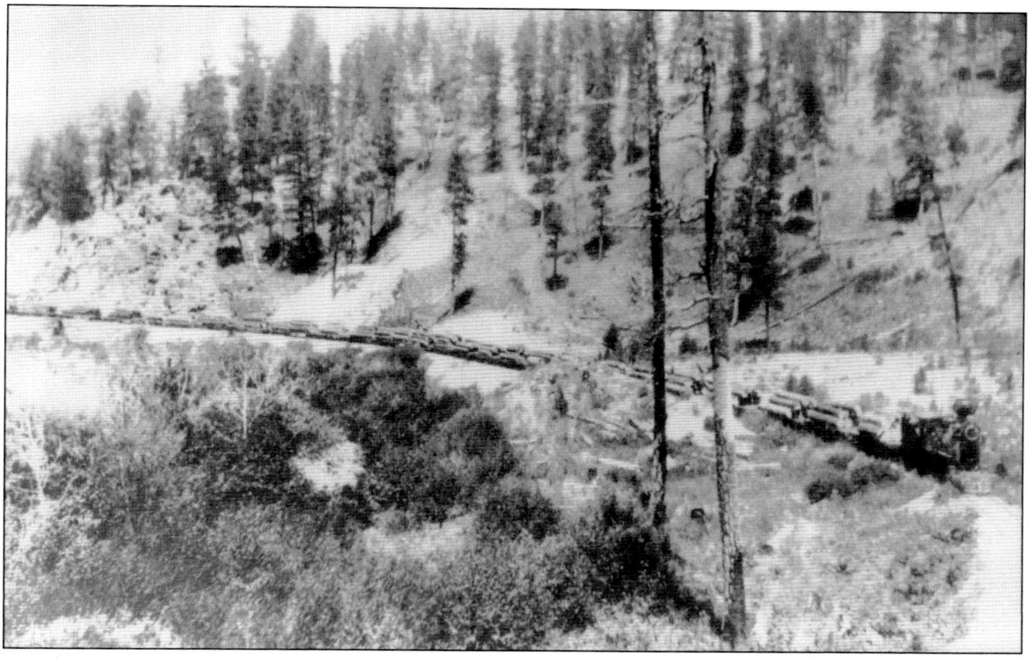

Brooks Mogul No. 2 with a log train bound for South Baker has paused below Boulder Gorge along the Powder River in 1897. This is now the route of the Elkhorn Scenic Highway. (Photograph by L. J. Hicks; Baker County Library, Baker City, Oregon, Image No. TR-15.)

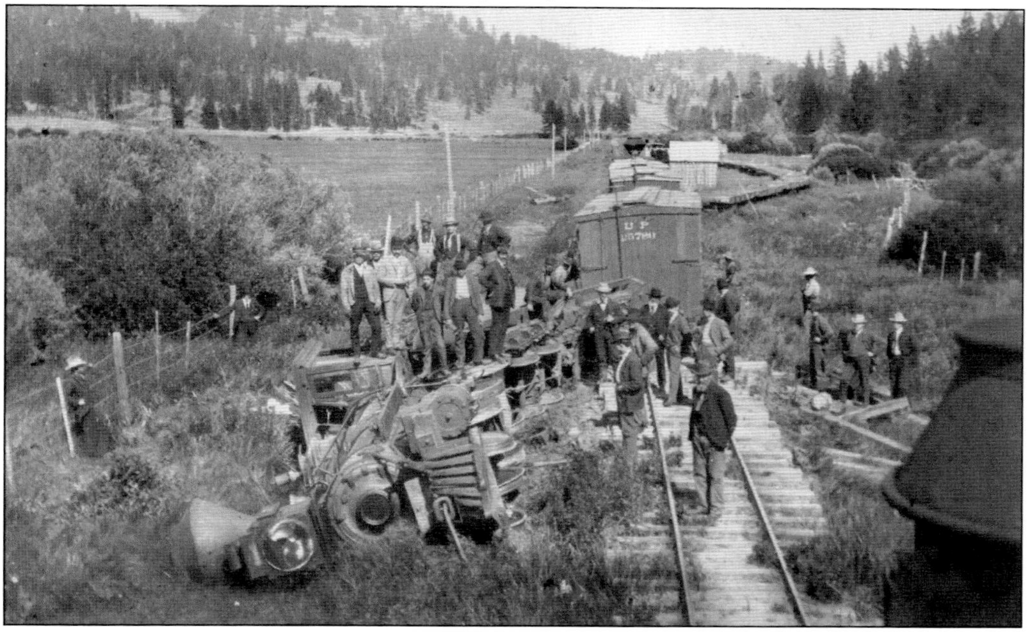

Shortly after 1900, an unidentified Brooks Mogul, possibly No. 5, lays on her side outside Bennett, between Salisbury and Lockhart, with several other locomotives standing by to help with her recovery. The Union Pacific flatcars in the background would have been from the first purchase of Utah and Northern rolling stock. (F. M. Shurtliff Collection; Sumpter Valley Railroad Restoration, Inc.)

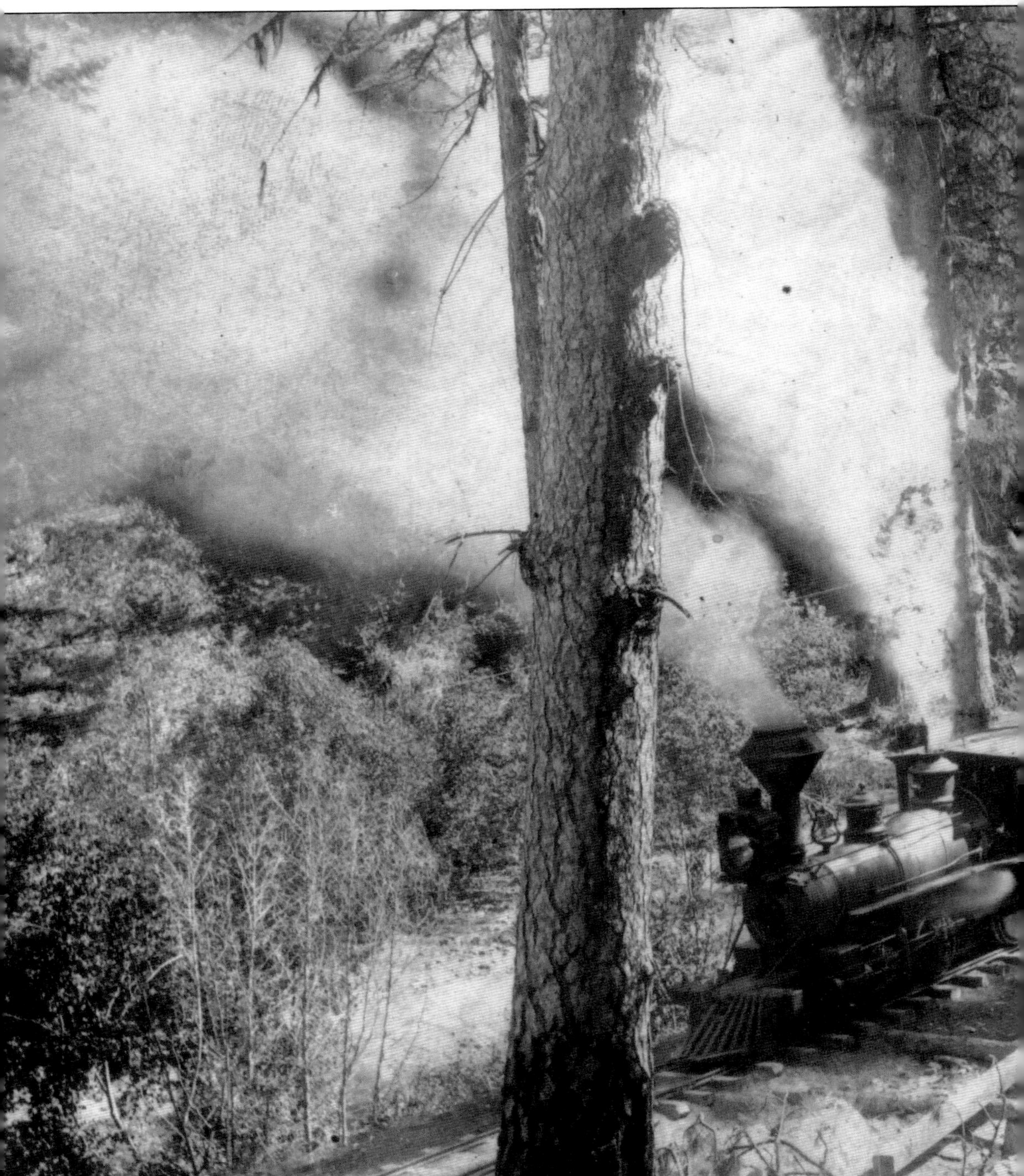

Brooks Mogul No. 5 in Boulder Gorge pulls a mixed train of passenger and flatcars around 1898. The first car behind the locomotive is a rare Brill narrow-gauge baggage car, noted by the round head windows and roof design. The crew appears to have taken a lunch break. This allowed them to gather a full head of steam for the uphill grade to McEwen. This is a good example of a

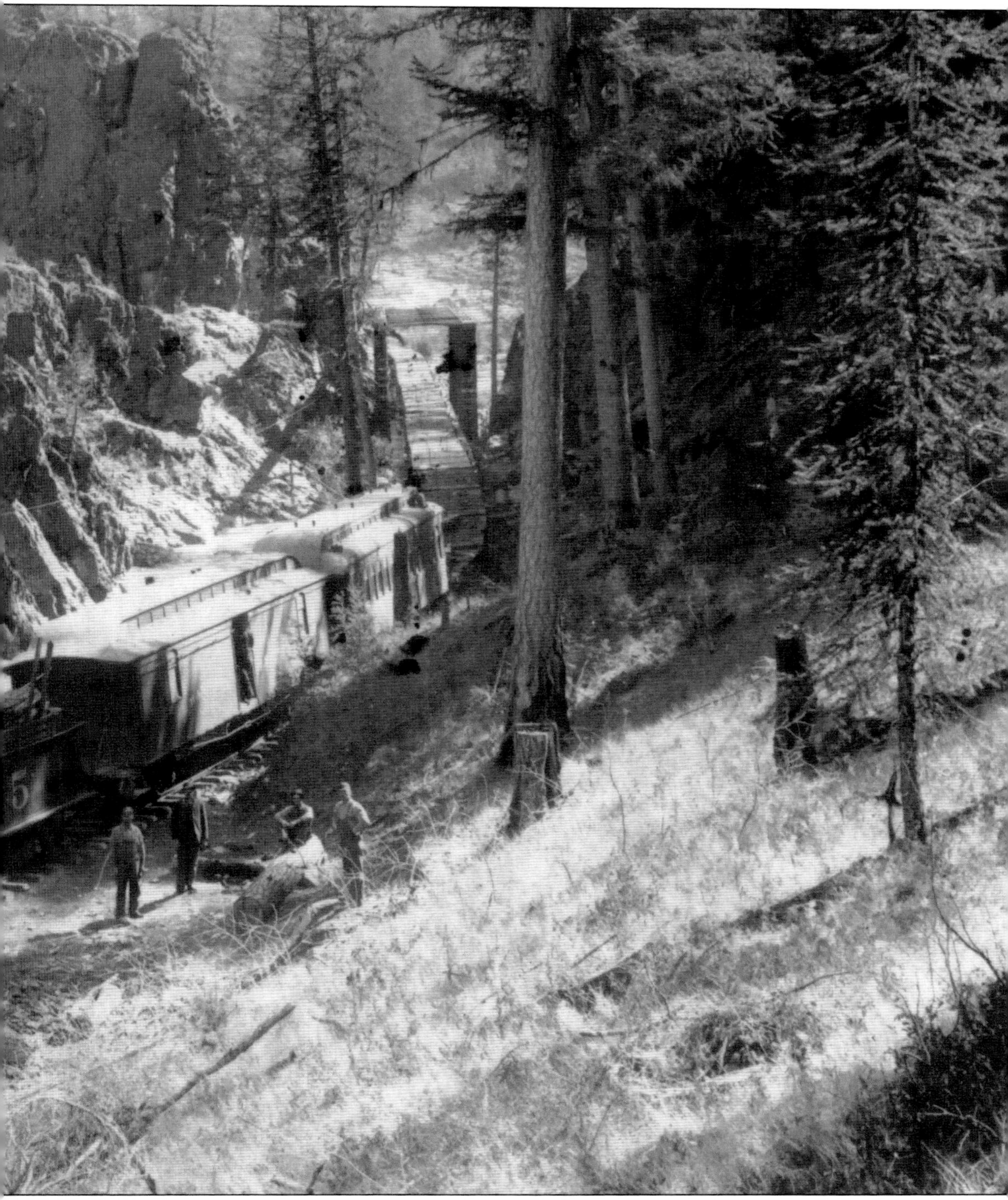

"squirrel tail" of steam. This was caused when the steam pressure exceeded the safety valve setting. (Possible C. R. Savage photograph; Oregon Historical Society, Negative No. 3833, Photograph No. 891-G[1].)

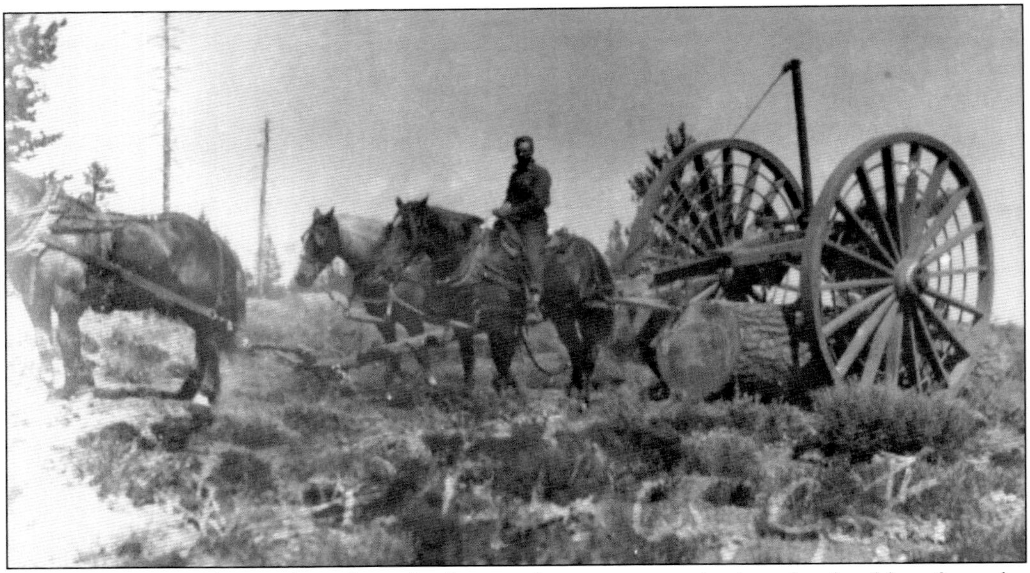

Four-horse log skidders with 10-foot wheels were the primary method used to haul logs from the woods to the trains until the 1920s, when tractors were introduced. (McCord Collection; Baker County Library, Baker City, Oregon, Image No. L-8.)

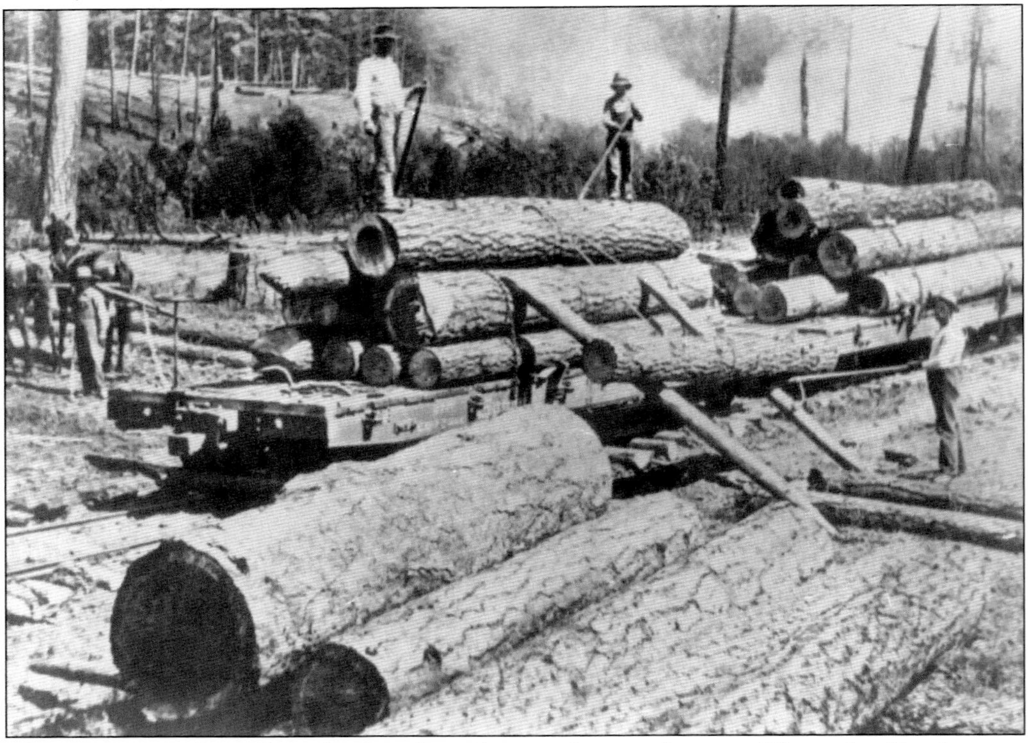

The next step to the mill was loading the railcars at the transfer point. This style of loading was called "haulback" loading. Horses were used to pull the logs onto the cars. This is one of the more dangerous jobs the loggers faced on a daily basis. (McCord Collection; Baker County Library, Baker City, Oregon, Image No. L-9.)

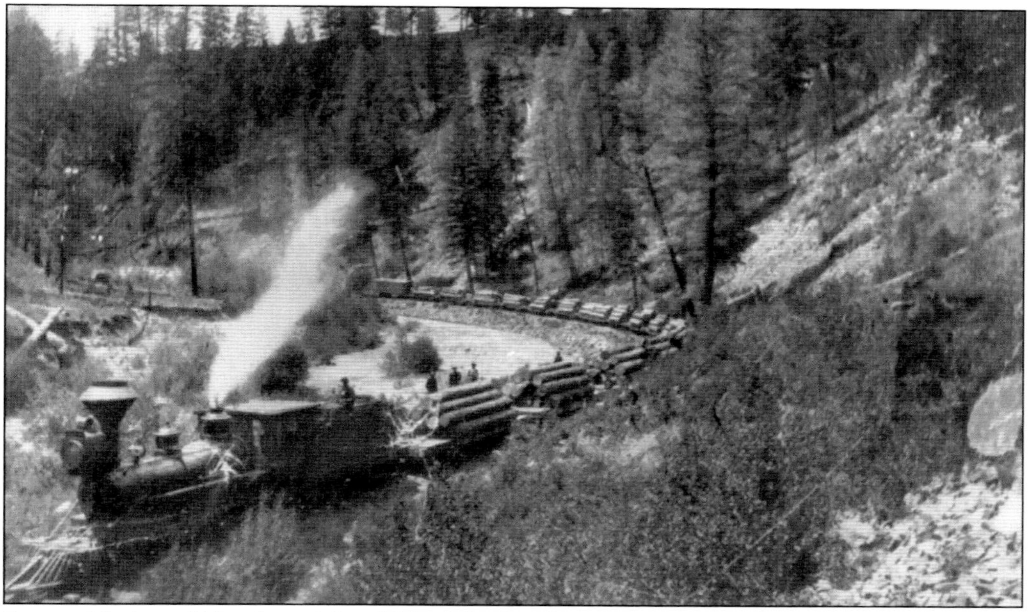

Former Utah and Northern Mogul No. 2 leads a log train to the mill at South Baker in this postcard image dating from 1897. Note the cupola-less waycar (caboose) at the rear of the train. (Photograph by L. J. Hicks, McCord Collection; Baker County Library, Baker City, Oregon, Image No. TR-3.)

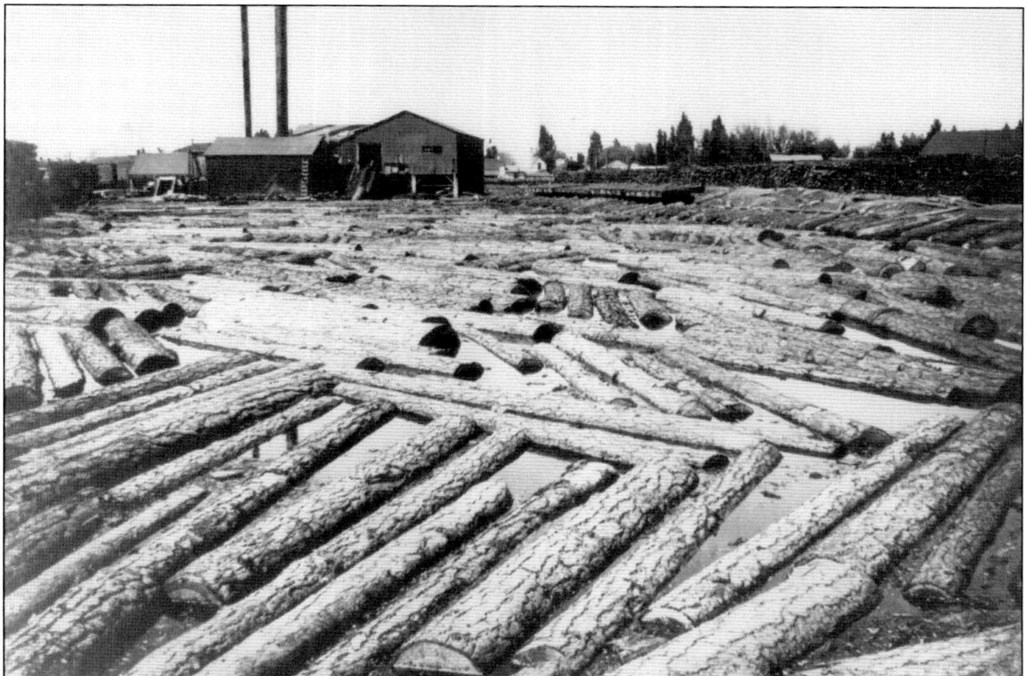

The Stoddard sawmill at South Baker was one of many mills along the Sumpter Valley Railway. (McCord Collection; Baker County Library, Baker City, Oregon, Image No. L-30.)

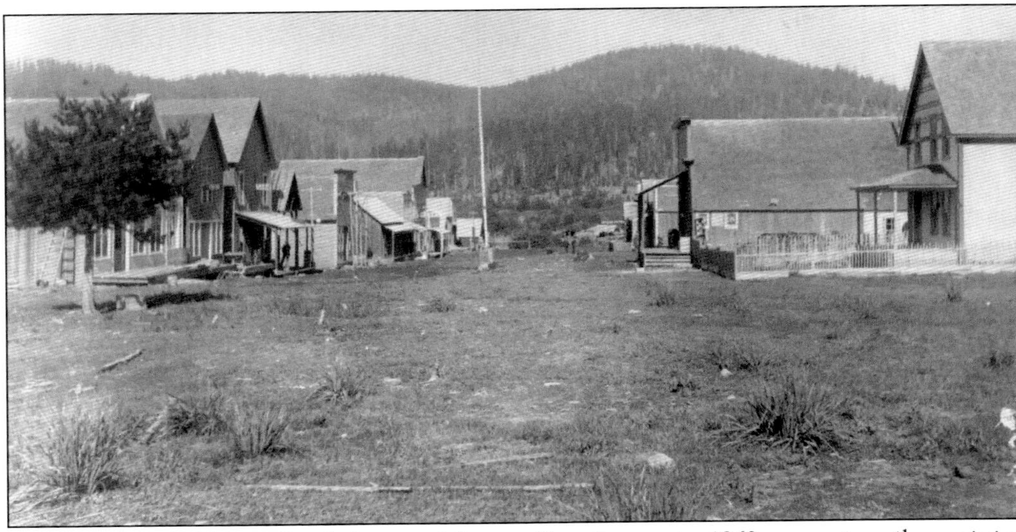

Sumpter, founded by ex-Confederate soldiers as Fort Sumter in 1862, was primarily a mining camp with limited placer claims. This photograph, taken in 1895 just before the Sumpter Valley Railway arrived, looks down Granite Street. (McCord Collection; Baker County Library, Baker City, Oregon, Image No. T-44.)

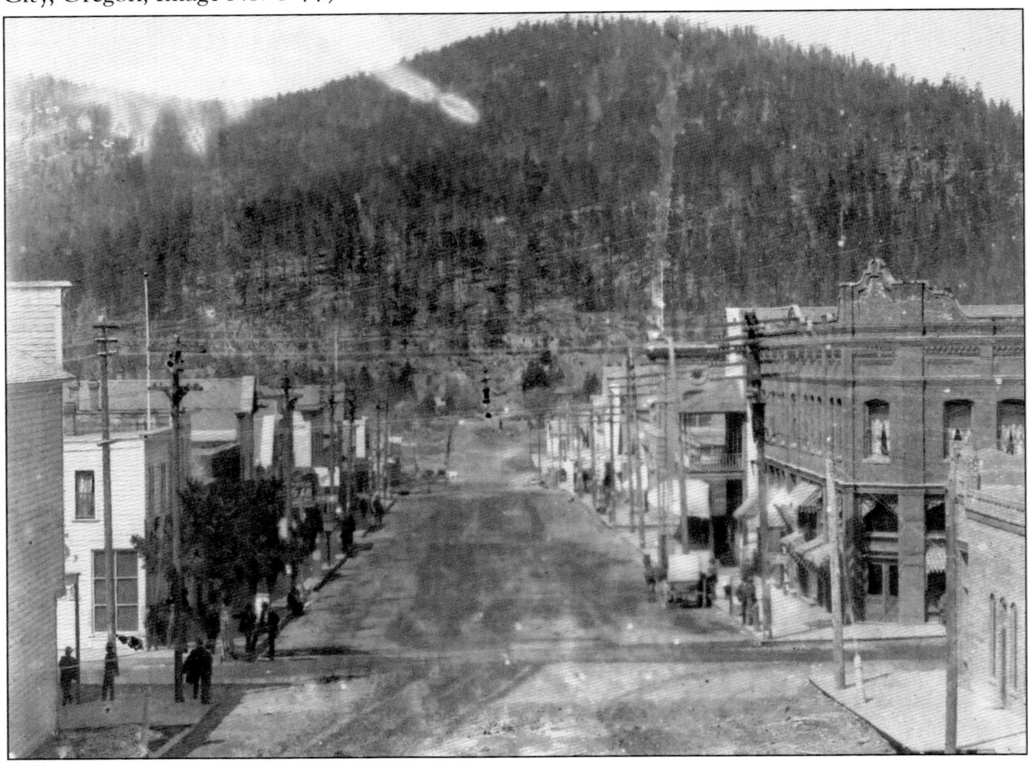

Looking from the same viewpoint as the previous photograph around 1908, this image shows (on the right) the Sumpter Hotel. At the intersection, one block farther down, sits the First National Bank. The bank is identifiable by the stonework and round windows. (Brooks Hawley Collection; Baker County Library, Baker City, Oregon, Image No. BH1b/1992.1.159.)

Two

Sumpter and Larch Hill (1898–1900)

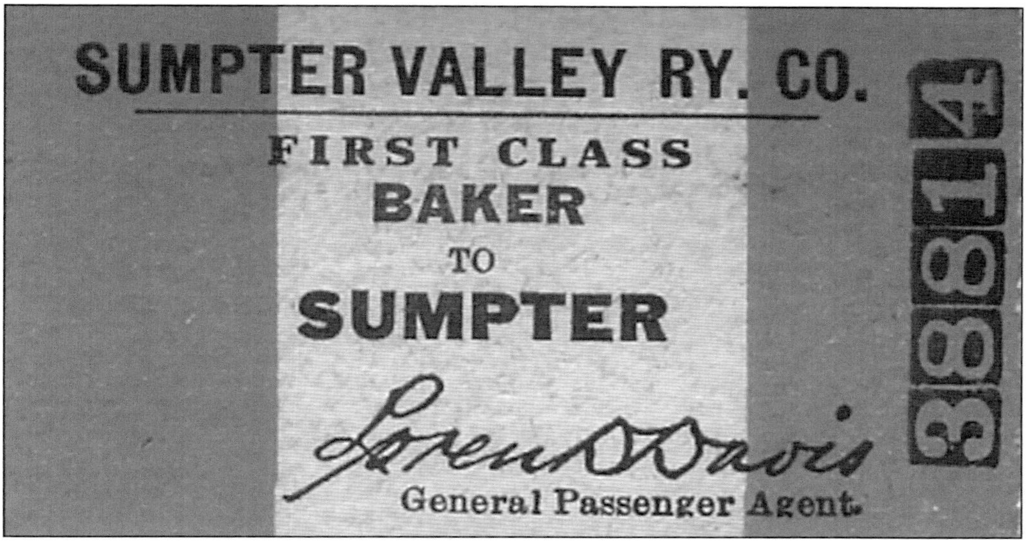

This is a copy of a 1930s original ticket to Sumpter. (Earl Emlaw Collection; National Railway Historical Society, Pacific Northwest Chapter.)

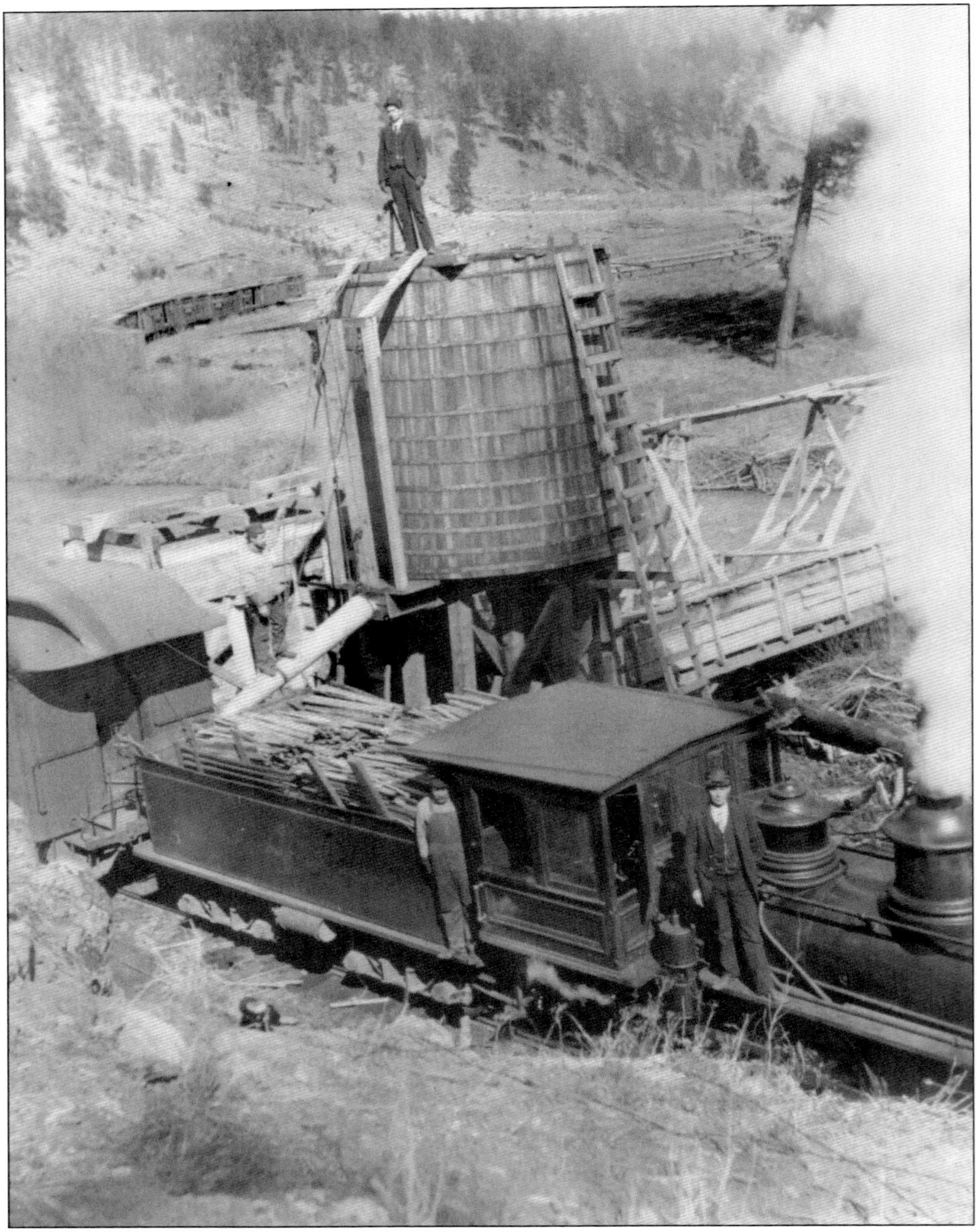

The well-dressed crew of Locomotive No. 4, an American (4-4-0), pauses to take on water at the Boulder Gorge water tank around 1903. (Photograph by L. J. Hicks, Ron Harr Collection; Sumpter Valley Railroad Restoration, Inc.)

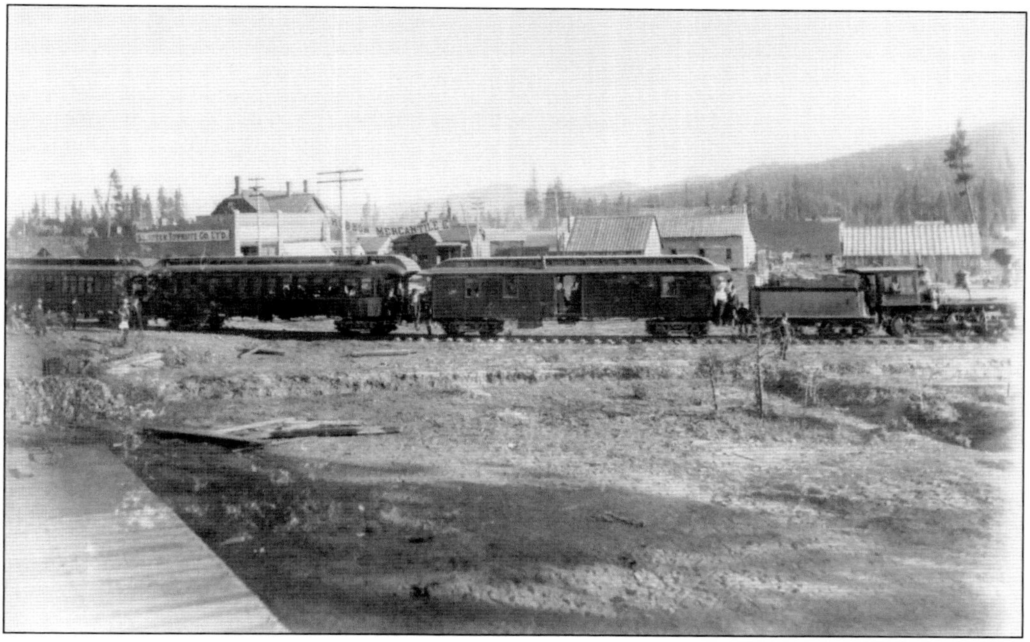

A passenger train is being turned at Sumpter around 1900. The railroad entered Sumpter in 1897, and its arrival heralded the apex of Sumpter's hard rock mining years, when gold, silver, and other precious metals flowed to the smelters. (McCord Collection; Baker County Library, Baker City, Oregon, Image No. TR-25.)

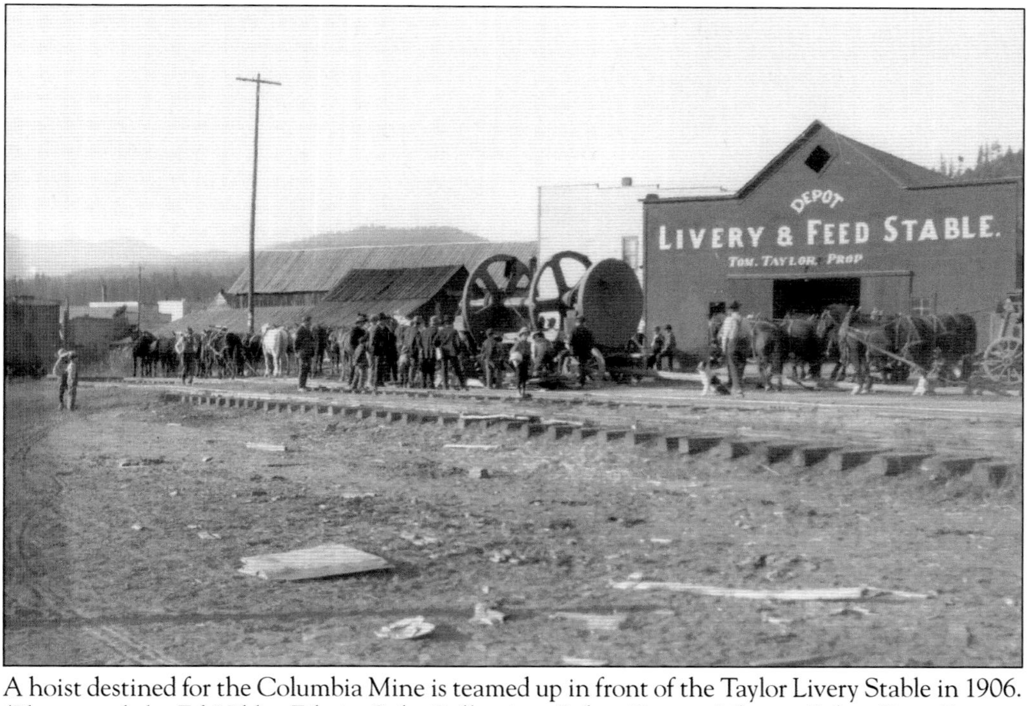

A hoist destined for the Columbia Mine is teamed up in front of the Taylor Livery Stable in 1906. (Photograph by Ed Hibbs, Edwin Culp Collection; Baker County Library, Baker City, Oregon, Image No. 31-A [B-H Coll] 1992.1.236b.)

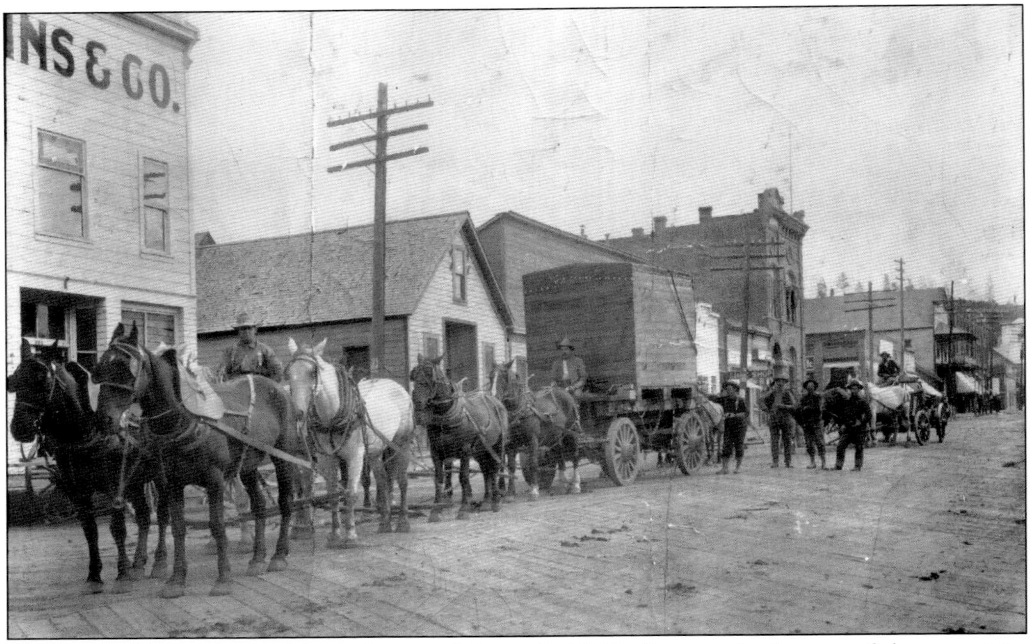

During the height of the mining boom of the early 1900s, Sumpter had many of the amenities of a modern city and a population of at least 4,000. (Pierce Library, Eastern Oregon University No. EOL00049.)

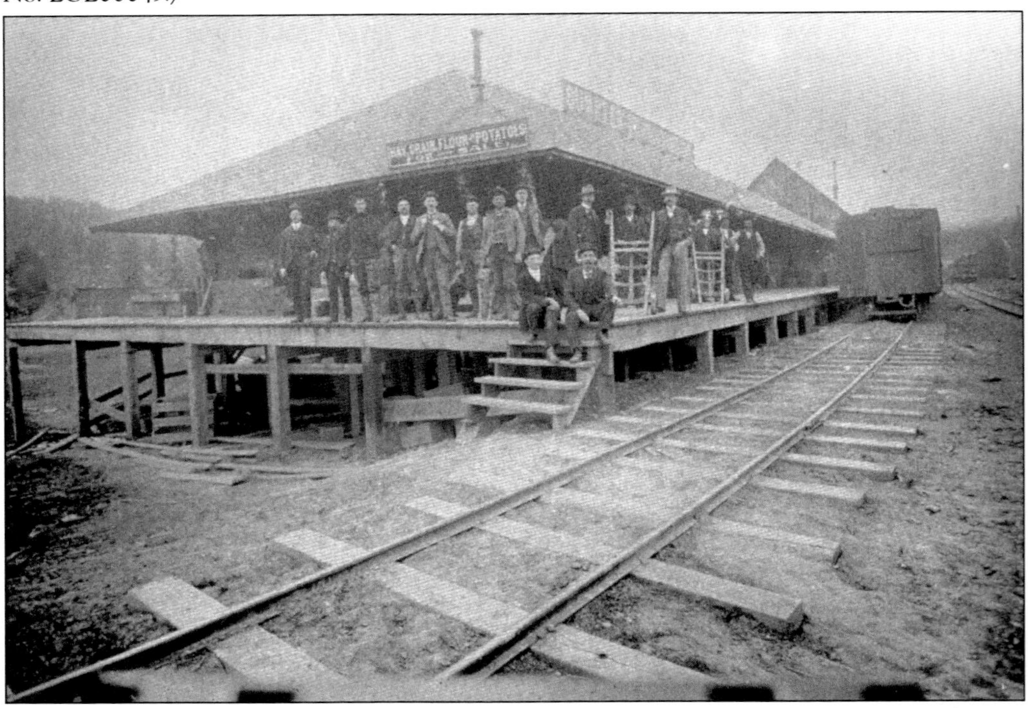

The staff of the Sumpter Forwarding Company stands on the loading dock. Several warehouses were located along the tracks in Sumpter. (Ron Harr Collection; Sumpter Valley Railroad Restoration, Inc.)

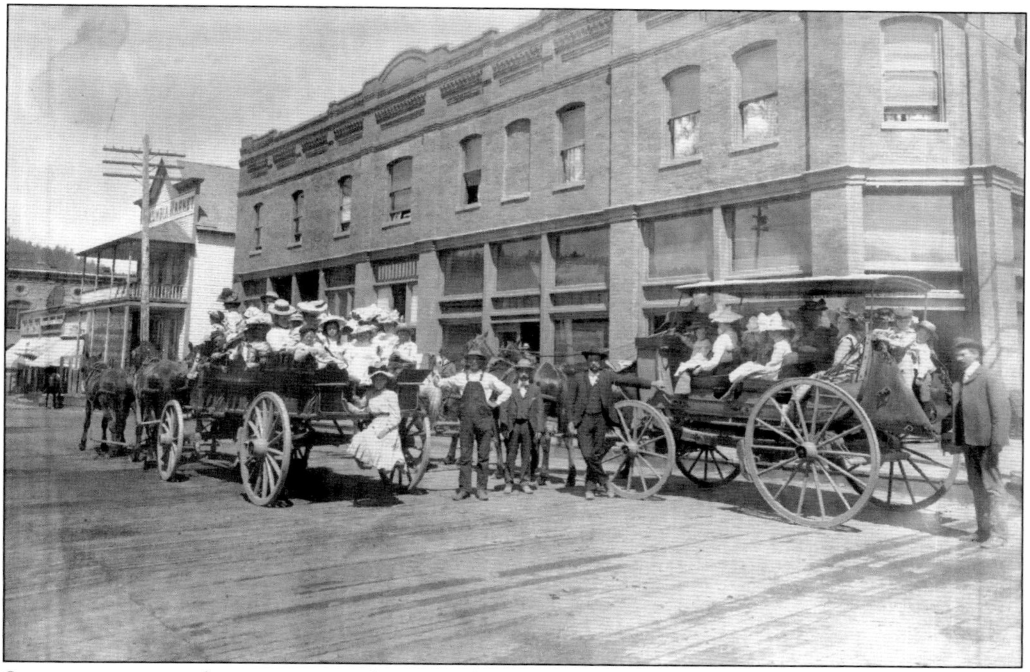

Sumpter gentry ride on two omnibuses in front of the Sumpter Hotel on Granite Street on a summer day in 1901. (Brooks Hawley Collection; Baker County Library, Baker City, Oregon, Image No. 1b/1992.1.206.)

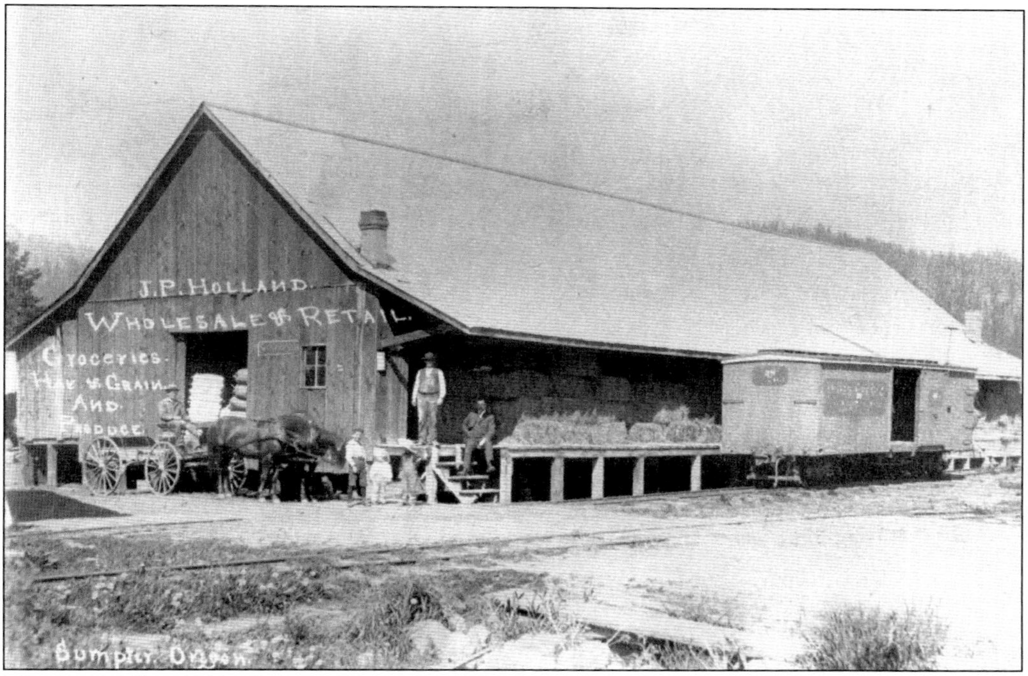

The J. P. Holland Warehouse in Sumpter is shown with hay, grain, and mining supplies around 1905. (Elizabeth Izatt [née Holland], Brooks Hawley Collection; Baker County Library, Baker City, Oregon, Image No. BH61-A/1992.1.237.)

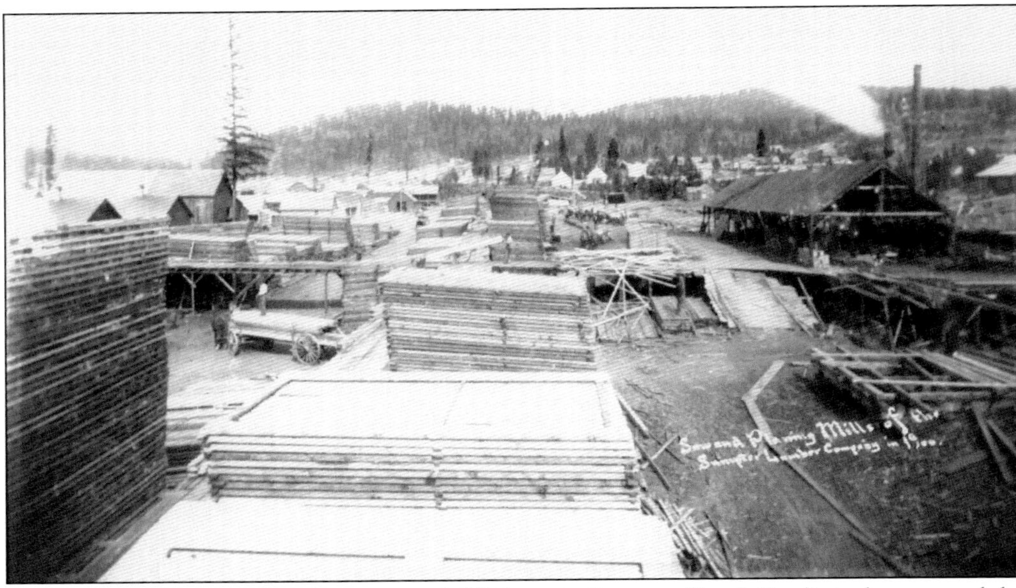

This is the Sumpter Lumber Company on Mill Street in Sumpter. Frank Gardinier later owned the mill before it was purchased by the Stoddard Lumber Company. (Ron Harr Collection; Sumpter Valley Railroad Restoration, Inc.)

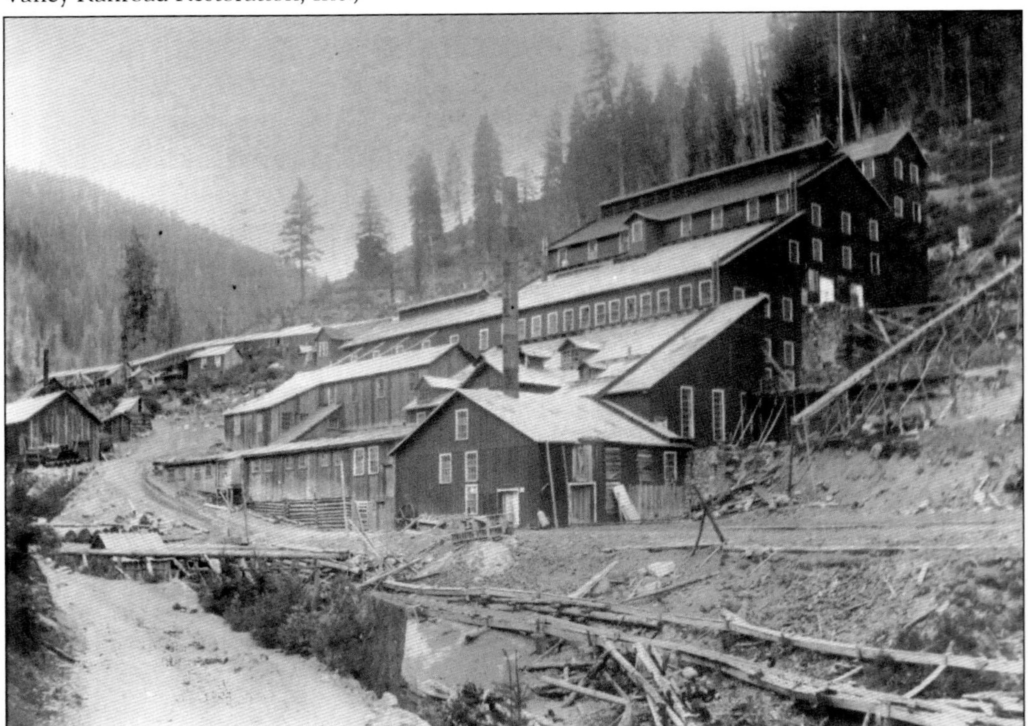

Pictured here is the Eureka and Excelsior Mine in Bourne. This mill was typical of the many mine complexes that covered the hills around Sumpter and the other nearby boom towns. (McCord Collection; Baker County Library, Baker City, Oregon, Image No. E17.)

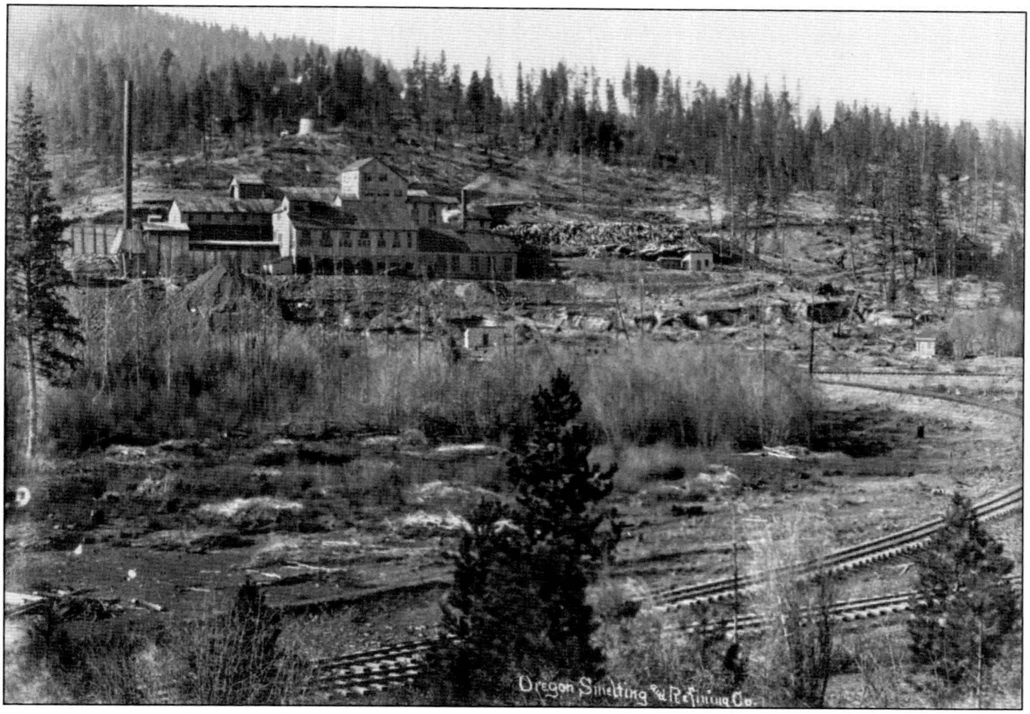

The Oregon Smelting and Refining Company was located on the mainline east of Sumpter. Far from a commercial success, it was completed just as the hard rock mining began playing out. (Ron Harr Collection; Sumpter Valley Railroad Restoration, Inc.)

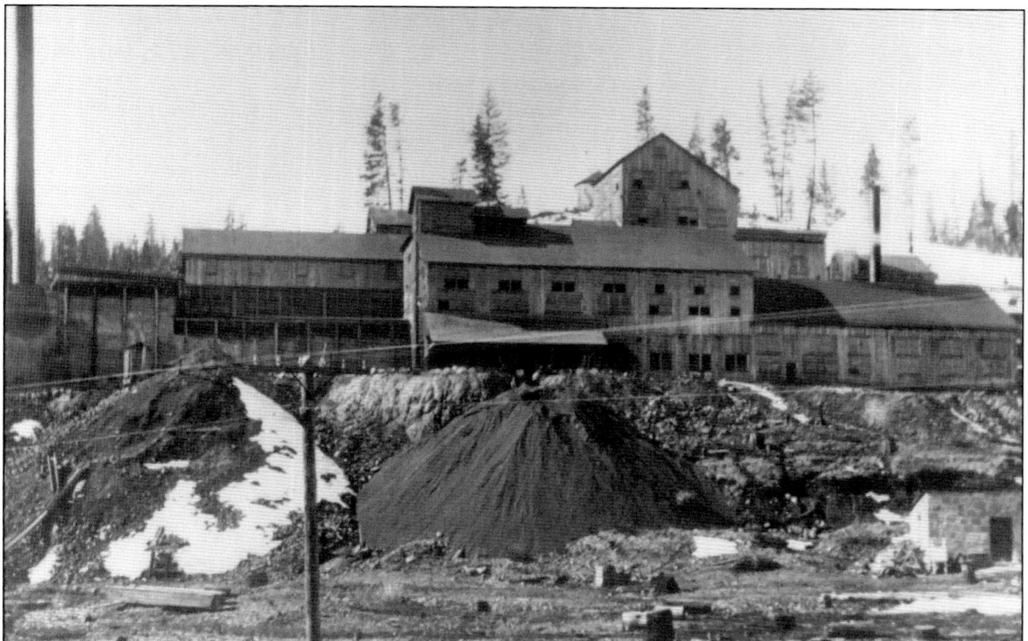
This is a closer view of the Oregon Smelting and Refining Company. (Ron Harr Collection; Sumpter Valley Railroad Restoration, Inc.)

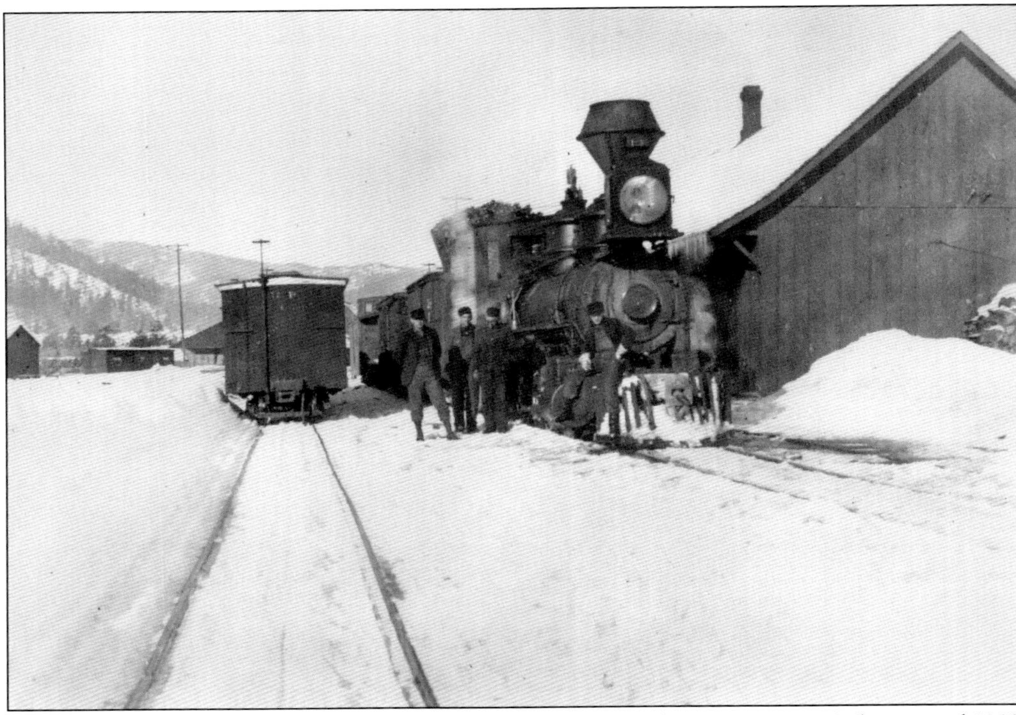

Consolidation No. 7 arrives with a freight train at the Sumpter depot on a winter's day around 1903. Note the link-and-pin couplers and the former Union Pacific boxcar on the siding. (Photograph by Ed Hibbs, Brooks Hawley Collection; Baker County Library, Baker City, Oregon.)

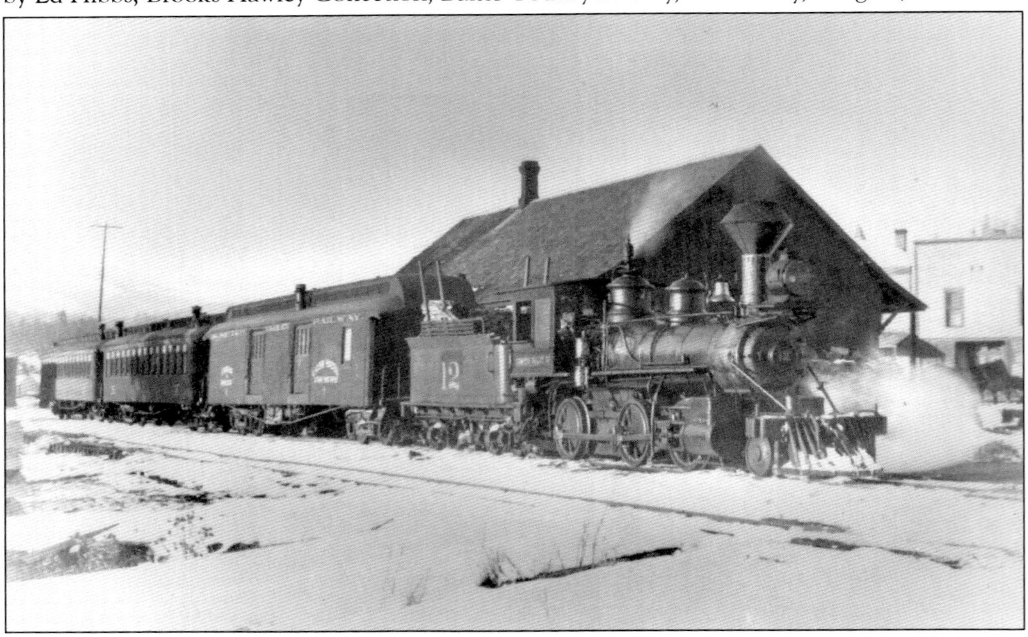

Mogul No. 12 with the daily passenger train, also known as the "Stump Dodger," is shown in front of the Sumpter depot in the winter of 1912. (Ron Harr Collection; Sumpter Valley Railroad Restoration, Inc.)

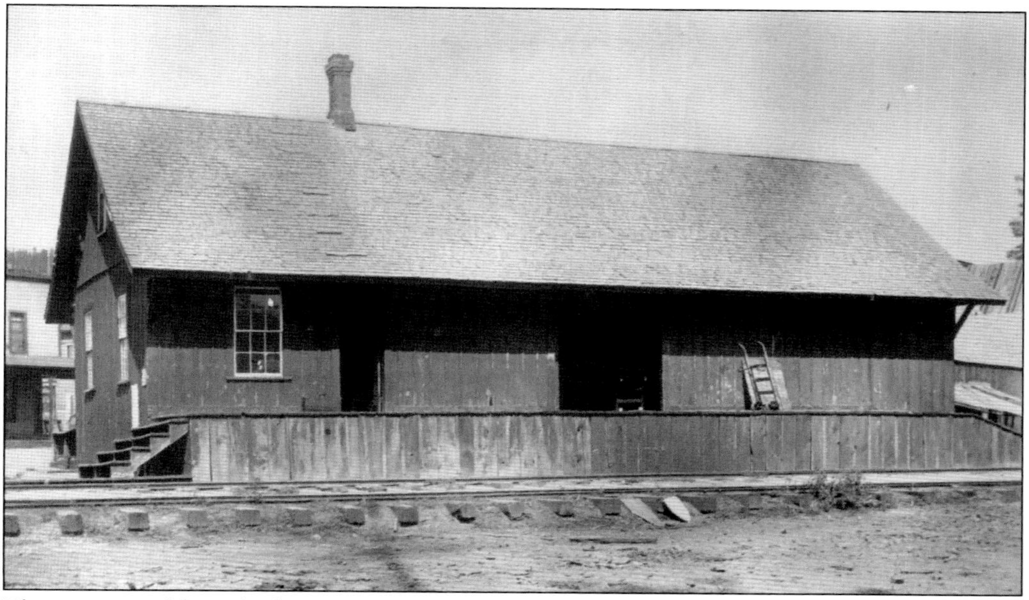

This is a view of the rail side at Sumpter Depot before 1911. The State Railway Commission ordered the upgrade of the depot and other railway facilities to conform to the American Association of Railroad Standards Act in 1911. (Brooks Hawley Collection; Baker County Library, Baker City, Oregon.)

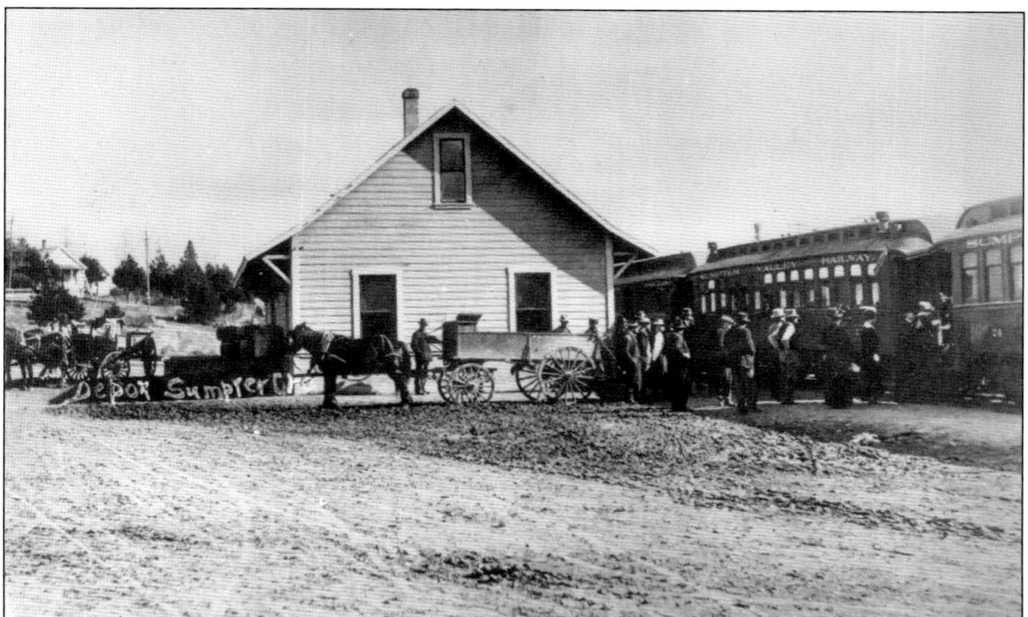

It's train time at Sumpter in 1912. The depot has been recently remodelled; note the new paint and horizontal siding. (Photograph by Ira Irwin, McCord Collection; Baker County Library, Baker City, Oregon.)

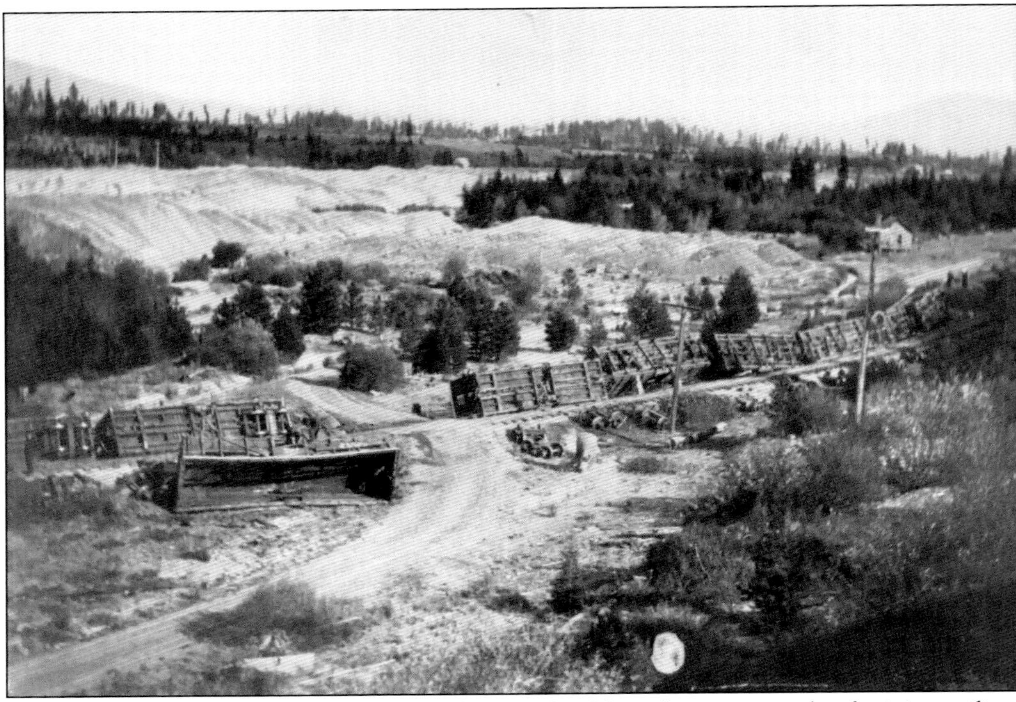

This is a view of the 1915 stock train wreck at S-Wye. Note the growing pile of mining tailings in the background. (Ron Harr Collection; Sumpter Valley Railroad Restoration, Inc.)

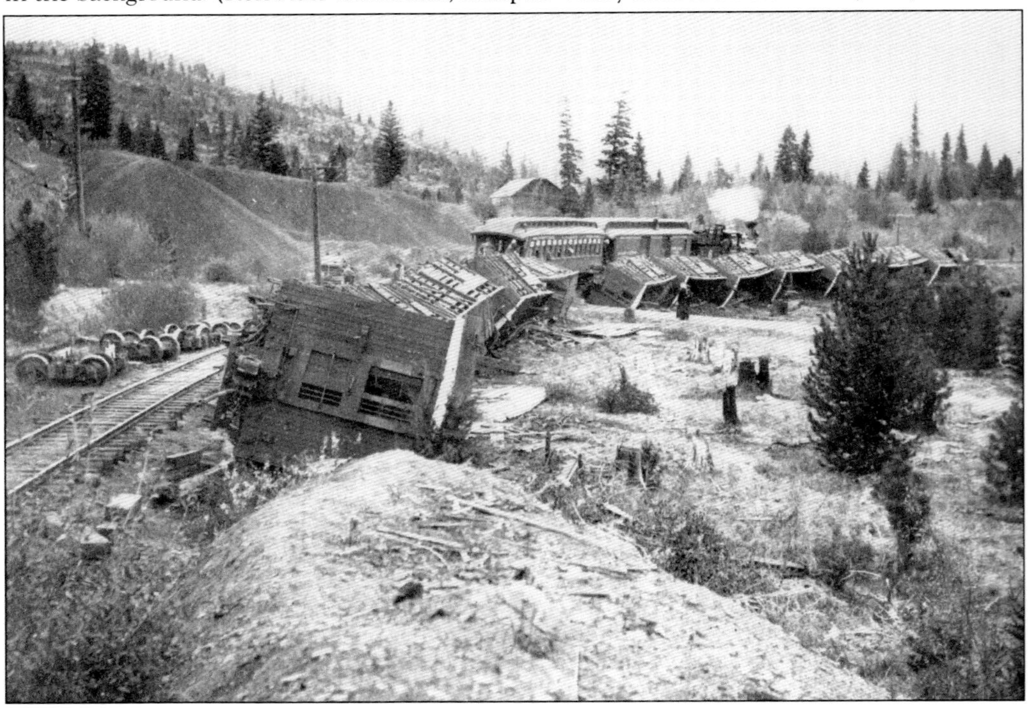

A passenger train passes the site of the 1915 stock train wreck at S-Wye in 1915. (Ron Harr Collection; Sumpter Valley Railroad Restoration, Inc.)

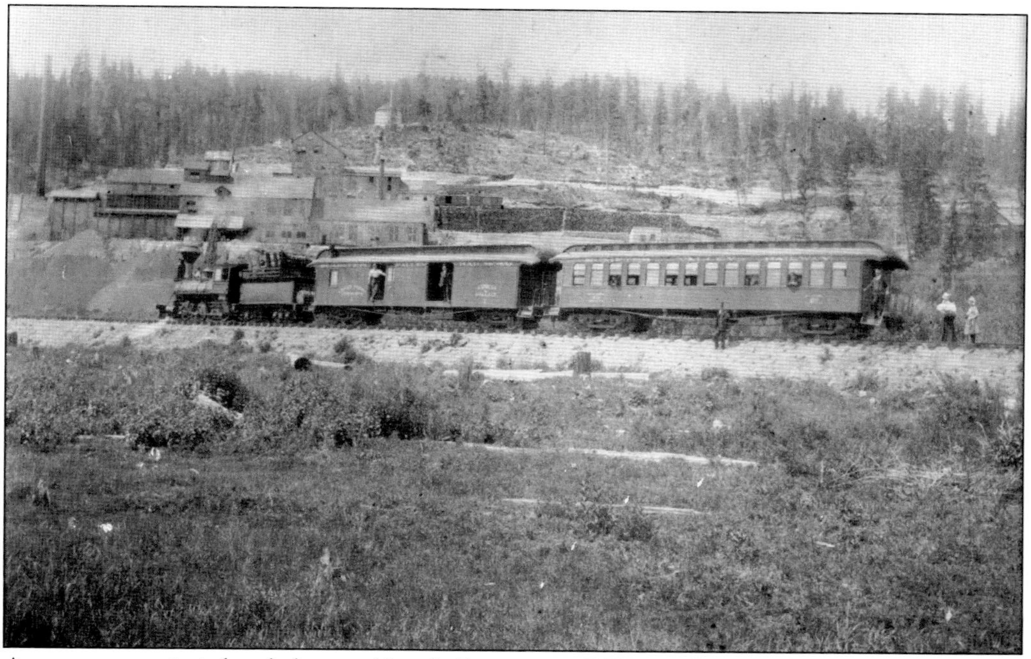

A passenger train is headed toward Larch Summit on S-Wye in front of the site of the Sumpter Smelting and Refining facility around 1904. (Pierce Library, Eastern Oregon University No. EOL00005.)

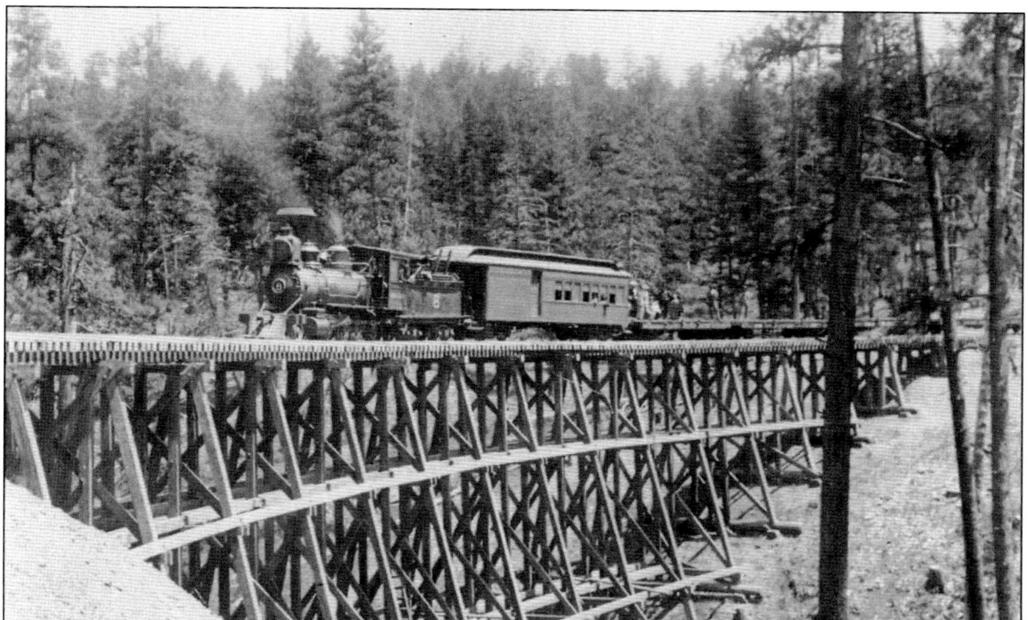

Baldwin Consolidation No. 8 has Brill combine No. 5 and a work train in tow. The newly completed trestle was located on the way to Larch Summit. This trestle was later replaced with fill and is not listed in the 1918 Interstate Commerce Commission (ICC) survey. (Ron Harr Collection; Sumpter Valley Railroad Restoration, Inc.)

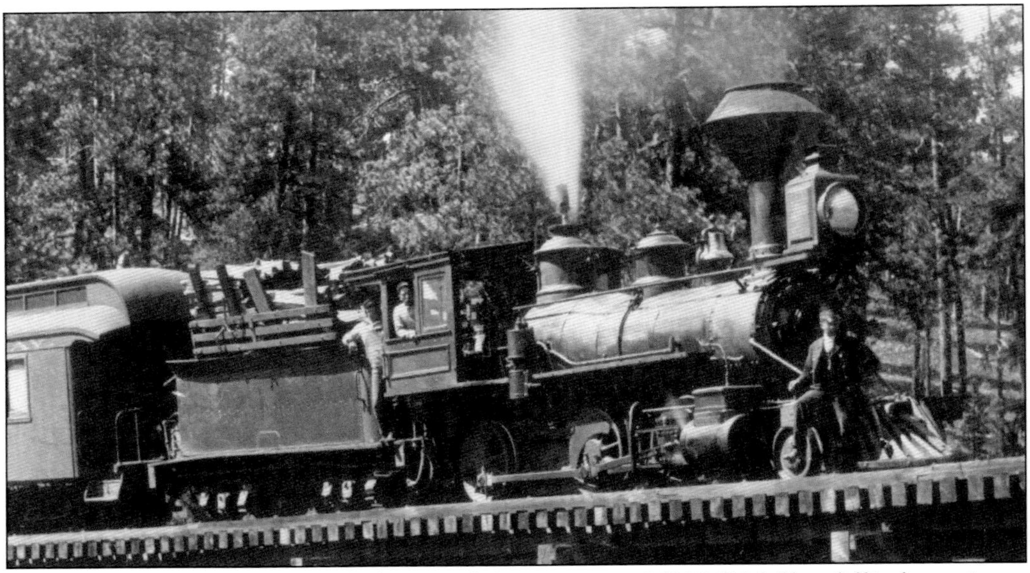

Mogul No. 1 is heading downgrade from Larch Summit around 1900. F. M. Shurtliff is the engineer. (Ron Harr Collection; Sumpter Valley Railroad Restoration, Inc.)

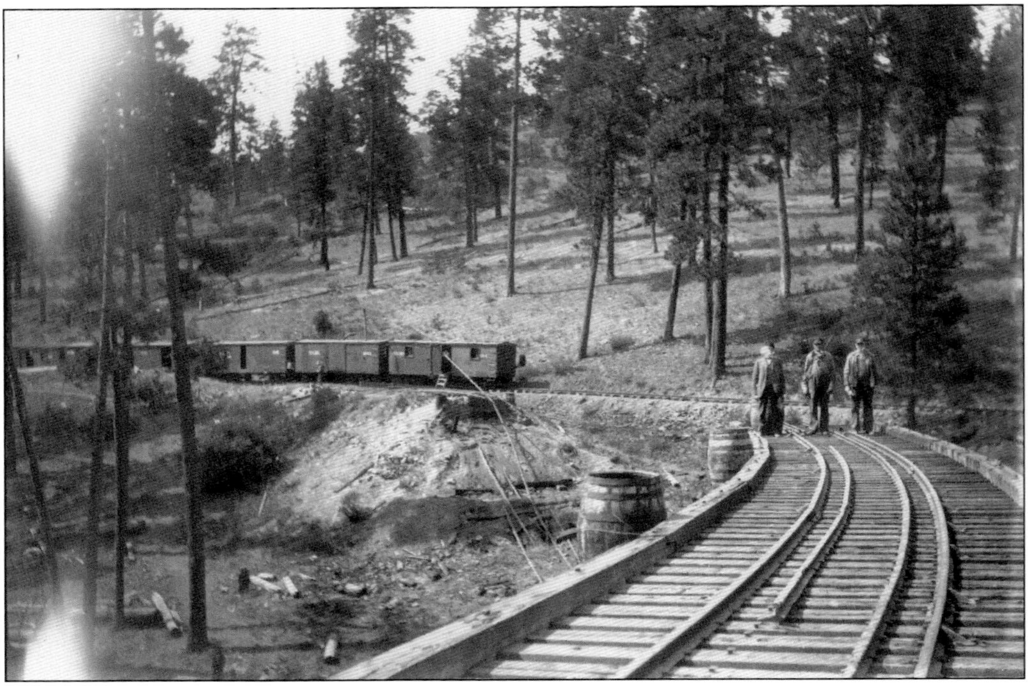

A work crew is busy rebuilding the Alder Creek Trestle around 1900. Note the fire-bent rails draped across the bottom of the gulch. In later years, this was a particularly popular photographic site on the west side of Larch Summit. (Pierce Library, Eastern Oregon University No. EOL00514a.)

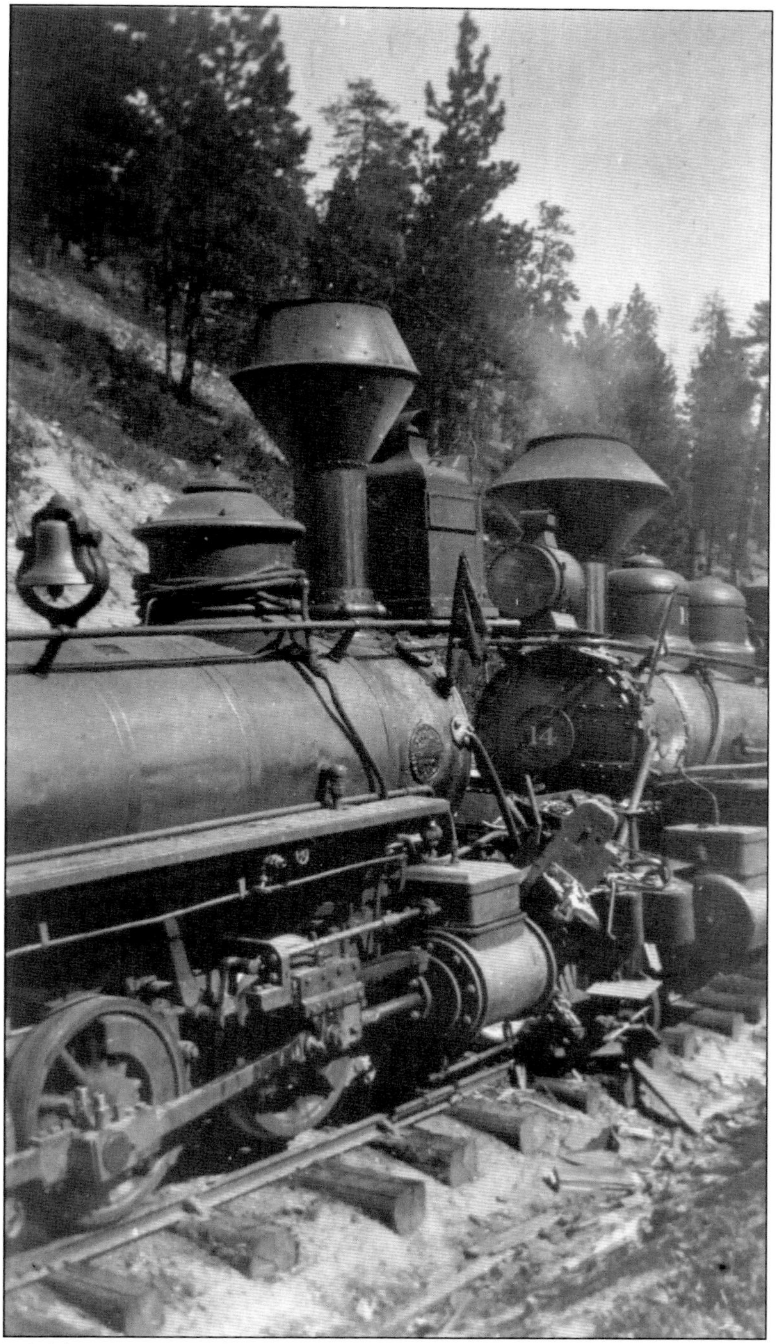

A minor cornfield meet occurred between engines No. 10 and 14 near Larch in September 1913. No. 14 is an outside-frame Consolidation that had been purchased from the Eureka and Palisades Railroad the previous year, while the No. 10 is a former Rio Grande Western Baldwin inside-frame Consolidation acquired in 1900. In later years, the ICC required the Sumpter Valley to adopt a more mainline standard of operations in an attempt to cut down on accidents. (Photograph by Ed Hibbs, Brooks Hawley Collection; Sumpter Valley Railroad Restoration, Inc.)

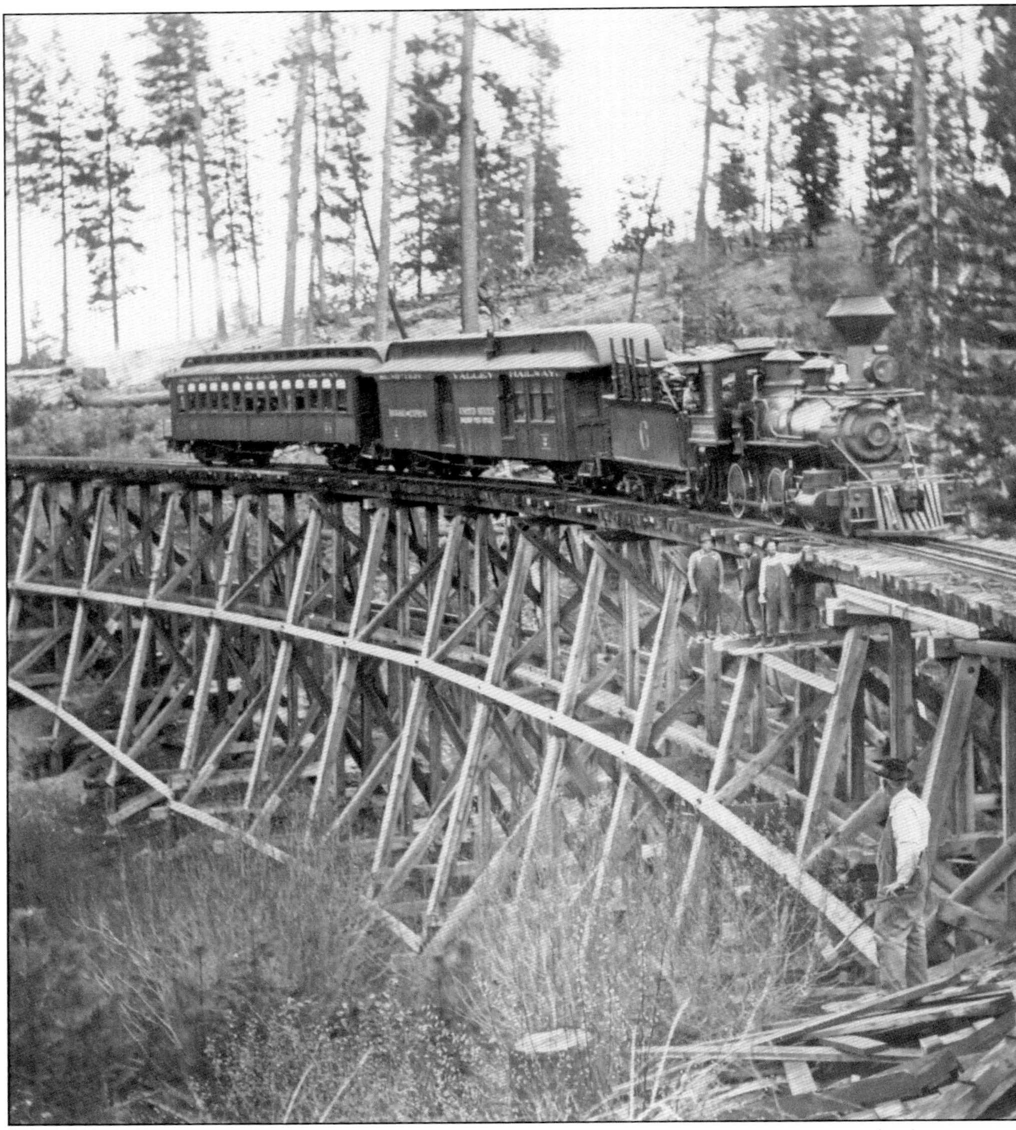

A train led by Mogul No. 6 pauses on the grade toward Sumpter in 1914. Trailing the locomotive are combine No. 2, an Ohio Falls product, and Coach No. 23. The trestle was located near Larch Summit and was replaced with fill in 1916 to accommodate the new Baldwin Mikados. (Ron Harr Collection; Sumpter Valley Railroad Restoration, Inc.)

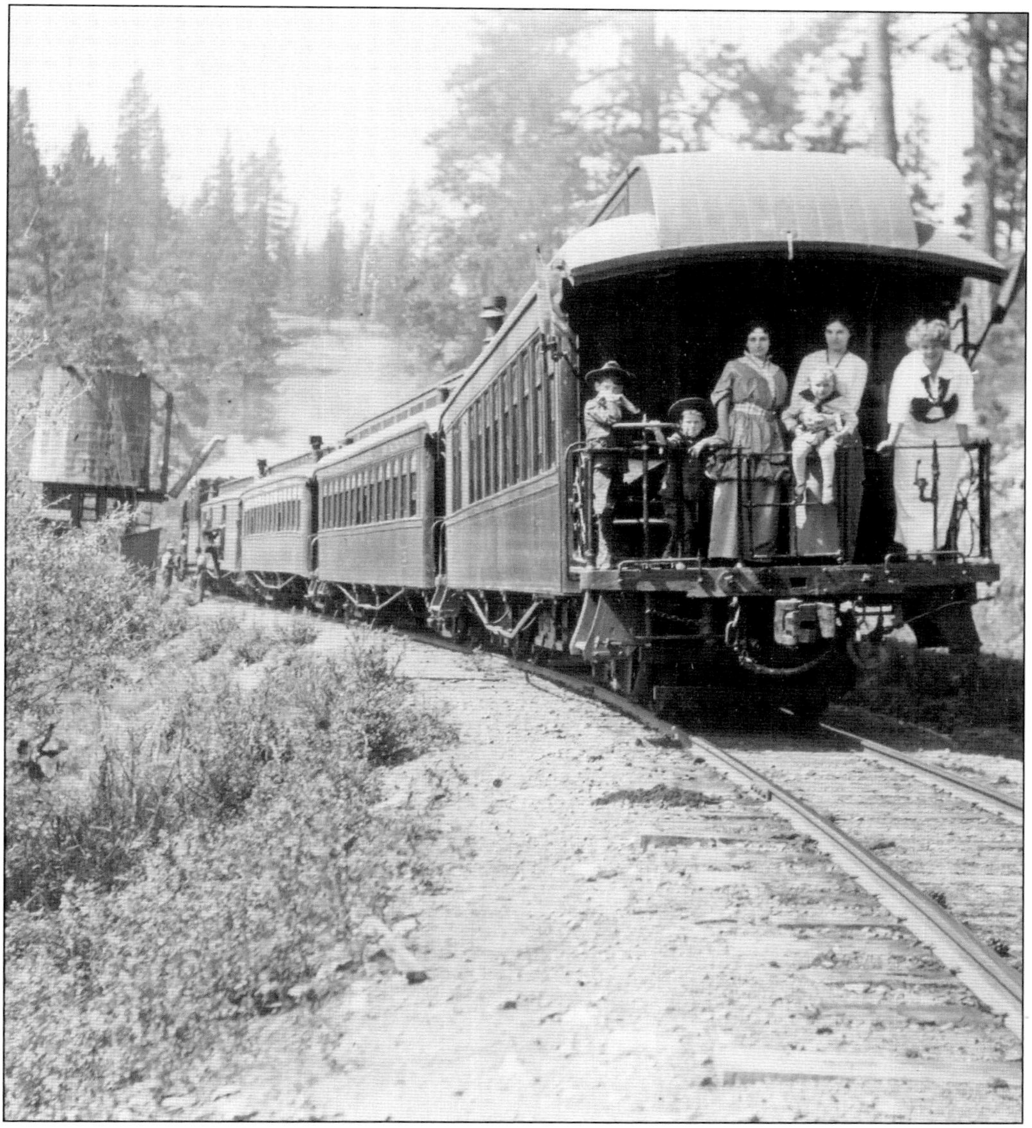

An excursion train takes on water at the Boulder Gorge tank around 1910. Car No. 1, the last car of the train, is the private car of the Eccles family. This car was acquired sometime between 1903 and 1908 and may have been a gift to David Eccles from the Union Pacific. (Pierce Library, Eastern Oregon University No. EOL00513.)

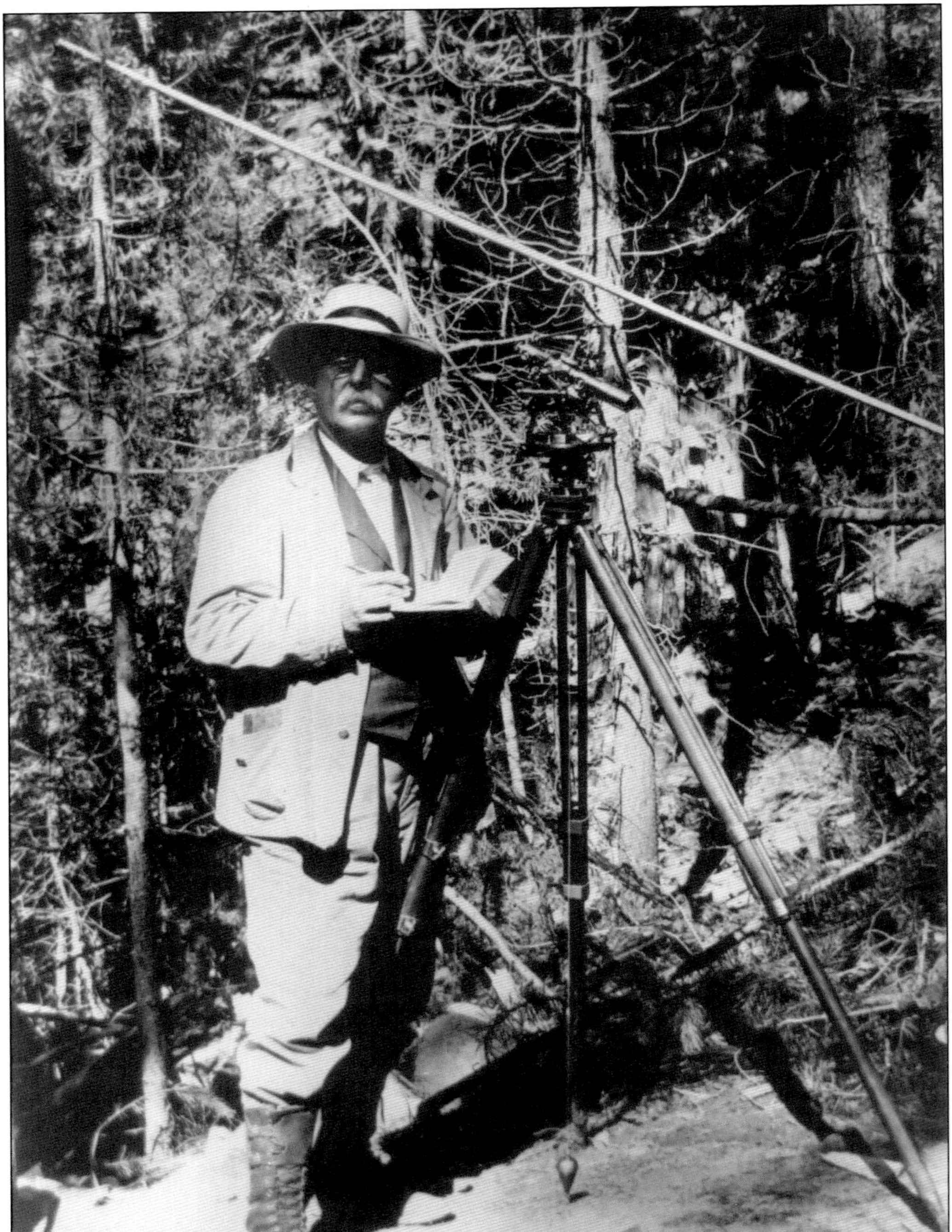

Joseph Barton, acting agent and surveyor for the Sumpter Valley Railway, is shown surveying the line through Bridge Creek. Note the surveying equipment; the transit was used to measure direction and distance. (Ron Harr Collection; Sumpter Valley Railroad Restoration, Inc.)

Three

WHITNEY, TIPTON, AUSTIN, AND BATESVILLE (1901–1907)

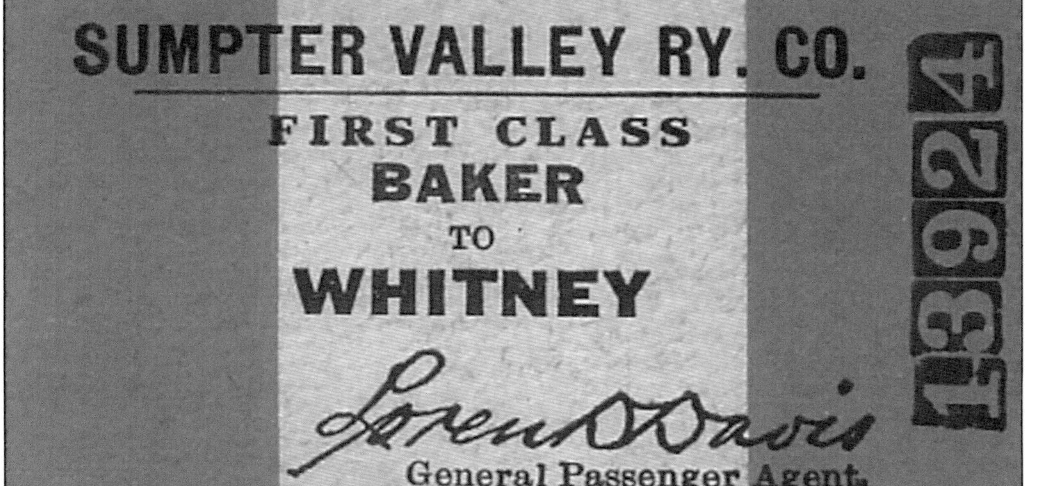

This is a copy of a 1930s original ticket to Whitney. (Earl Emlaw Collection; National Railway Historical Society, Pacific Northwest Chapter.)

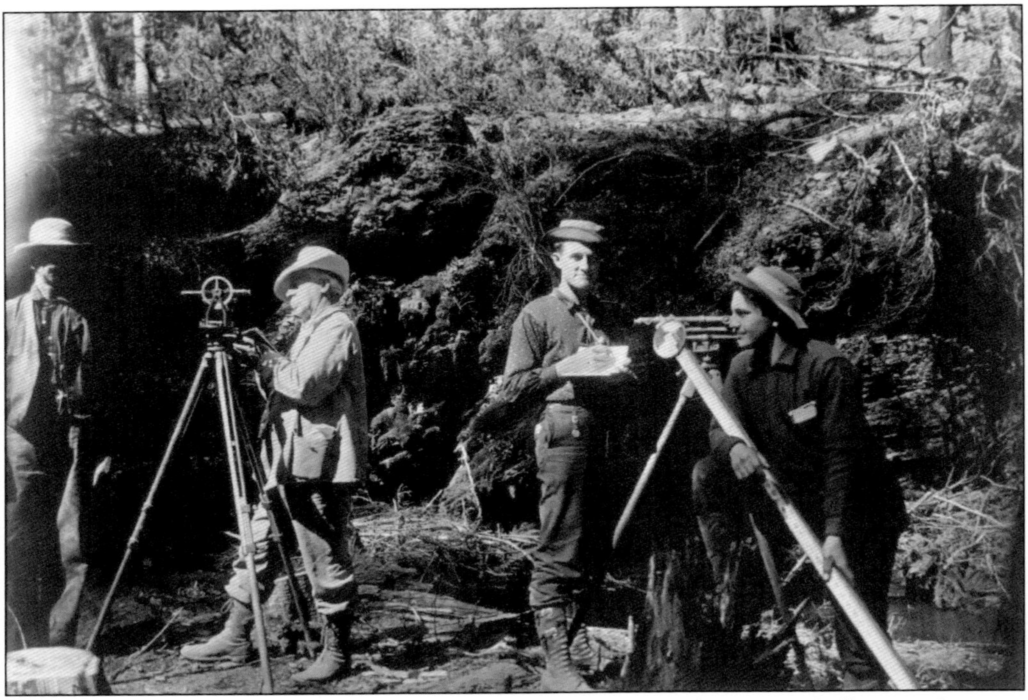

Here the Barton Survey Team works along Bridge Creek in 1910. (Ron Harr Collection; Sumpter Valley Railroad Restoration, Inc.)

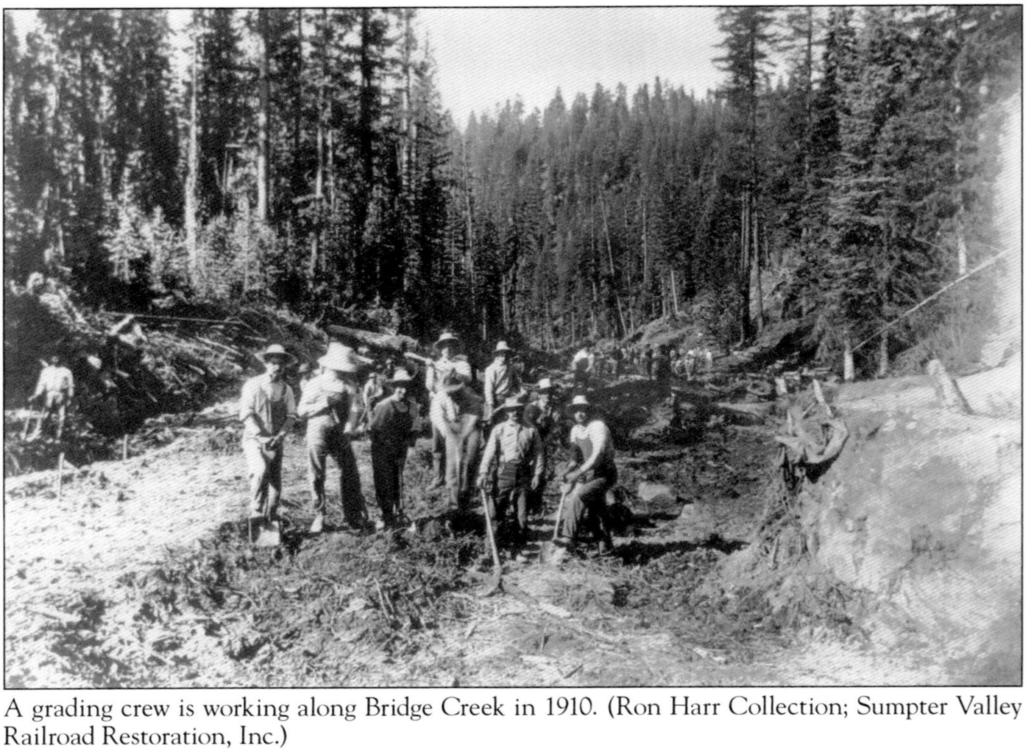

A grading crew is working along Bridge Creek in 1910. (Ron Harr Collection; Sumpter Valley Railroad Restoration, Inc.)

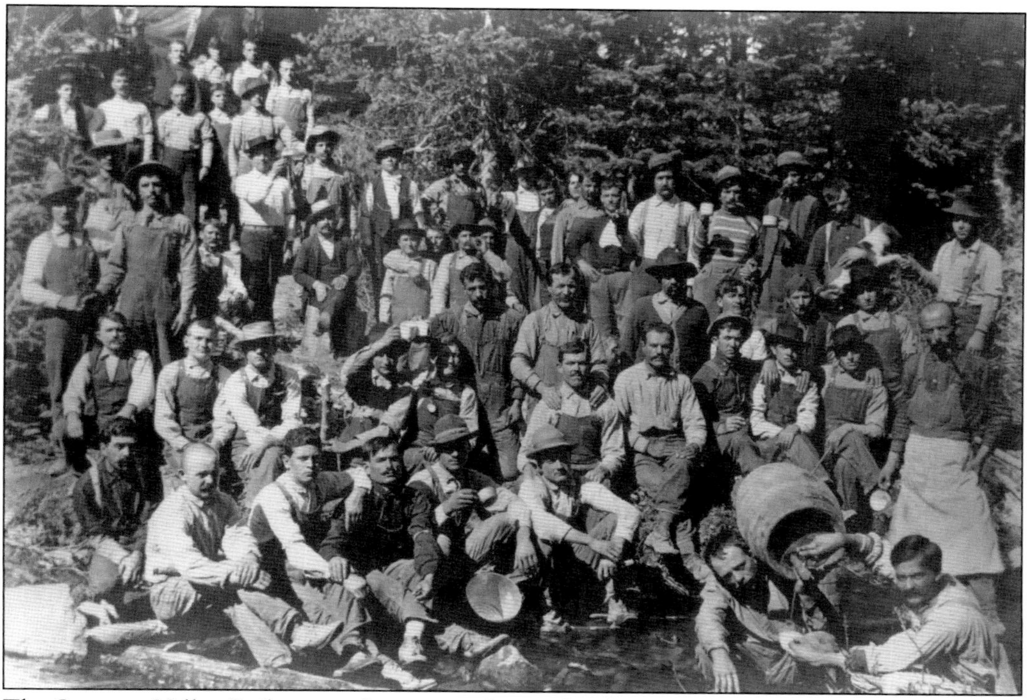

The Sumpter Valley Railway track gang is taking a break on Bridge Creek in 1910. (Ron Harr Collection; Sumpter Valley Railroad Restoration, Inc.)

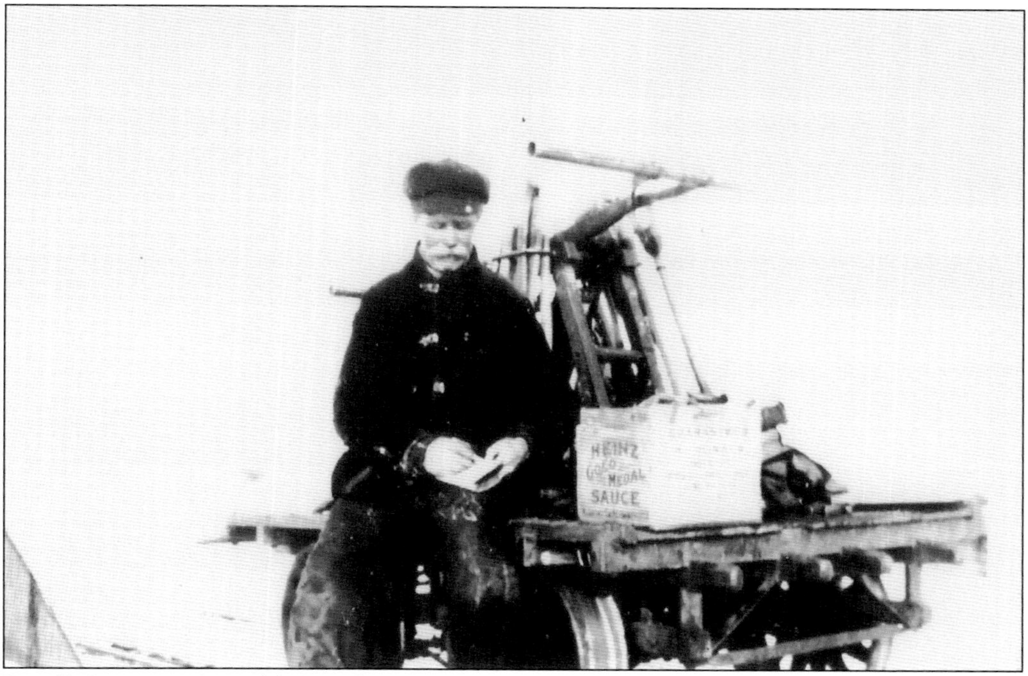

Bundled against the cold, Joseph Barton pauses to take notes alongside one of the railway's handcars. Note the Heinz box on the deck. (Ron Harr Collection; Sumpter Valley Railroad Restoration, Inc.)

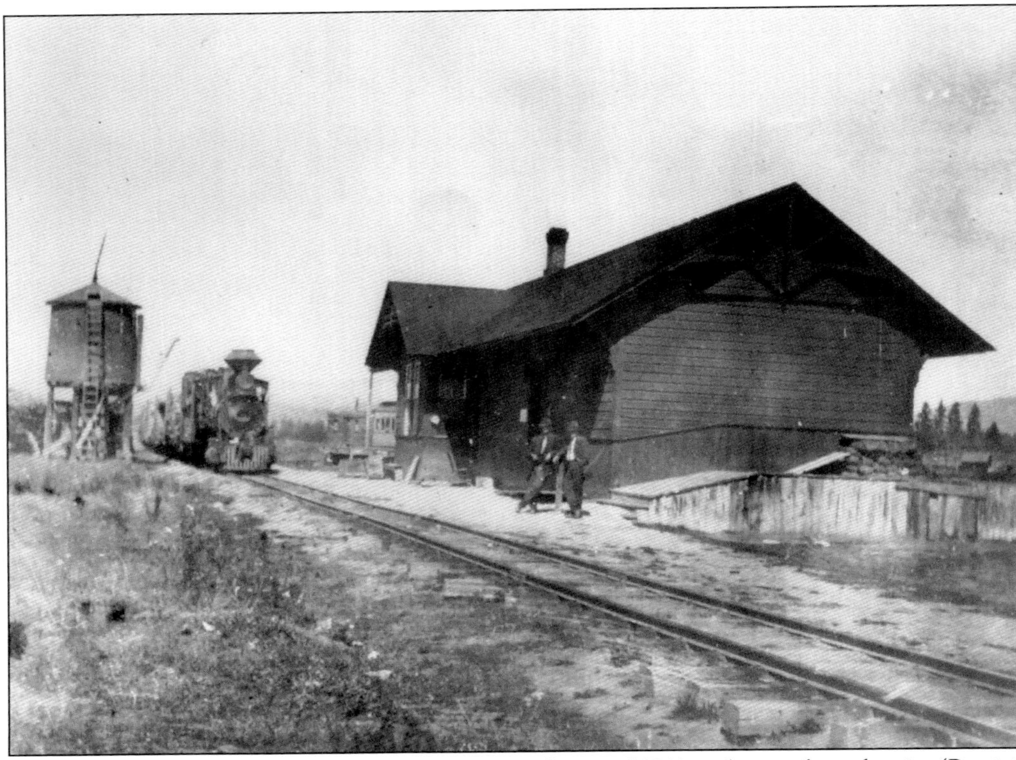

The Whitney Depot and its water tank are pictured around 1911 with a cordwood train. (Patricia Stewart Baker Collection, Sumpter Valley Railroad Restoration, Inc.)

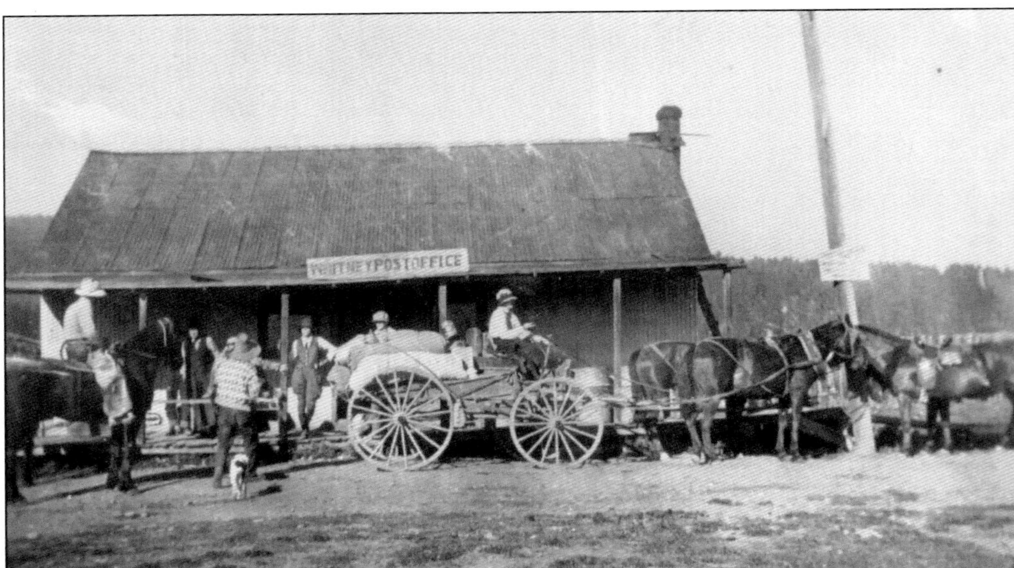

In this image of the Whitney Post Office on a summer day around 1905, one can see the loaded wagons in use at the time. Also note the cowboy in chaps. (McCord Collection; Baker County Library, Baker City, Oregon, Image No. T273-1992.1.63.)

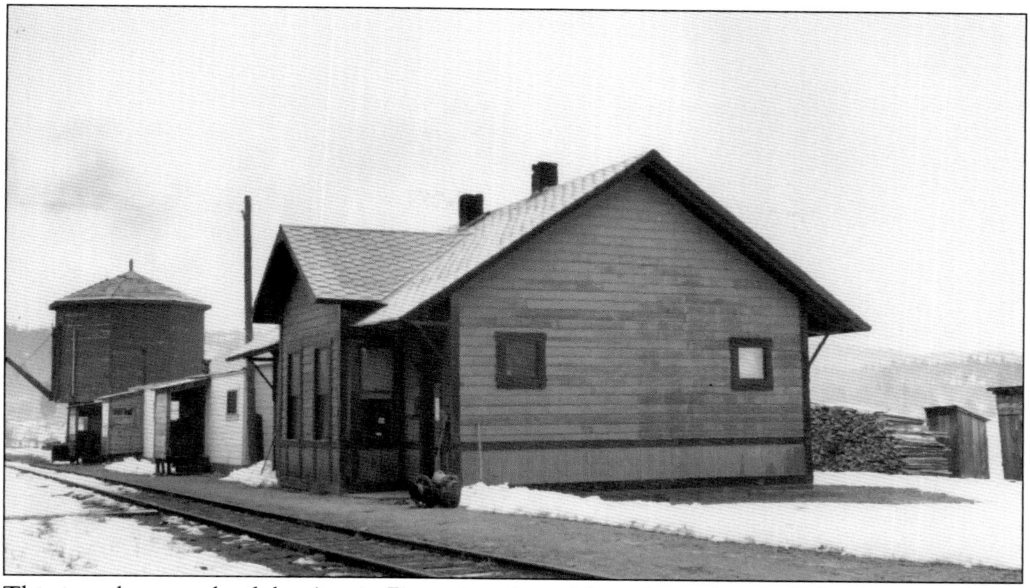

This is a photograph of the Austin Depot in winter. Note the outhouses behind the cordwood piles on the right and the other support structures on the left. (Ron Harr Collection; Sumpter Valley Railroad Restoration, Inc.)

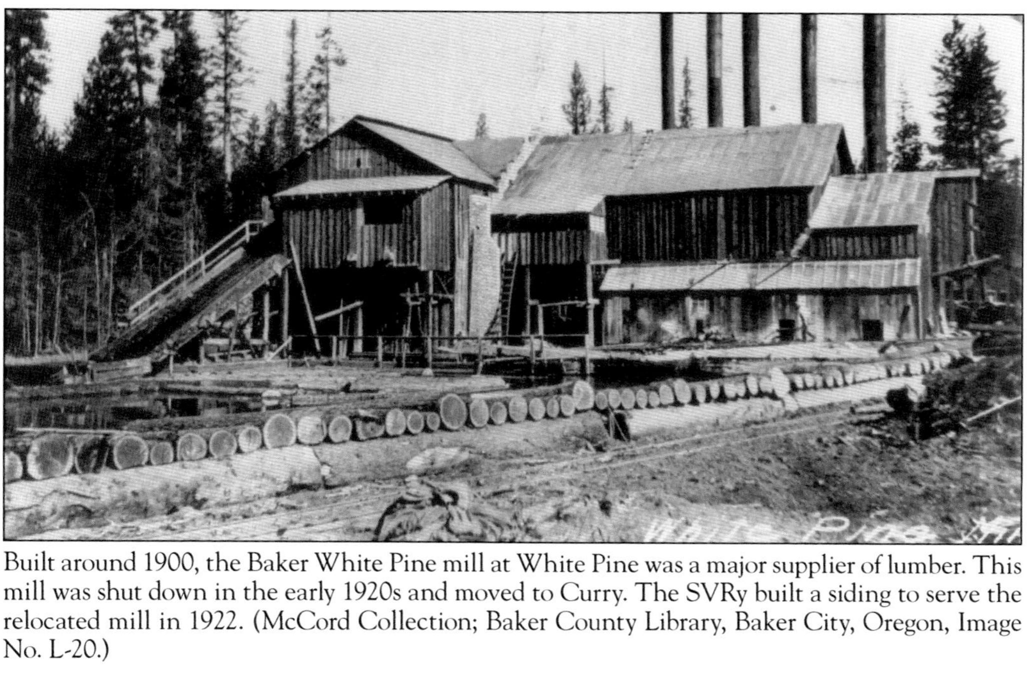

Built around 1900, the Baker White Pine mill at White Pine was a major supplier of lumber. This mill was shut down in the early 1920s and moved to Curry. The SVRy built a siding to serve the relocated mill in 1922. (McCord Collection; Baker County Library, Baker City, Oregon, Image No. L-20.)

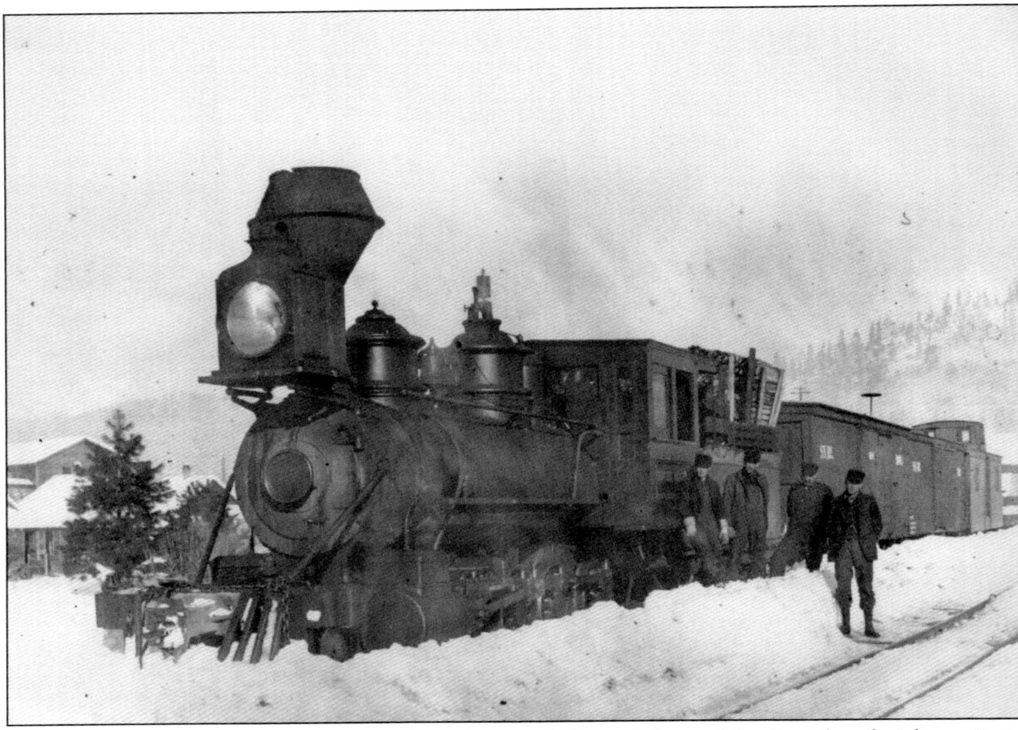

Winter in Sumpter finds the crew gathered around Consolidation No. 7 with a freight train in tow. (Brooks Hawley Collection; Sumpter Valley Railroad Restoration, Inc.)

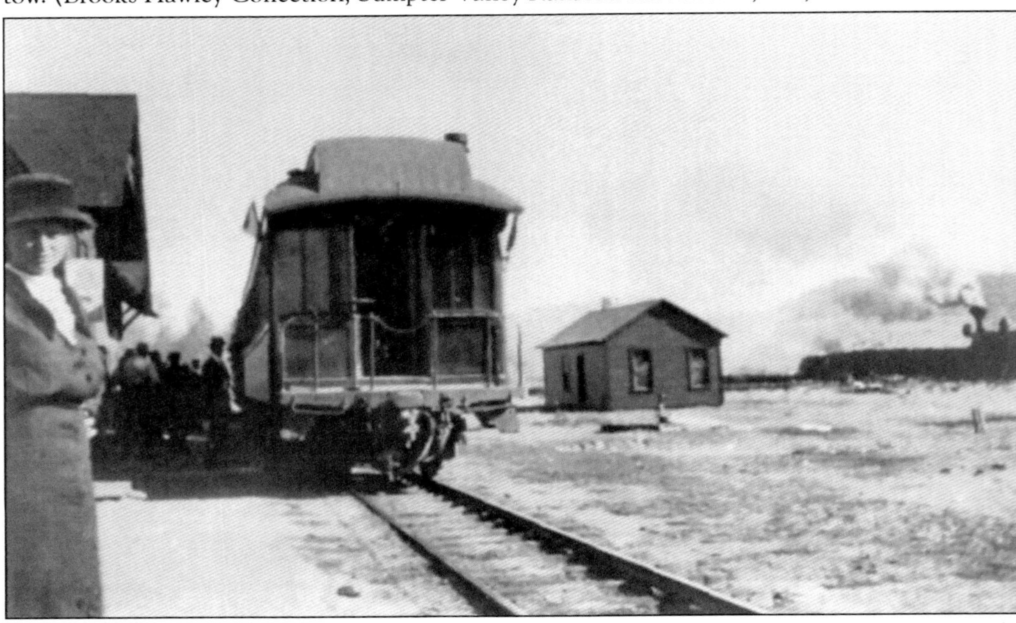

A passenger train pauses at Whitney around 1910. Many believe this to be one of the gold spike picnic trains headed to Bridge Creek to celebrate the opening of the line to Prairie City. Note the extra flags on the sides of the passenger car that signal more passenger train sections will follow. (Bret Bane Collection.)

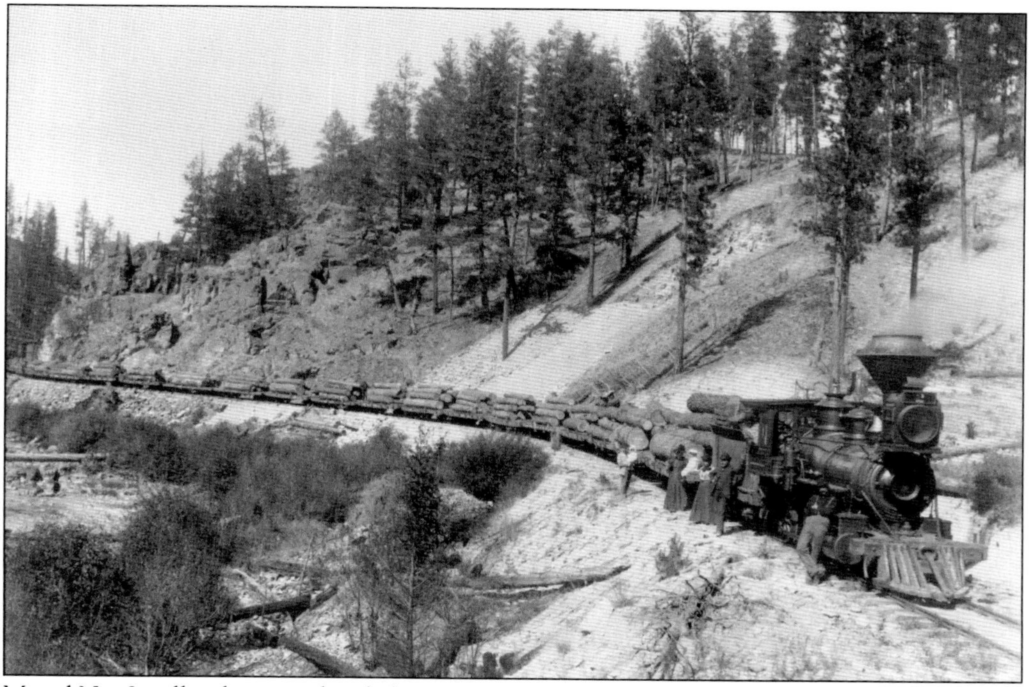

Mogul No. 2 pulls a log train headed east just past Devils Gate (Red Bridge) around 1902. (L. J. Hicks Collection; Sumpter Valley Railroad Restoration, Inc.)

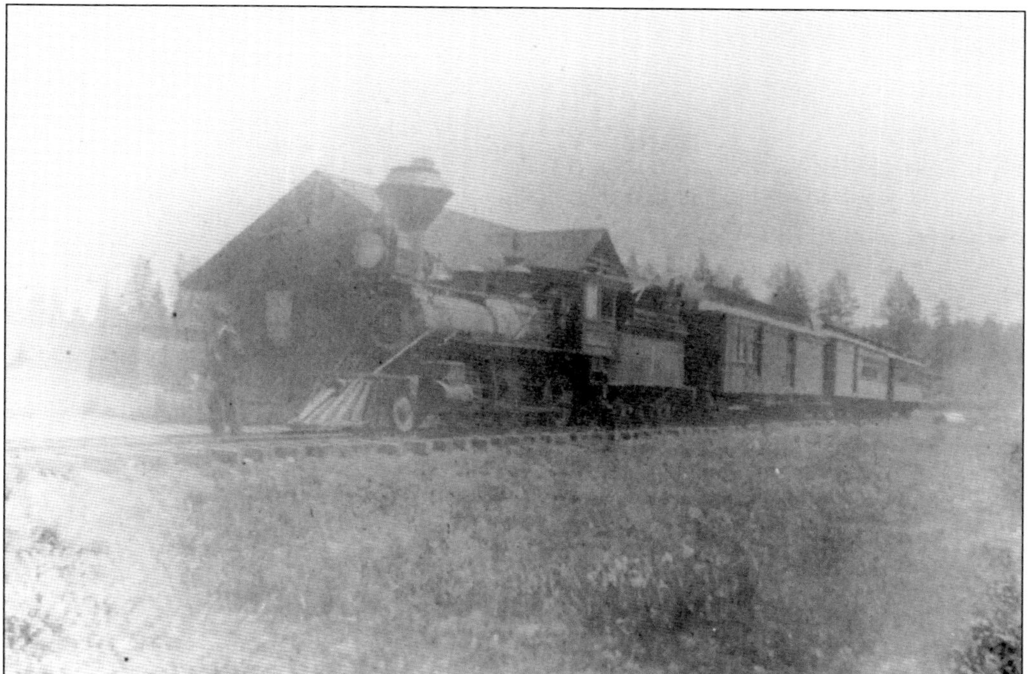

A South Baker–bound passenger train arrives at the Tipton Depot around 1903. The train is made up of Locomotive No. 1, baggage car No. 02, a combine, and coach. (Ron Harr Collection; Sumpter Valley Railroad Restoration, Inc.)

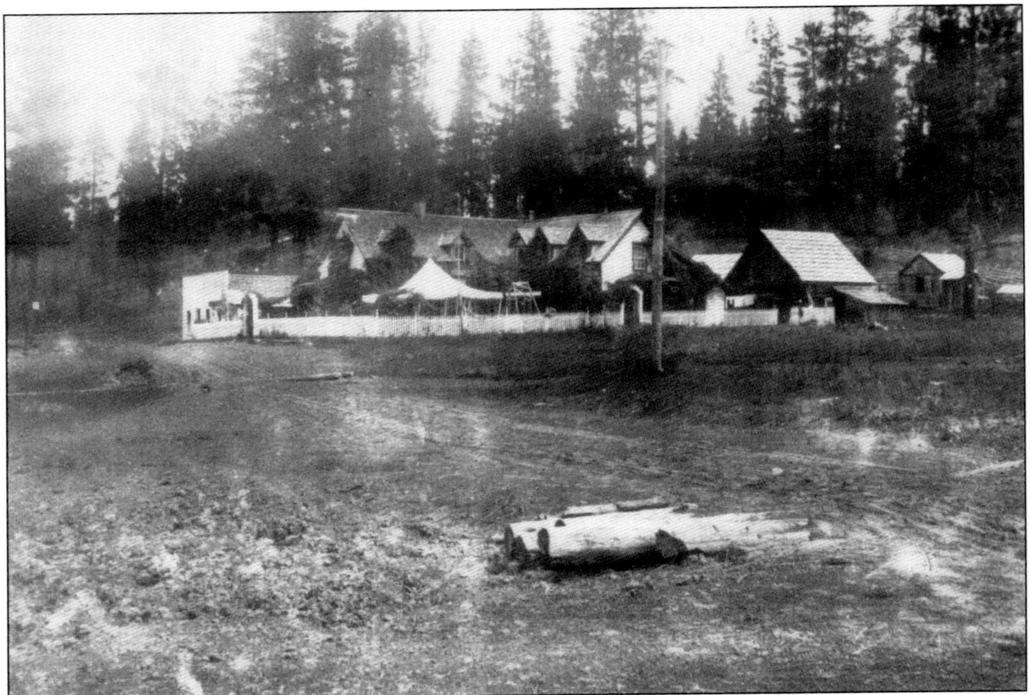

The famous Austin House was a popular lunch and stage stop for many years during and prior to passenger service on the Sumpter Valley Railway. (Baker County Library, Baker City, Oregon, Image No. 1981.1.2084/LT263B.)

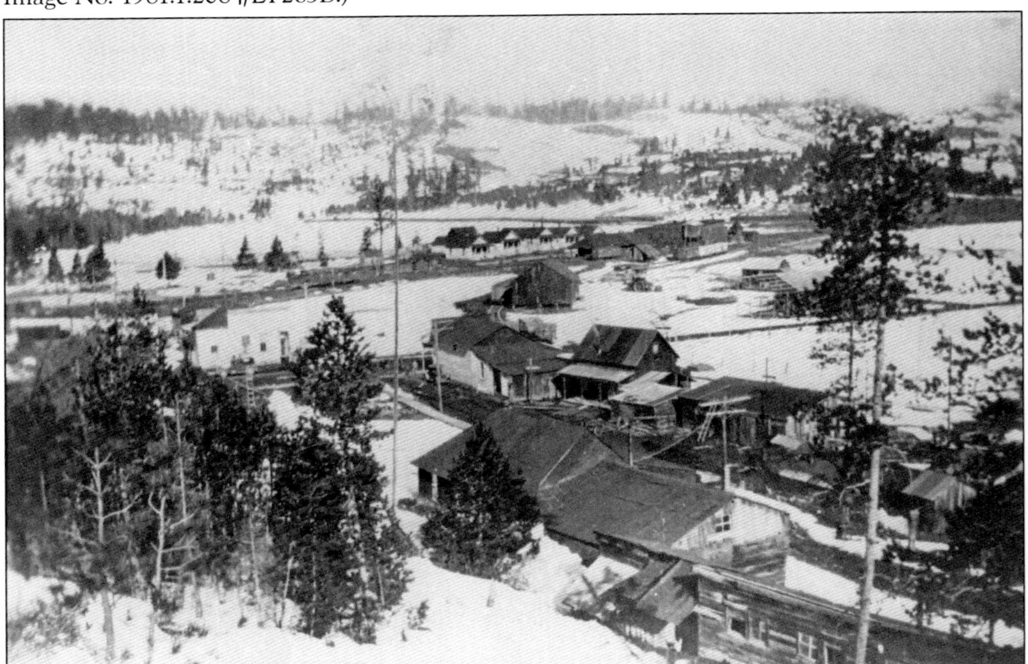

This photograph of a winter day around 1912 in Austin looks toward the Sumpter Valley Railway depot and service facilities. (Ron Harr Collection; Sumpter Valley Railroad Restoration, Inc.)

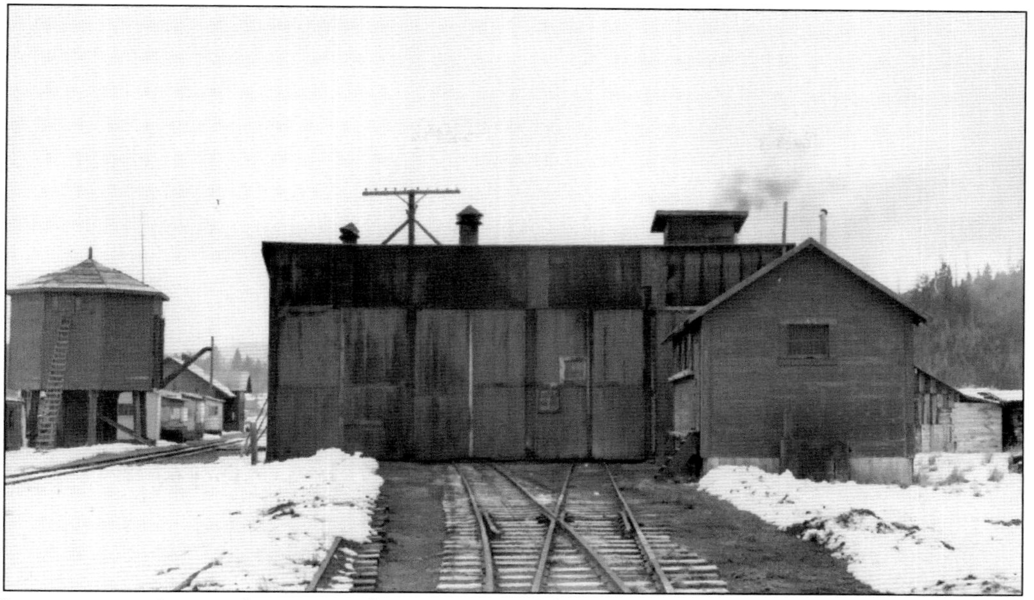

It is winter in Austin, the western division point of the Sumpter Valley Railway in 1946. Pictured is the three-stall engine house along the mainline; the water tower and depot are on the left. (H. R. Griffiths Collection; Sumpter Valley Railroad Restoration, Inc.)

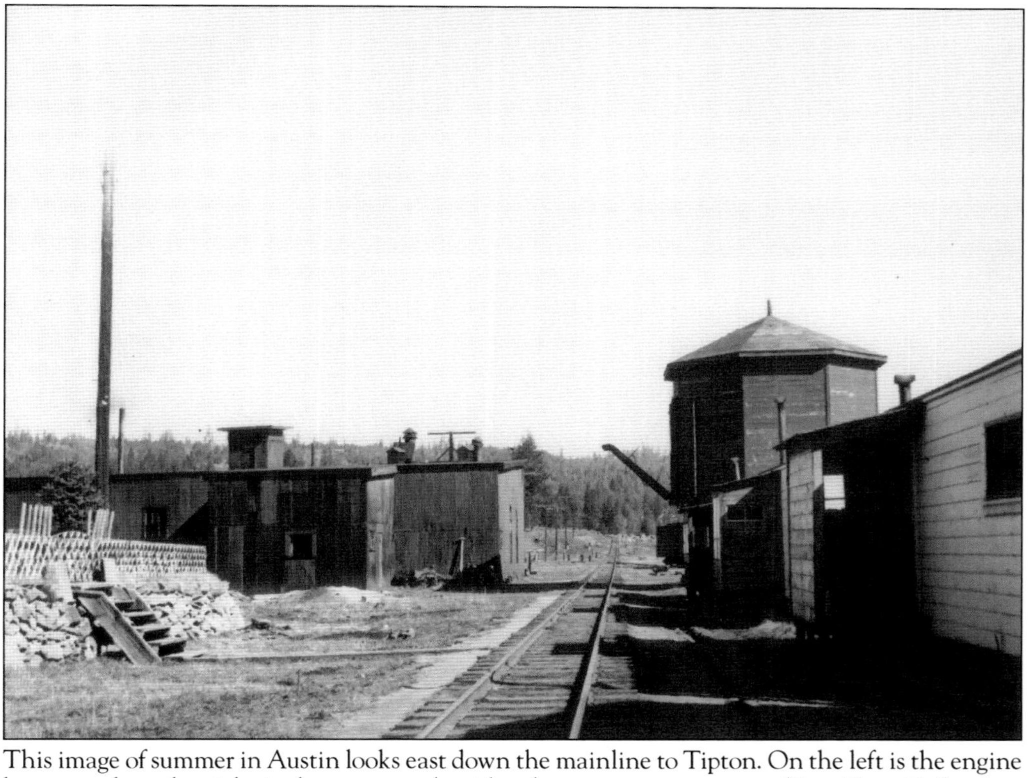

This image of summer in Austin looks east down the mainline to Tipton. On the left is the engine house, and on the right is the water tank with other support structures. (Ron Harr Collection; Sumpter Valley Railroad Restoration, Inc.)

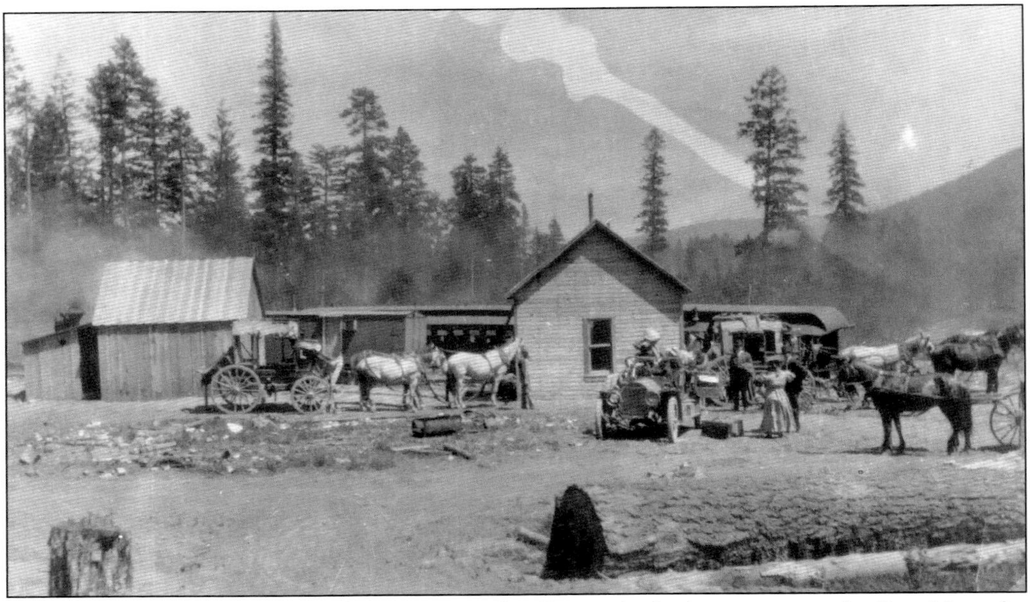

It is 1910, and a passenger train has just arrived at Dixie, the highest point on the line. Note the stagecoaches and the Pierce touring car awaiting the train's arrival. (McCord Collection; Baker County Library, Baker City, Oregon.)

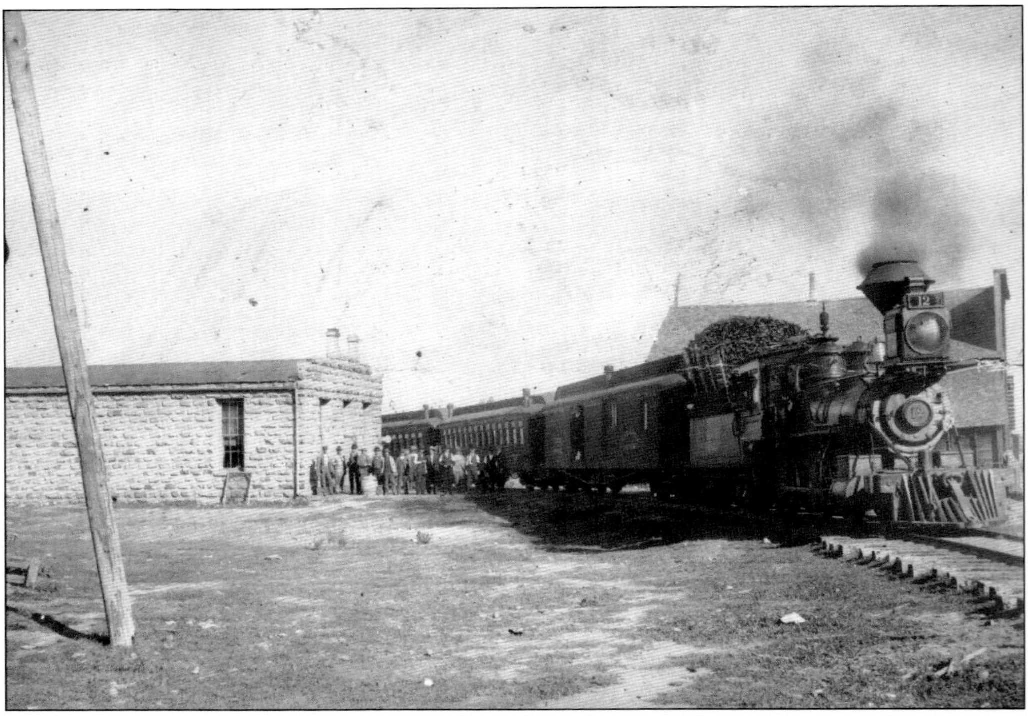

Locomotive No. 12, a Brooks Mogul (2-6-0), stops in front of the South Baker Office Building with an up-bound train for Sumpter between 1903 and 1906. (Oregon Historical Society, Negative No. OrHi3836.)

Four

Renumbering, Prairie City, and New Equipment (1907–1917)

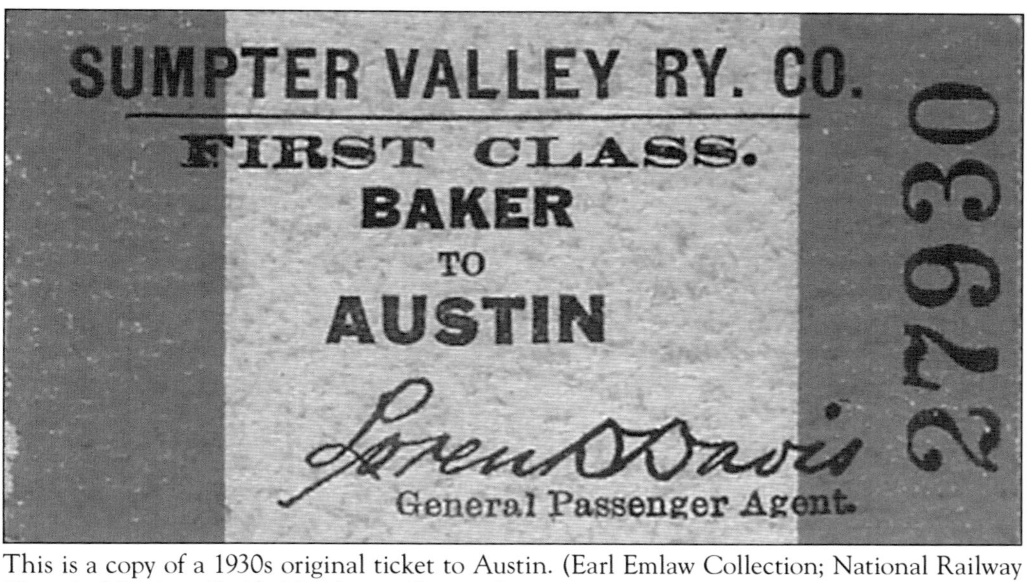

This is a copy of a 1930s original ticket to Austin. (Earl Emlaw Collection; National Railway Historical Society, Pacific Northwest Chapter.)

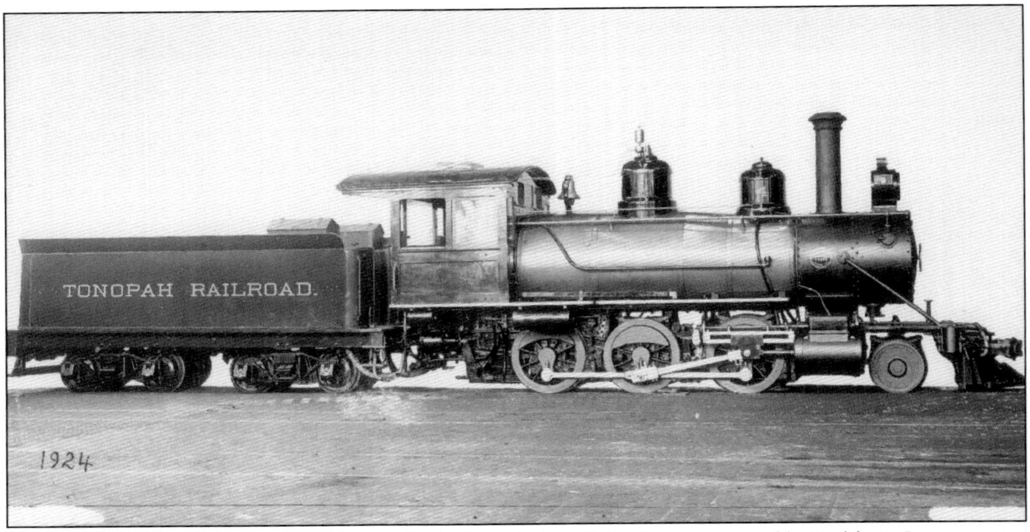

This is a builder's photograph of Tonopah Railroad Mogul No. 4, constructed by Baldwin Locomotive Works in 1904. The Sumpter Valley Railway retained the original number when the locomotive was purchased from the Tonopah Railroad in 1906. (H. L. Broadbelt from original Baldwin Railroad negative; Sumpter Valley Railroad Restoration, Inc.)

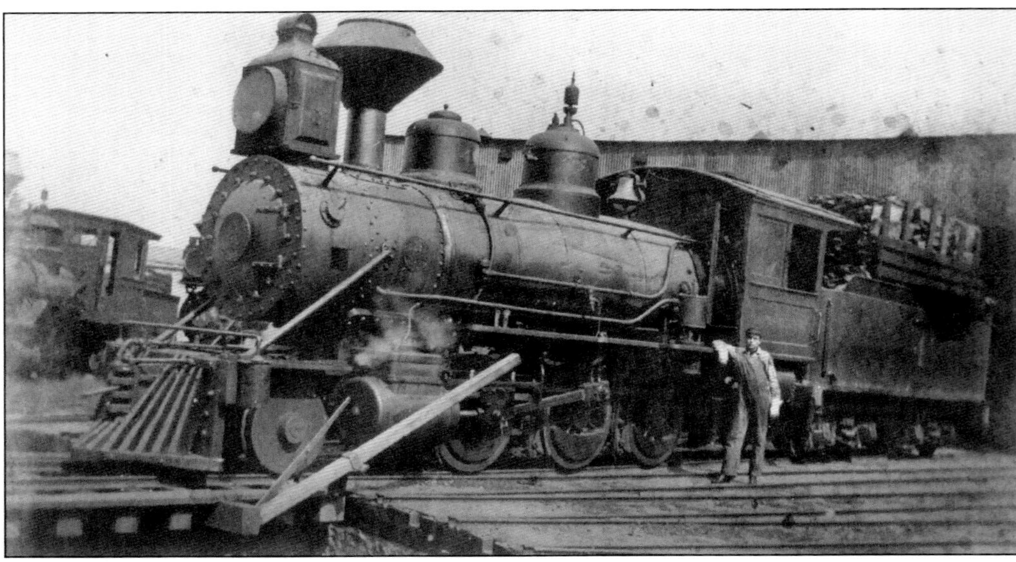

Locomotive No. 4 is captured outside the roundhouse at South Baker. Note the Armstrong turntable. A diamond stack has replaced the shotgun stack, as she has been converted to a wood burner. The locomotive now sports the older-style box headlight. Compared to the crewman, the size of the Tonopah Moguls is clearly shown. (Photograph by Bill Roundy, Ron Harr Collection; Sumpter Valley Railroad Restoration, Inc.)

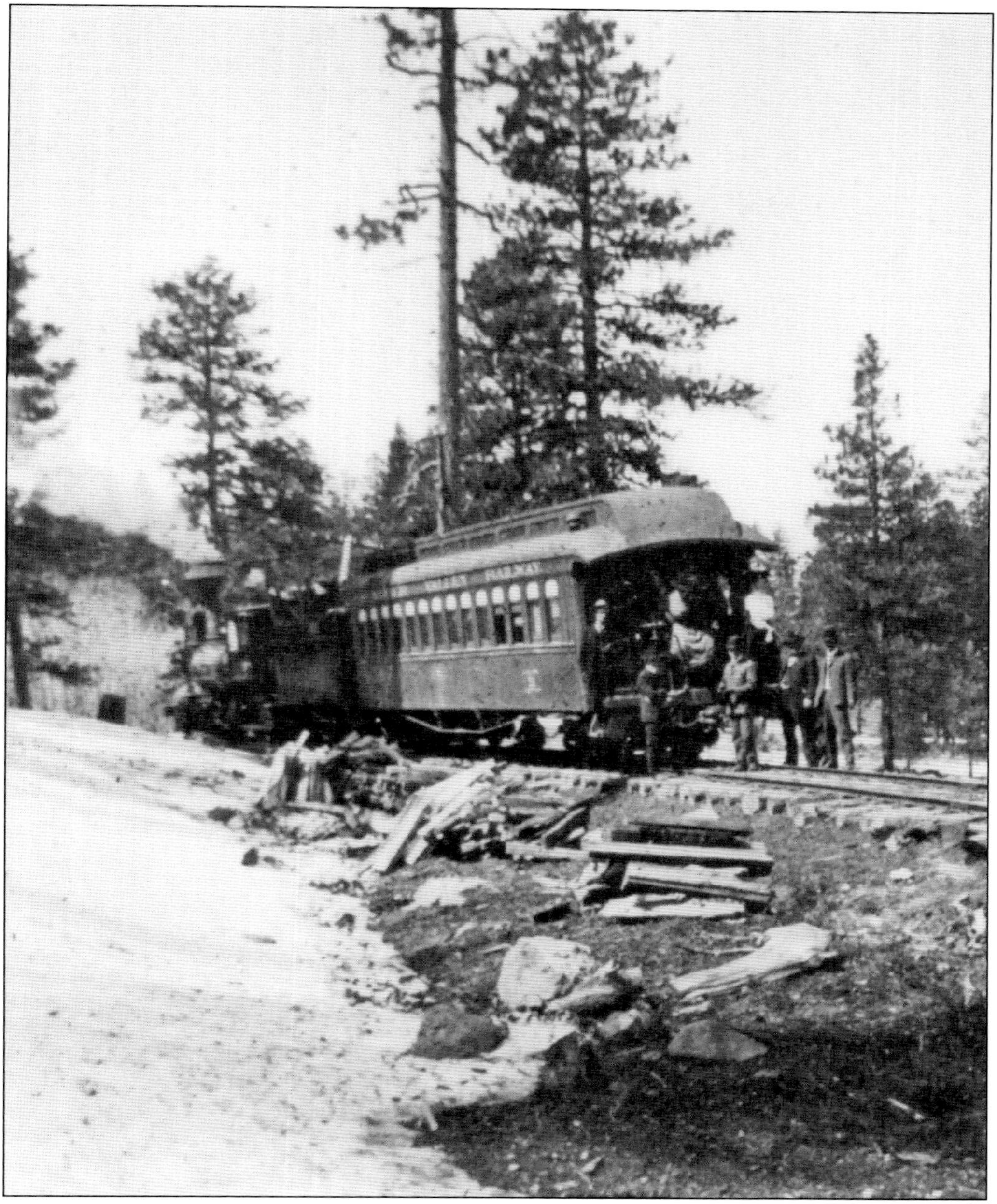

The Eccles family poses on the platform of their excursion train near Dixie around 1911. The engine is most likely Mogul No. 1, and the coach is No. 21. (Ron Harr Collection; Sumpter Valley Railroad Restoration, Inc.)

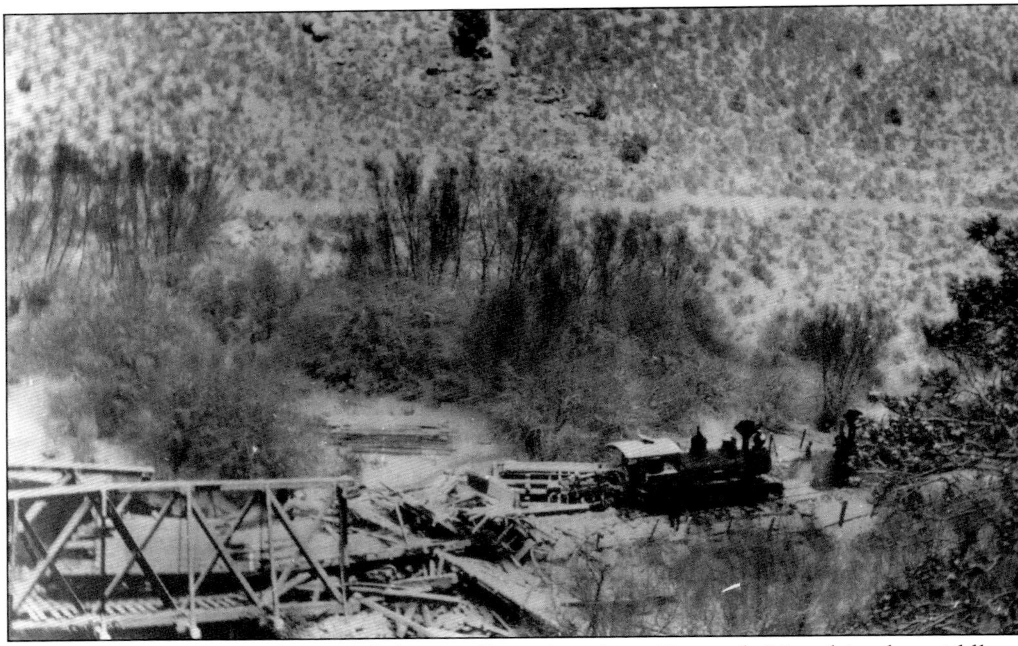

The old Howe truss bridge at Salisbury collapsed under a Tonopah Mogul in the middle of winter. The two wood-burners shown on the right are struggling to haul the damaged engine out of the Powder River and back onto the rails. (Ron Harr Collection; Sumpter Valley Railroad Restoration, Inc.)

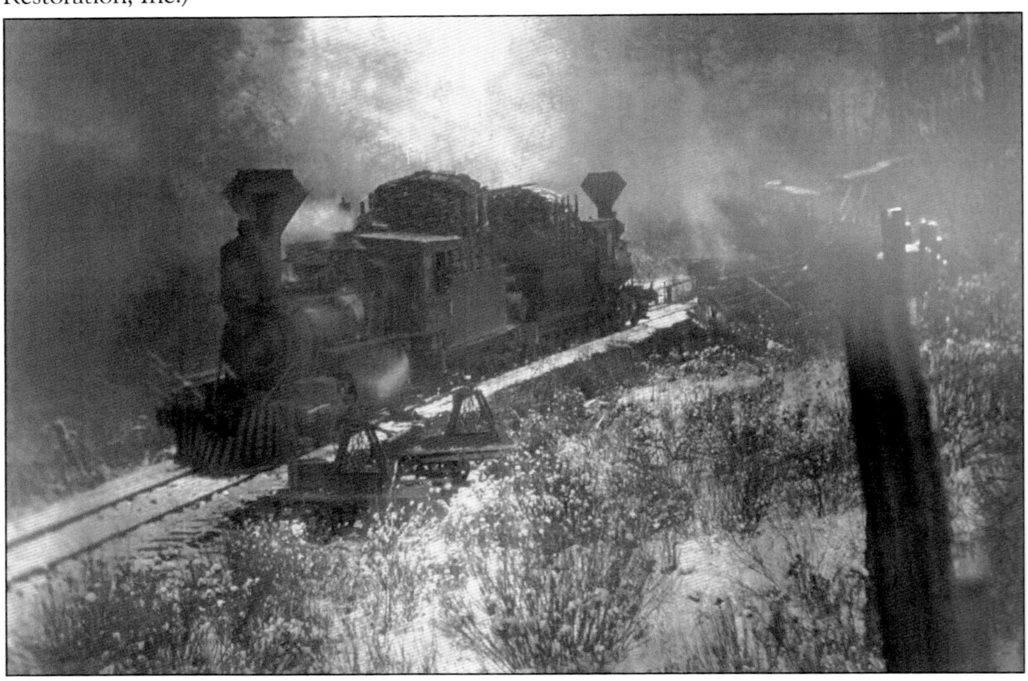

This is another photograph of the two locomotives that are working to pull the Tonopah Mogul out of the Powder River at Salisbury. (Ron Harr Collection; Sumpter Valley Railroad Restoration, Inc.)

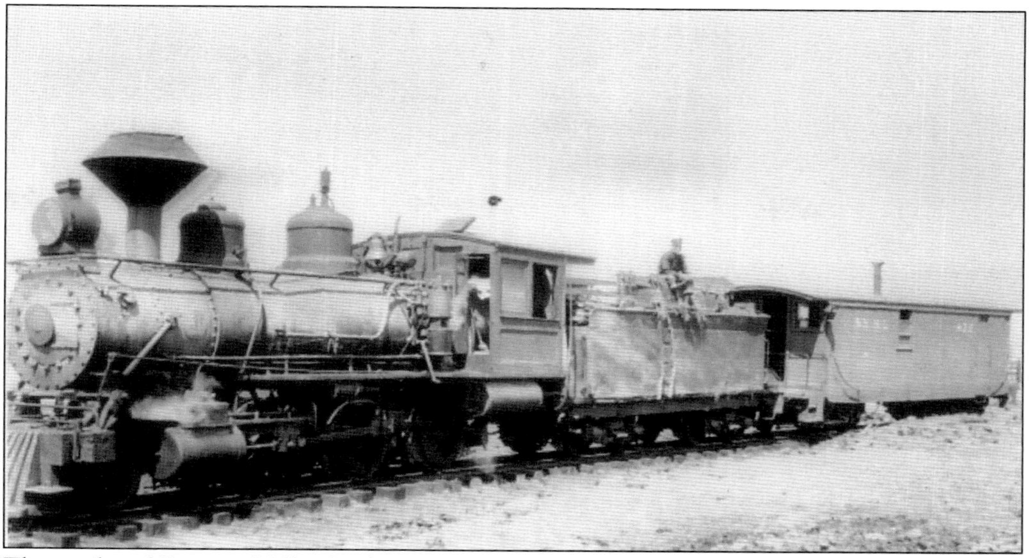

The tender of Sumpter Valley Railway's second No. 1, a former Tonopah Railroad Mogul, bears the signs of a very recent derailment. The unusual car behind the locomotive is a former Utah and Northern waycar that has been rebuilt into work caboose No. 072. (Ron Harr Collection; Sumpter Valley Railroad Restoration, Inc.)

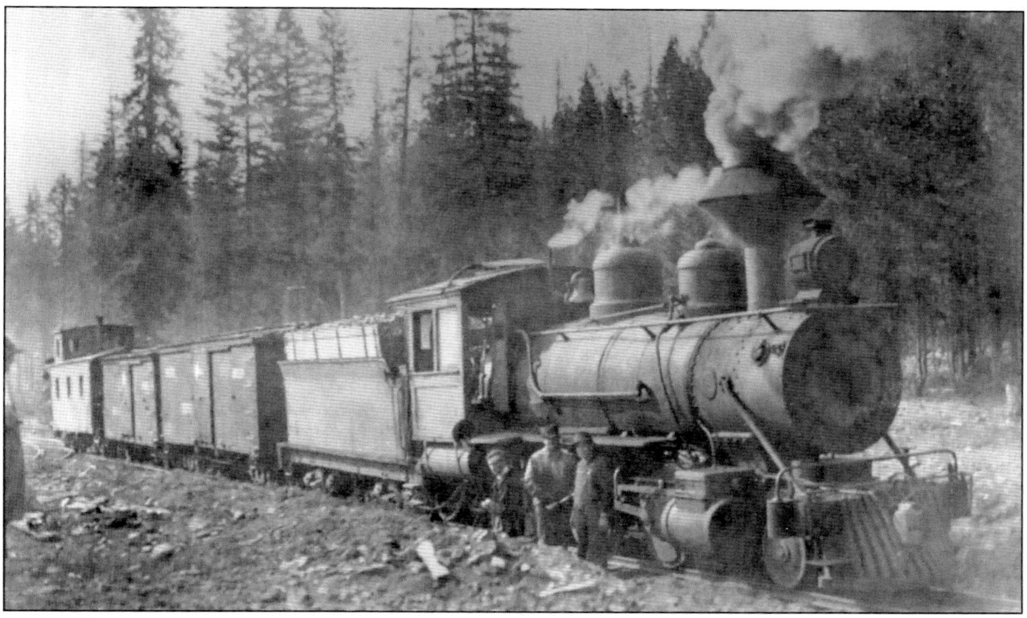

Tonopah No. 4 pauses at Bridge Creek with a short freight around 1910. Note that No. 4 appears to be burning coal rather than the usual wood. The story is that Emmett Endecott took this picture just after proposing to his future wife (just visible on the left). (Photograph by Emmett Endecott, Elvin Endecott Collection; Casey Carlson.)

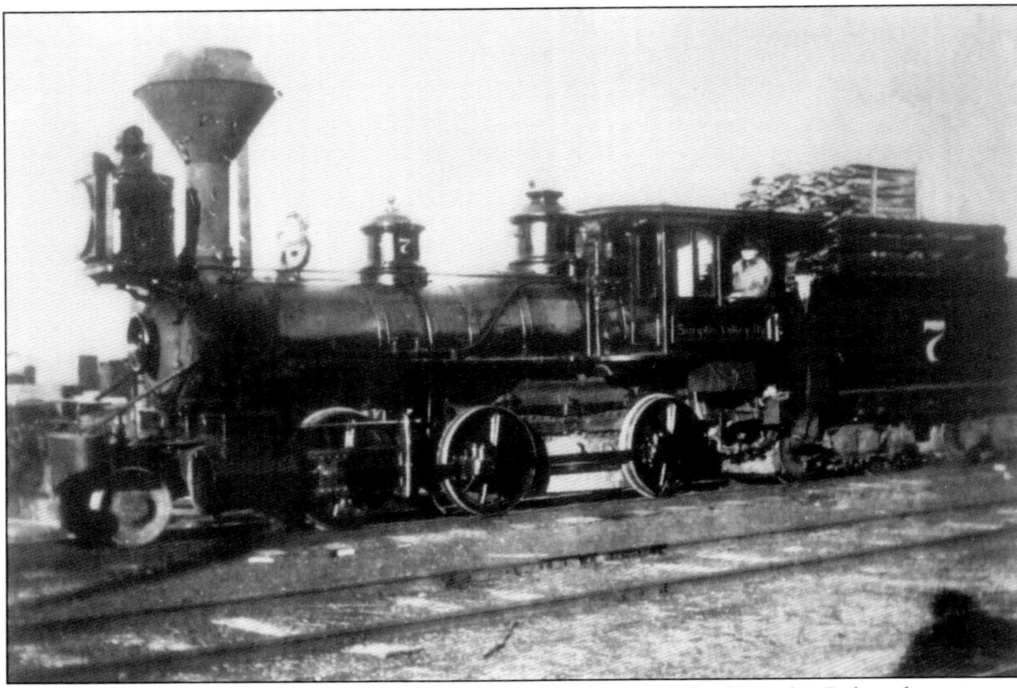

Brooks Mogul No. 7 rests in the South Baker yard. She was rebuilt at the Baker shops into a switcher after 1906; note the step pilot rather than the more traditional road pilot. (Ron Harr Collection; Sumpter Valley Railroad Restoration, Inc.)

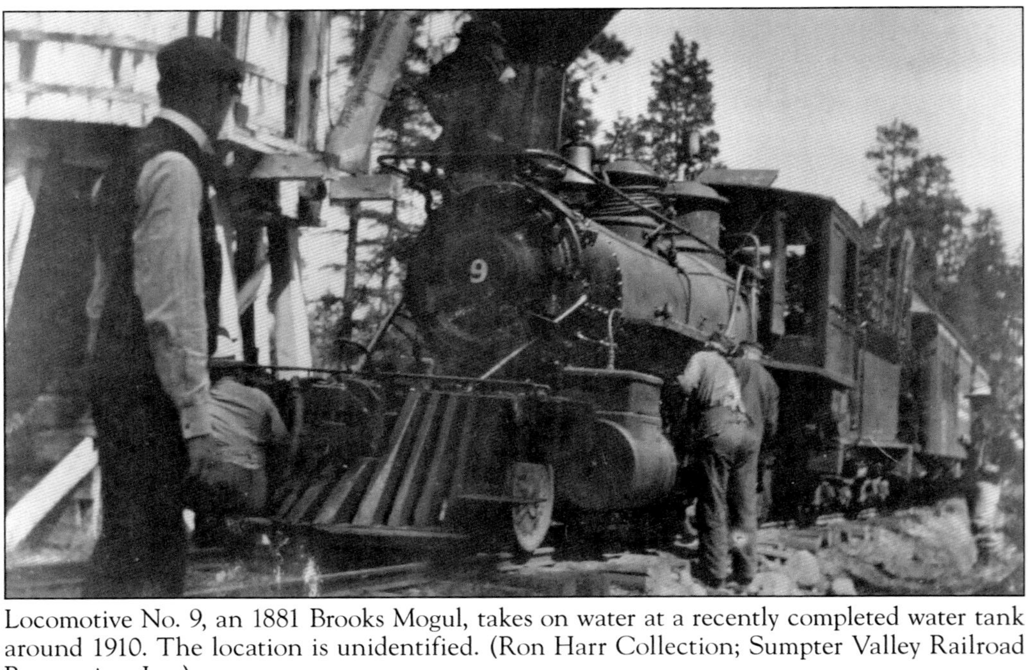

Locomotive No. 9, an 1881 Brooks Mogul, takes on water at a recently completed water tank around 1910. The location is unidentified. (Ron Harr Collection; Sumpter Valley Railroad Restoration, Inc.)

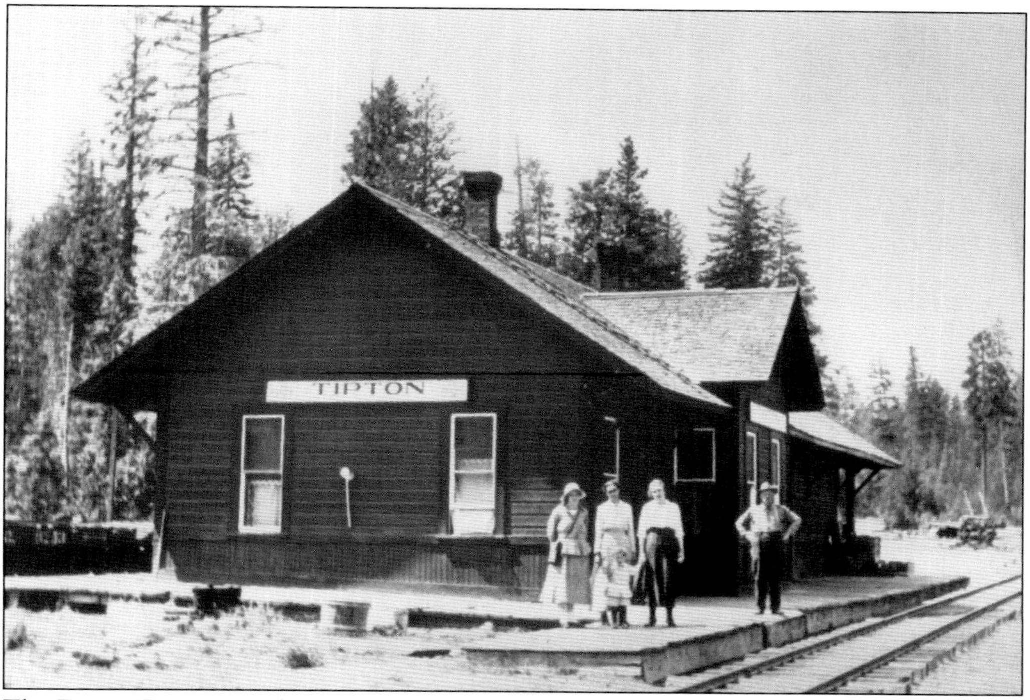

The Tipton Depot served as a station agent location for the Greenhorn mines as well as the local timber interests and cattle ranches. Due to the unballasted condition of the mainline, this photograph was most likely taken shortly after the building's completion in 1904. (Ron Harr Collection; Sumpter Valley Railroad Restoration, Inc.)

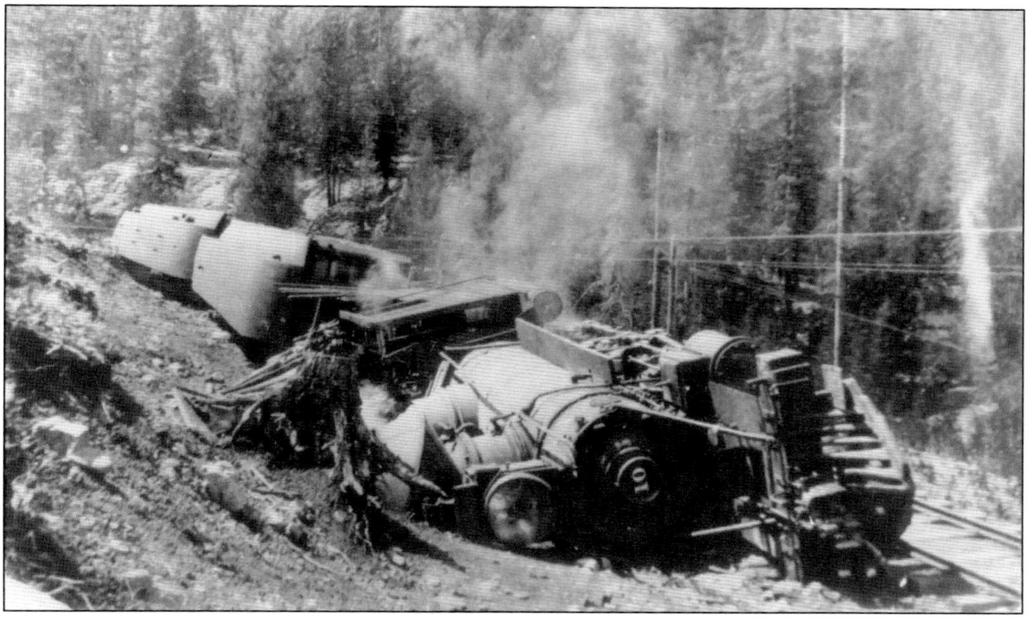

Soft track plagued the Sumpter Valley Railway every spring, and 1915 was no exception. Consolidation No. 10 and her passenger train are on their sides at Dixie on this March day. (Ron Harr Collection; Sumpter Valley Railroad Restoration, Inc.)

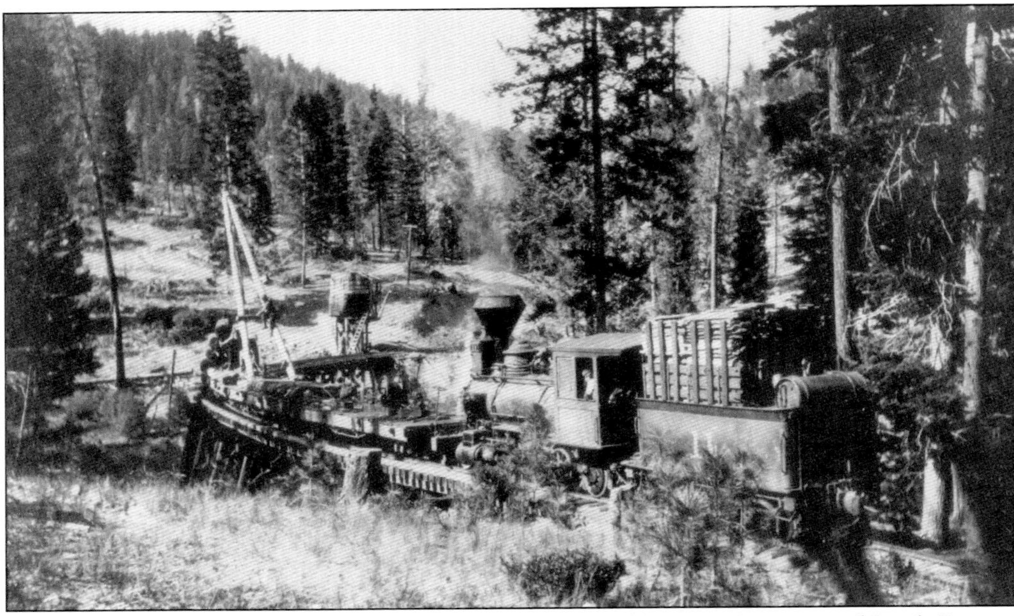

Consolidation No. 11 is pictured at Johnson Jump-off, located between Sumpter and Larch Summit, with a work train sometime after 1906. No. 11 was purchased from the Rio Grande Western in 1901. (Ron Harr Collection; Sumpter Valley Railroad Restoration, Inc.)

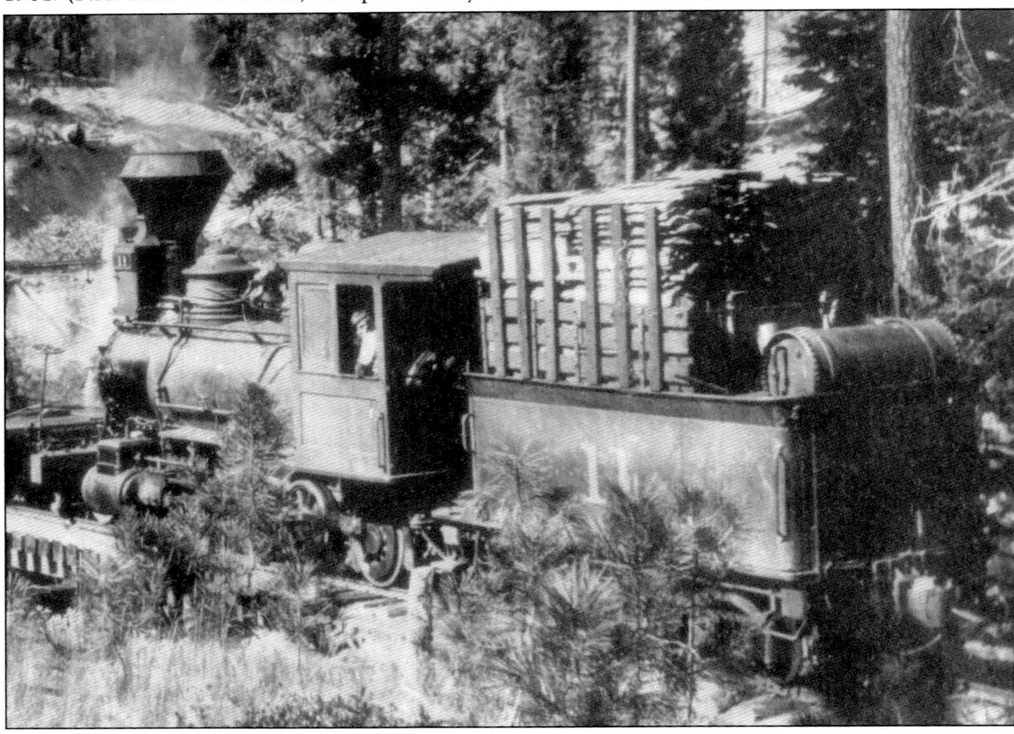

A close-up of No. 11 shows the wood loads for which the Sumpter Valley Railway was legendary. On a run from South Baker to Prairie City, a locomotive could use as much as 16 cords of wood. (Ron Harr Collection; Sumpter Valley Railroad Restoration, Inc.)

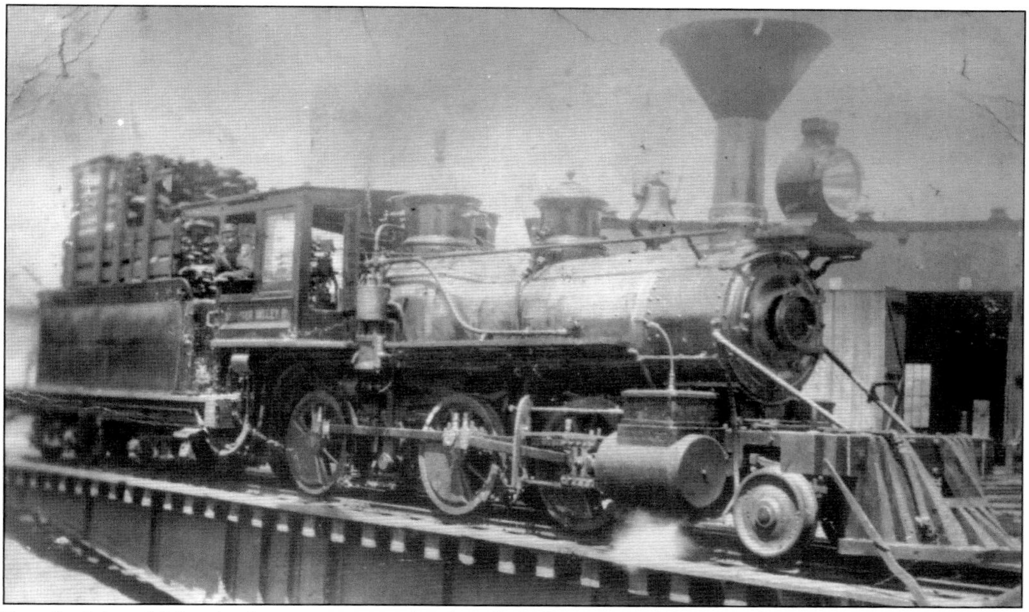

Brooks Mogul No. 6 takes a turn on the South Baker turntable. This locomotive was acquired from the Utah and Northern in 1903 and carried the same number through her entire life at the Sumpter Valley Railway. (Photograph by Bruce Morehead, Ron Harr Collection; Sumpter Valley Railroad Restoration, Inc.)

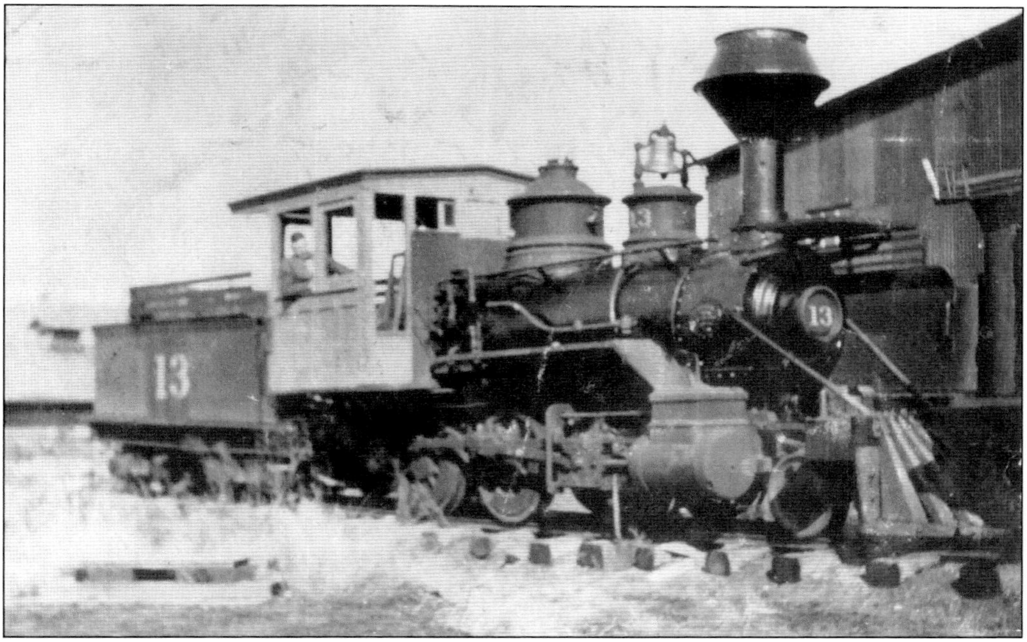

Locomotive No. 13 sits idle beside the South Baker roundhouse around 1910. This locomotive was originally from the Minneapolis, Lyndale, and Minnetonka Railroad and was purchased by the Sumpter Valley Railway in 1893. The locomotive proved to be too light for anything but the lightest work train duties and was scrapped in 1915. (Ron Harr Collection; Sumpter Valley Railroad Restoration, Inc.)

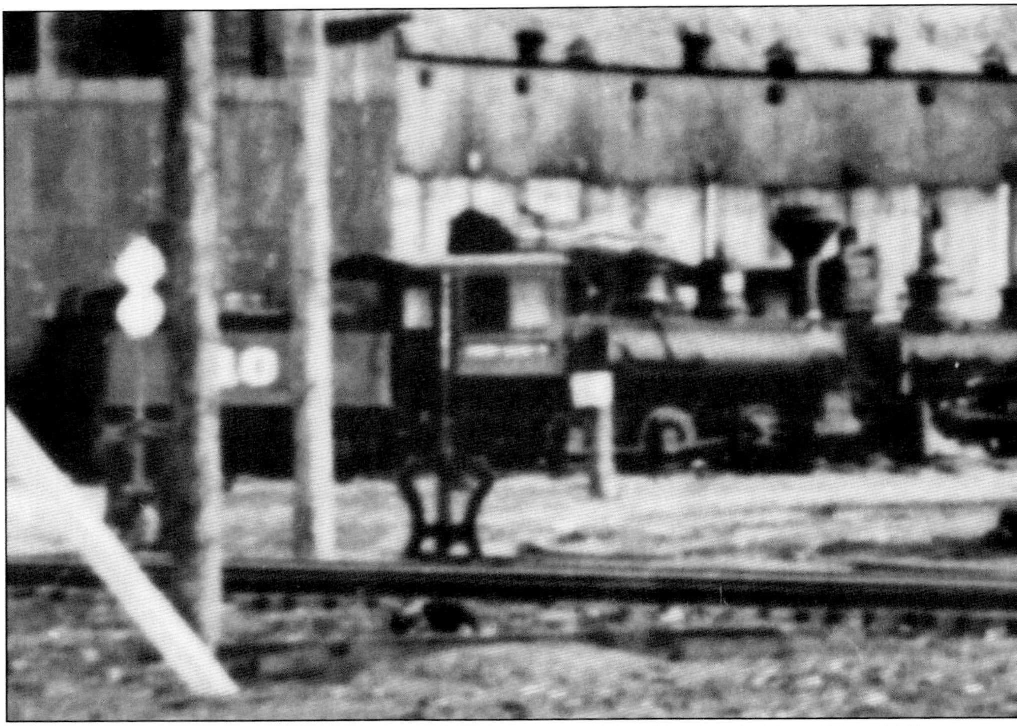

This is the only known photograph of Locomotive No. 10, the "Wharf Rat." She was an ex–Connotton Valley 0-6-0T that was rebuilt by the San Pete Railroad into a Mogul. Never a very effective engine, she spent a good deal of her life as a stationary steam plant. (Ron Harr Collection; Sumpter Valley Railroad Restoration, Inc.)

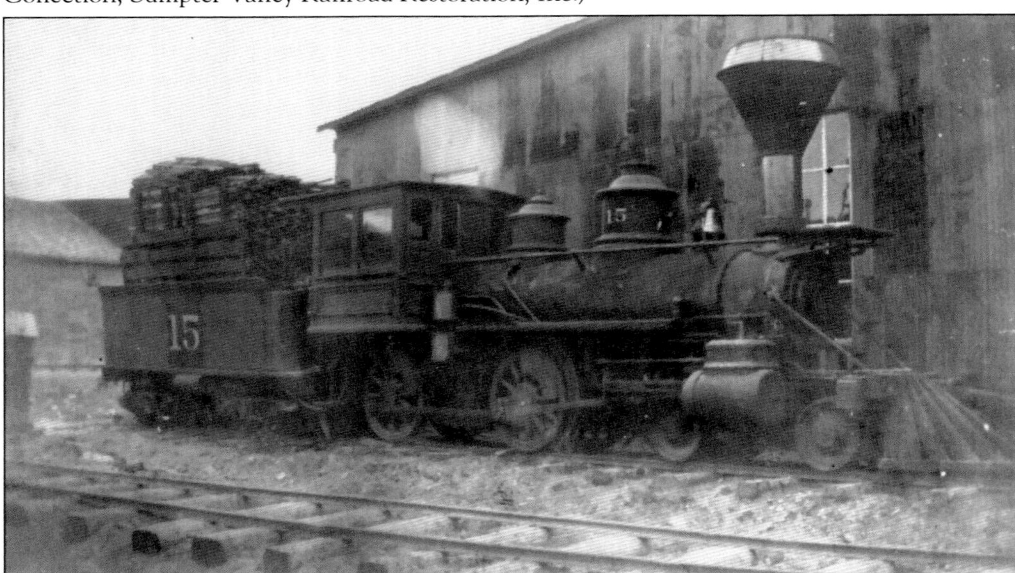

Locomotive No. 15, a Baldwin 4-4-0, serves as a boiler for the roundhouse in South Baker around 1906. She was purchased from the Utah and Northern in 1890. She was sold to the Eureka-Nevada Line in 1912. (Ron Harr Collection; Sumpter Valley Railroad Restoration, Inc.)

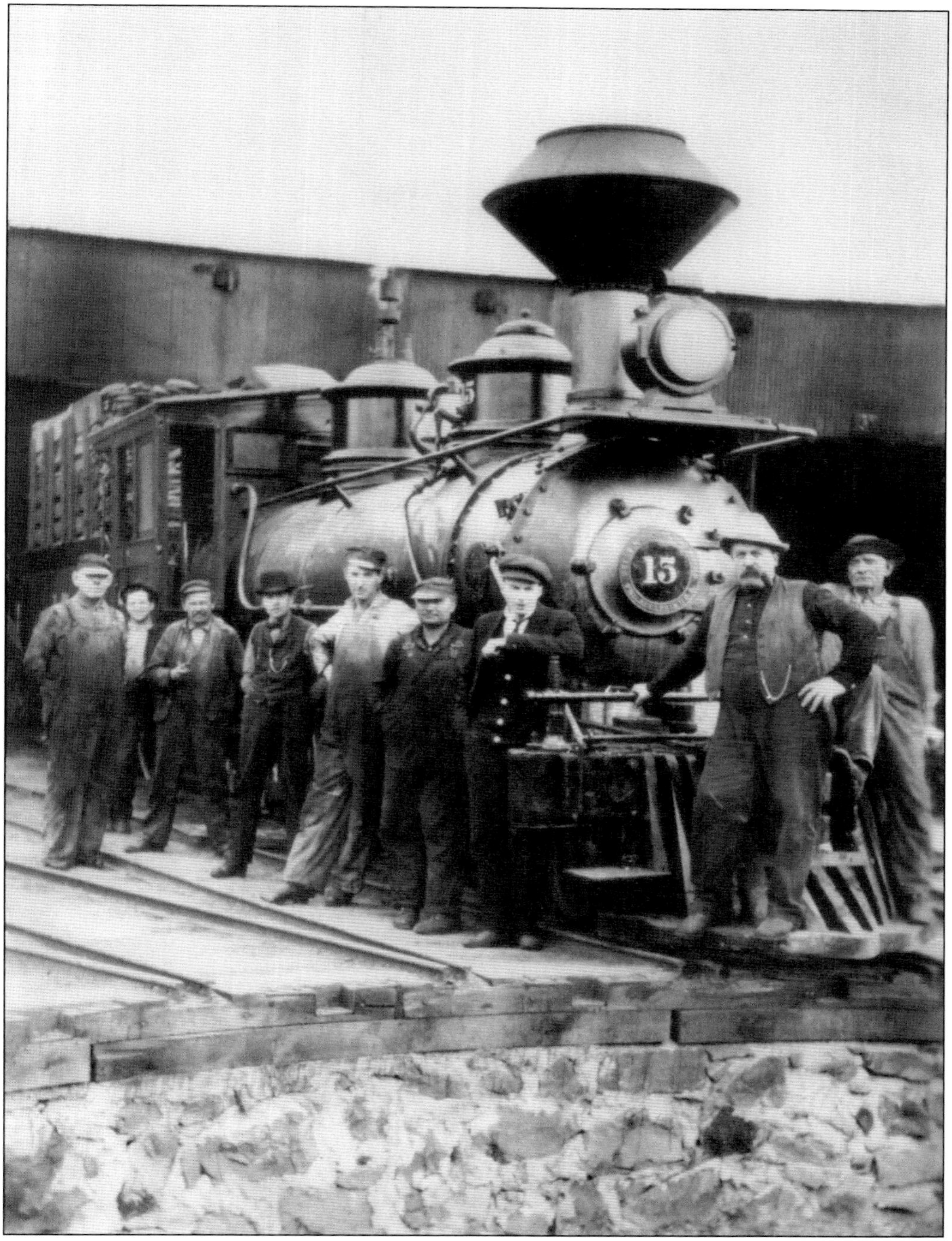

Locomotive No. 15, formerly Alberta Railway and Coal Company No. 7, a Baldwin Consolidation, stands in front of stall 6 of the South Baker roundhouse. She is the backdrop for this photograph of the Sumpter Valley Railway's South Baker shop crew. F. M. Shurtliff stands on the pilot. (F. M. Shurtliff Collection; Sumpter Valley Railroad Restoration, Inc.)

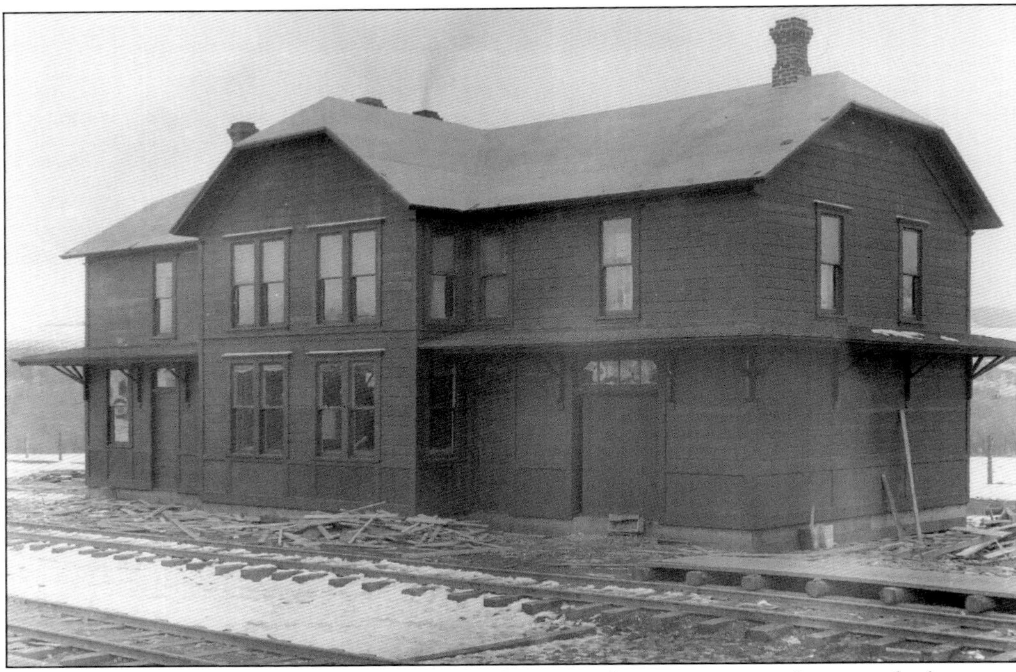

This 1910 photograph shows the Prairie City Depot under construction. It was a dual-purpose building serving both as a station and as the station agent's home. (Ron Harr Collection; Sumpter Valley Railroad Restoration, Inc.)

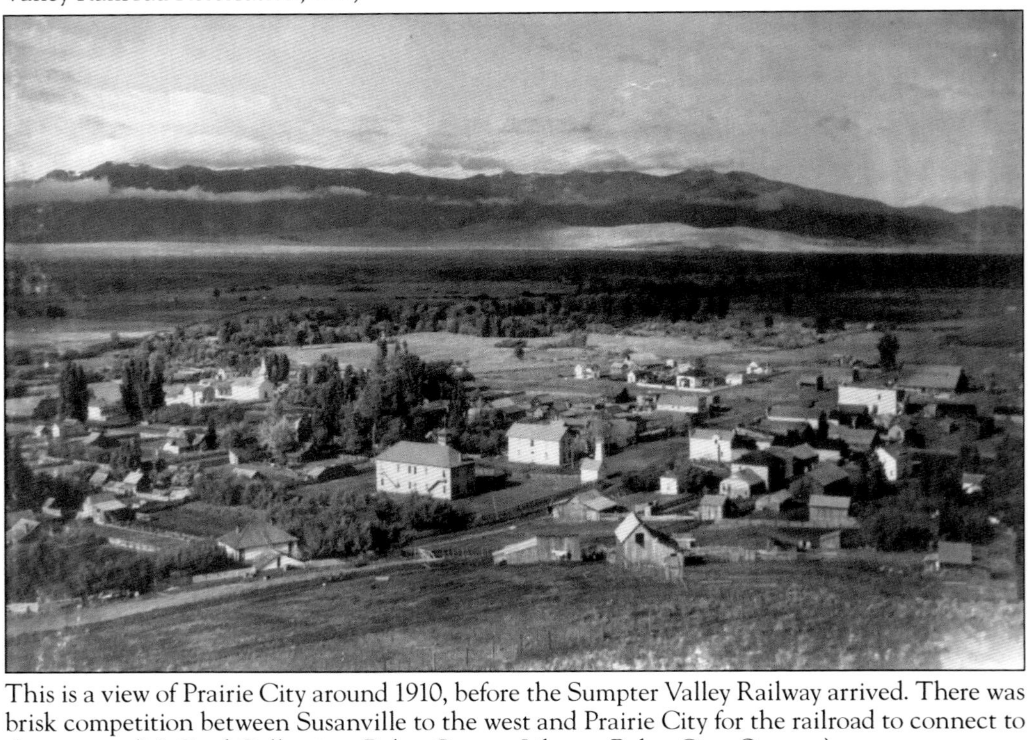

This is a view of Prairie City around 1910, before the Sumpter Valley Railway arrived. There was brisk competition between Susanville to the west and Prairie City for the railroad to connect to their town. (McCord Collection; Baker County Library, Baker City, Oregon.)

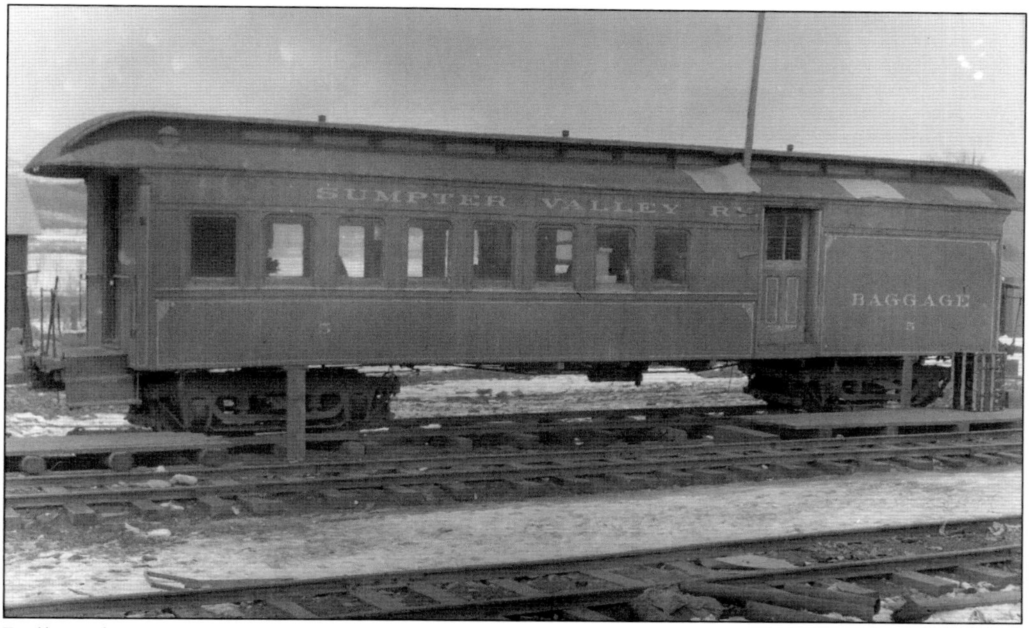

Brill combine No. 5 is serving as the temporary Prairie City Depot while the permanent structure is being built. If you follow the boardwalk to the top of page 62, you will see the complete view of this scene. Note the elaborate scrollwork and striping on the car. (Ron Harr Collection; Sumpter Valley Railroad Restoration, Inc.)

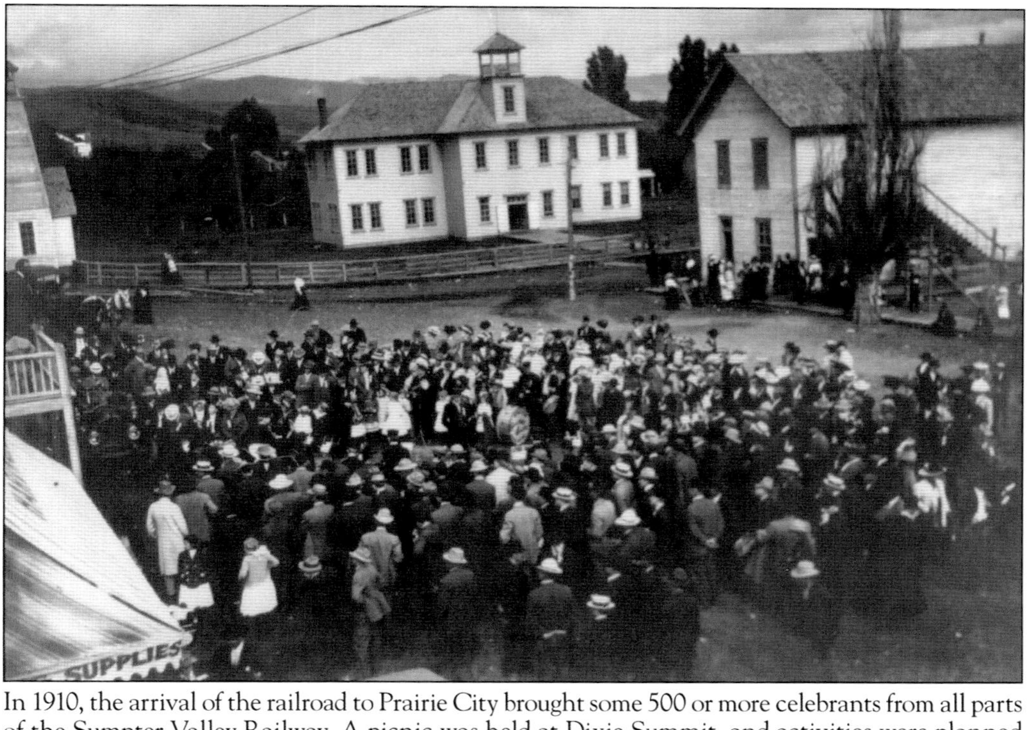

In 1910, the arrival of the railroad to Prairie City brought some 500 or more celebrants from all parts of the Sumpter Valley Railway. A picnic was held at Dixie Summit, and activities were planned in town. (McCord Collection; Baker County Library, Baker City, Oregon, Image No. T-129.)

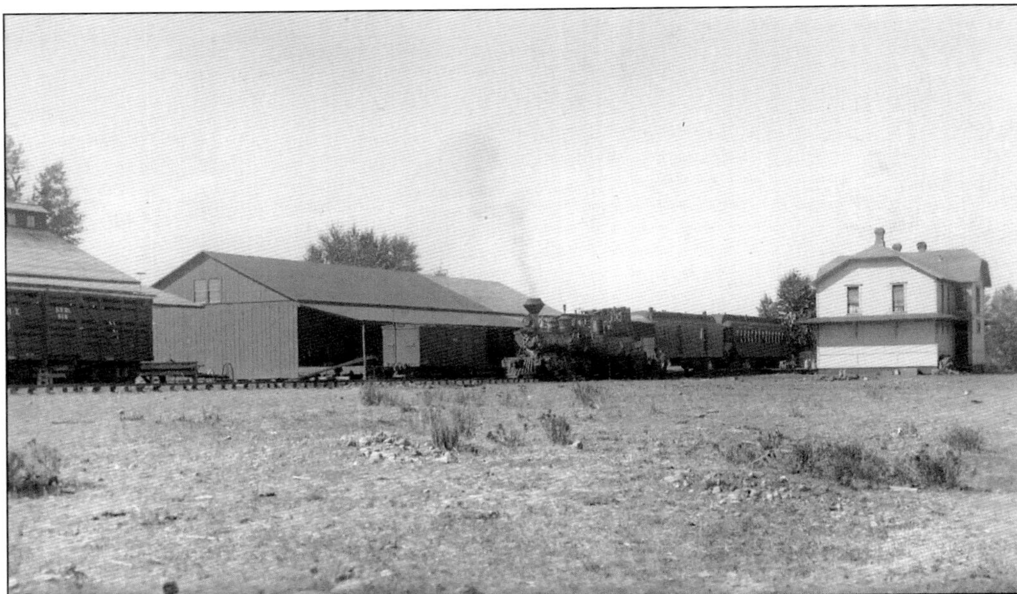

Mogul No. 8 is almost ready to depart Prairie City with the daily passenger train around 1912. This photograph also captures an unidentified boxcar at the Sumpter Valley Railway Warehouse that stood opposite the station, as well as stockcar No. 816 alongside the H. T. Halls Warehouse. (Taylor Rush Collection.)

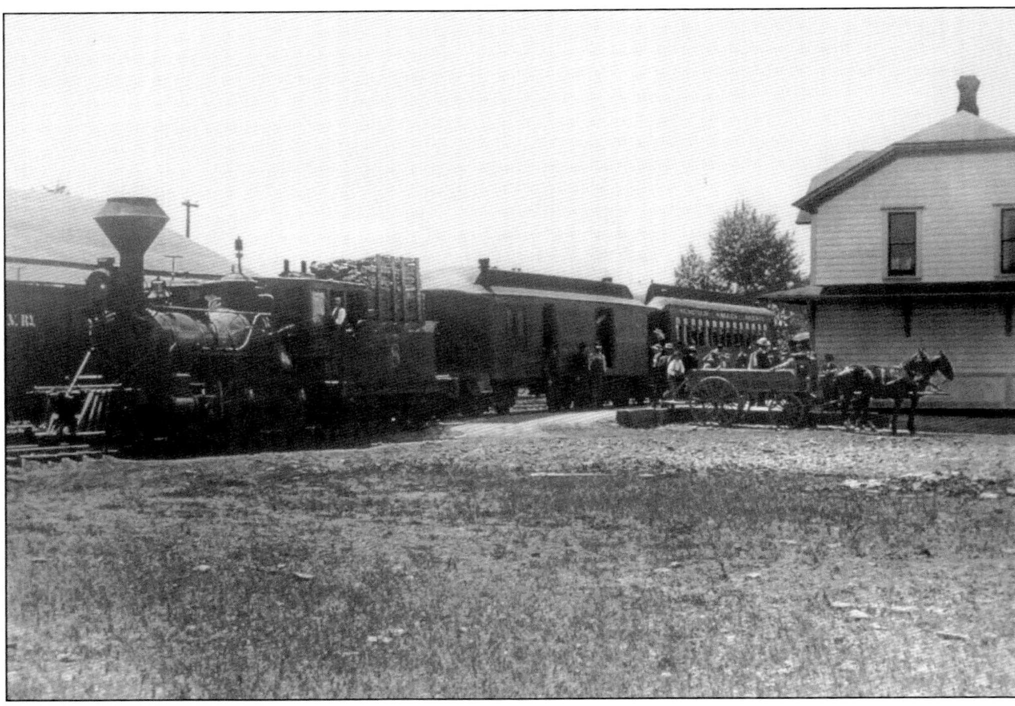

This is another photograph of the Prairie City Depot with the daily "Stump Dodger" passenger train taken earlier the same day. This shows the traffic of passengers boarding and freight being transferred. (Ron Harr Collection; Sumpter Valley Railroad Restoration, Inc.)

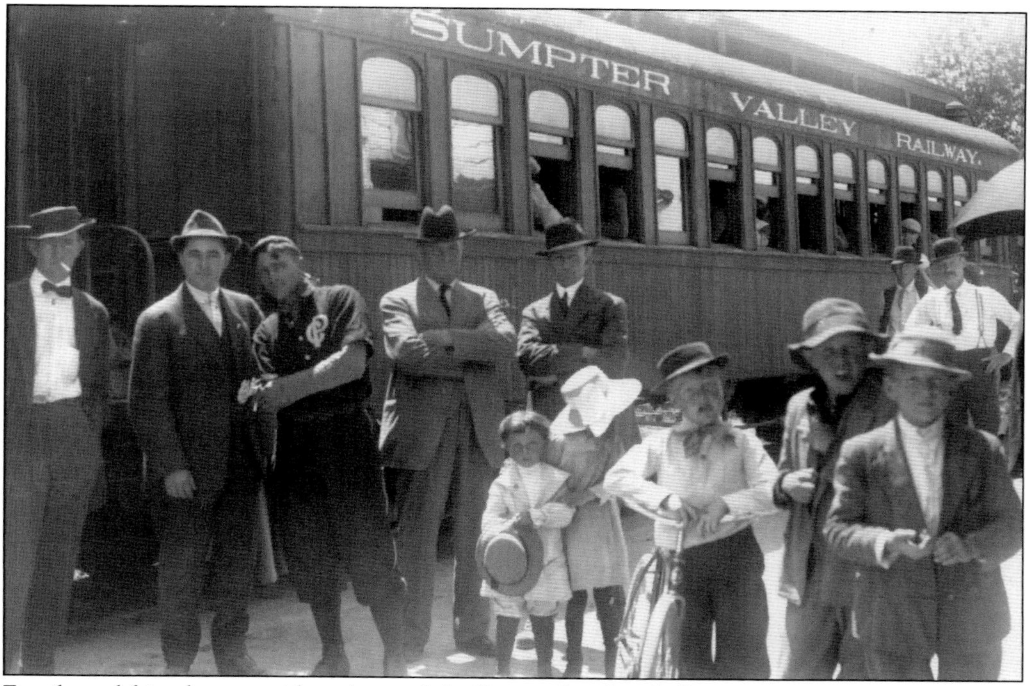

Family and friends pose with a player of the Prairie City baseball team, most likely en route to a game in Sumpter or Baker. As a major source of pride during this era, nearly every community boasted of at least one team, and they would regularly meet and play. (Ron Harr Collection; Sumpter Valley Railroad Restoration, Inc.)

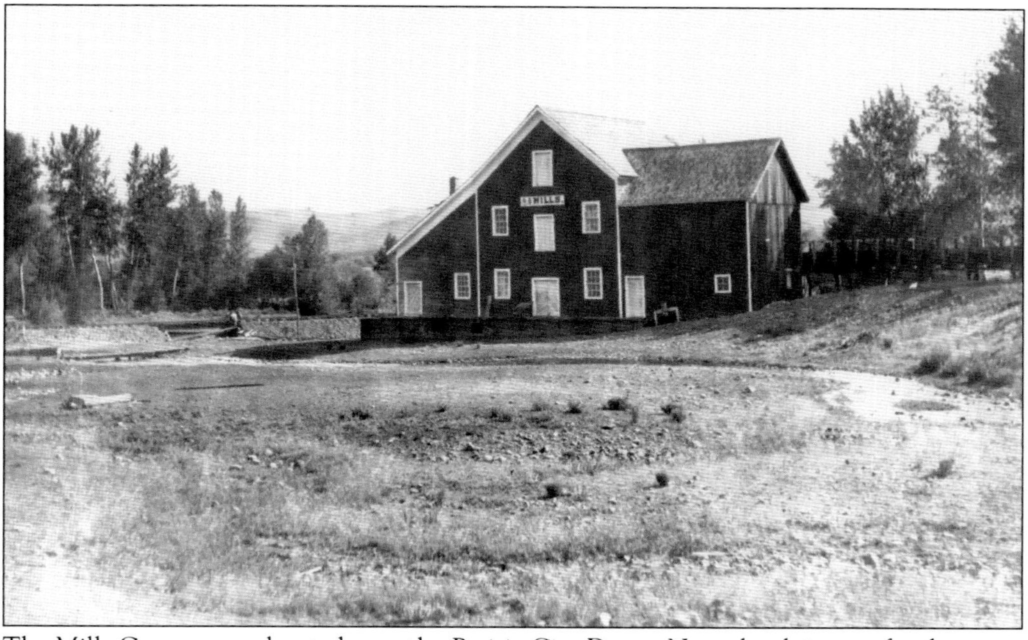

The Mills Granary was located near the Prairie City Depot. Note the sluiceway for the water wheel in the background and the railroad roadbed in the foreground. (McCord Collection; Baker County Library, Baker City, Oregon, Image No. T130.)

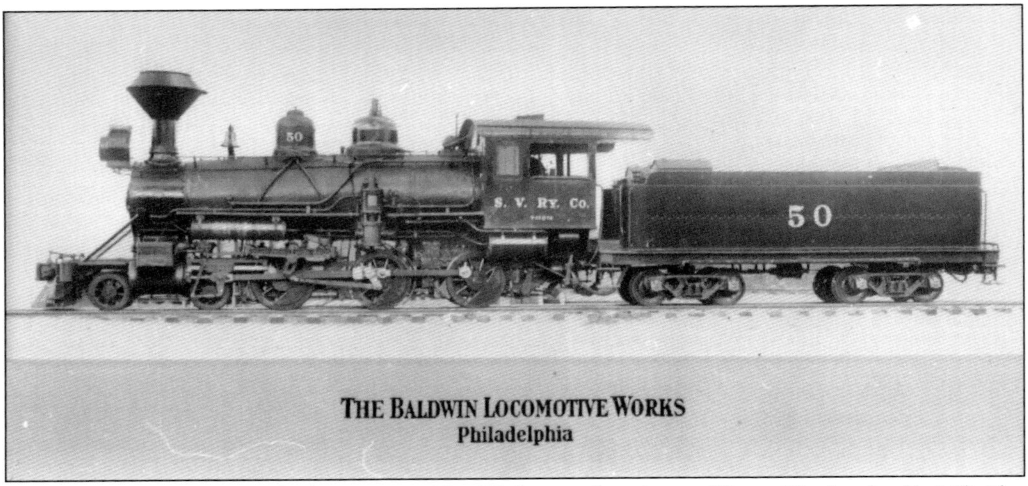

The builder's photograph for locomotive No. 50 shows a handsome 57-ton 10-wheeler (4-6-0). She was purchased new from Baldwin Locomotive Works in 1916 for use in both freight and passenger service. She was sold to the Peruvian government in 1946. (H. L. Broadbelt from original Baldwin Railroad negative; Sumpter Valley Railroad Restoration, Inc.)

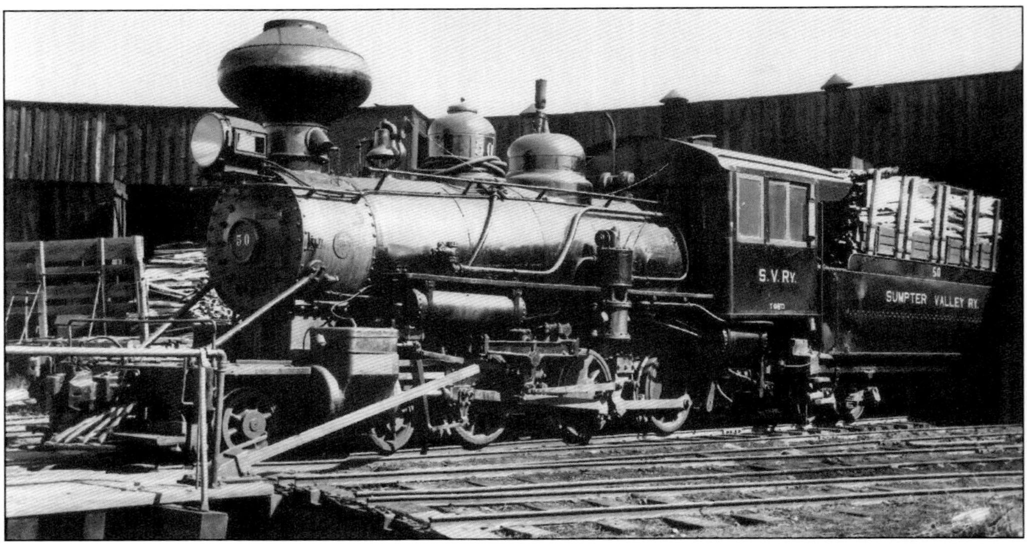

The year is 1934, and No. 50 is fresh out of the shops in South Baker. Besides the addition of the Rushton or "Onion" stack and some minor changes to the pilot and headlight, the locomotive is almost unchanged in appearance from her builder's photograph. (H. R. Griffiths Collection; National Railway Historical Society, Pacific Northwest Chapter.)

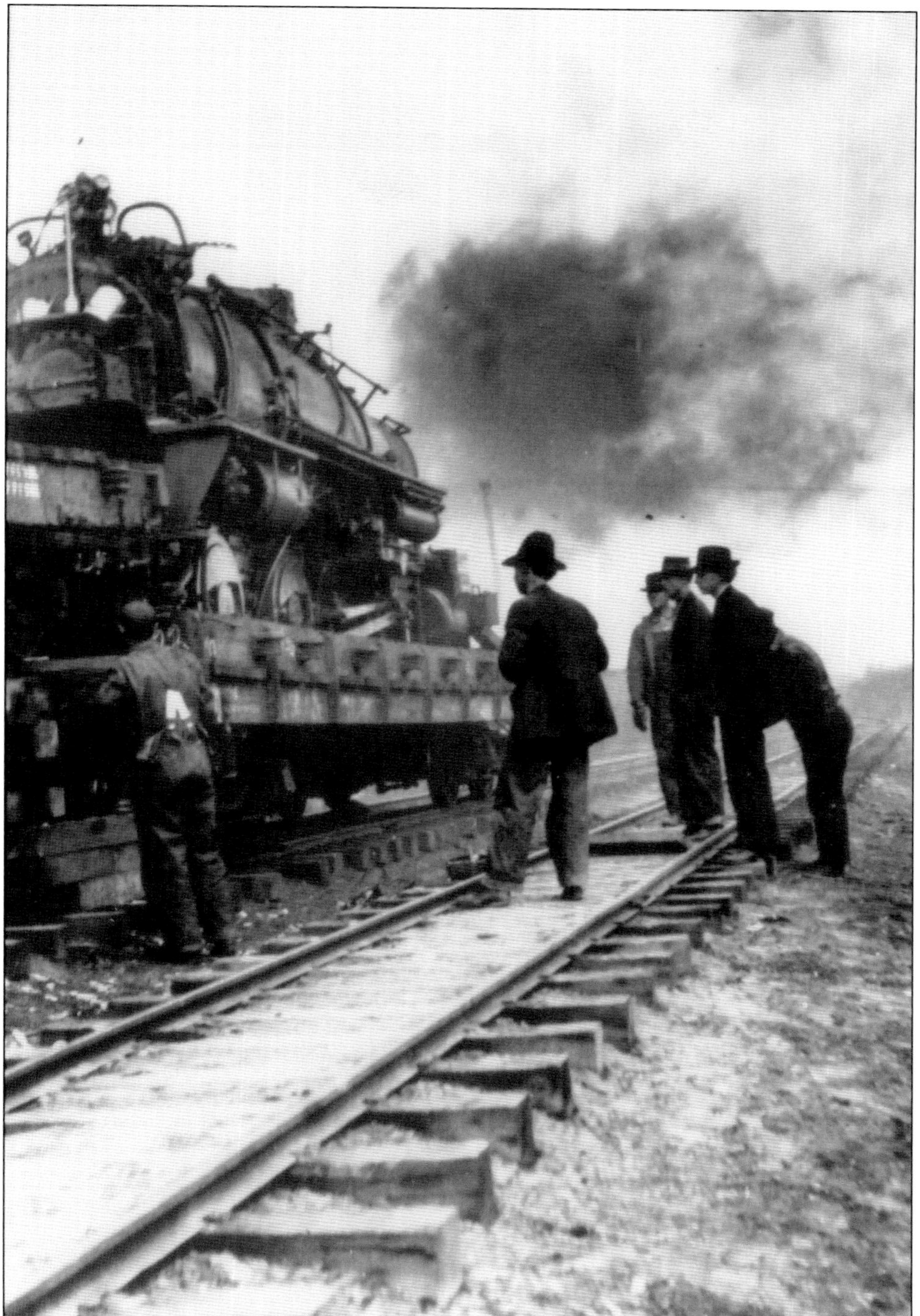

Locomotive No. 50 is being delivered to the Sumpter Valley Railway. Because of her size, she was partially dismantled for shipment. Notice the cribwork that the standard-gauge flatcar is abutted to and the narrow-gauge flatcar being used as an idler. A supervisory crew stands by to insure the job is done correctly. (Elvin Endecott Collection; Casey Carlson.)

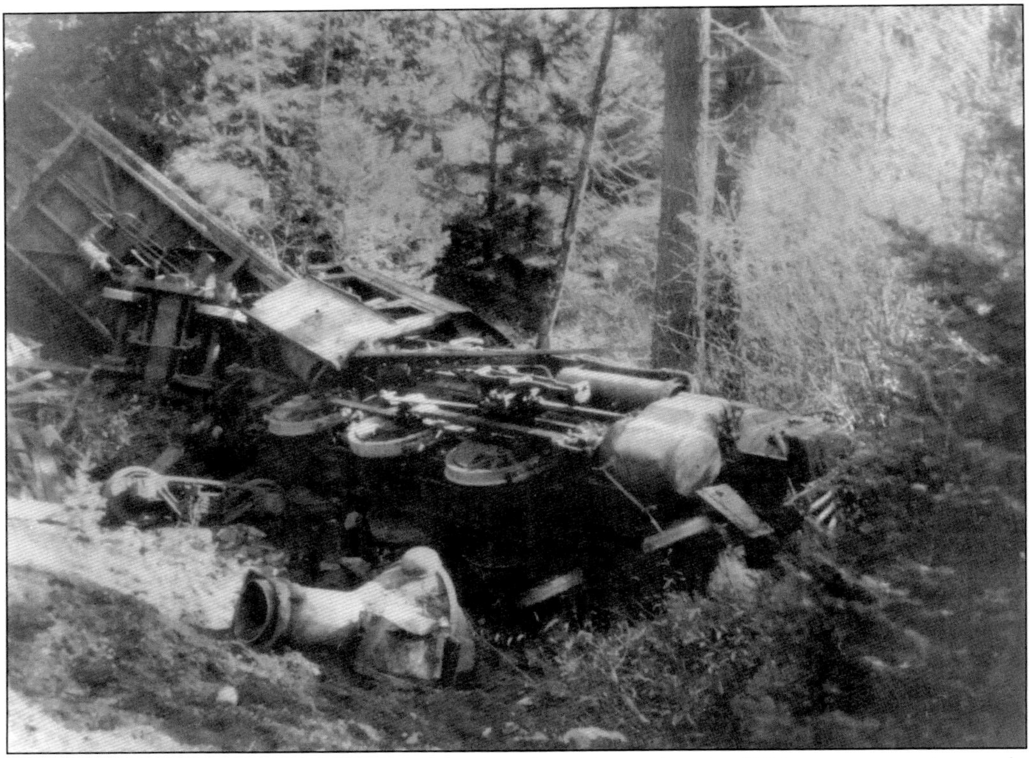

Locomotive No. 50 is on her side near Kights Trestle at Dixie after the 1922 passenger train wreck. There were no fatalities, though a number of people were seriously injured. No. 50 was recovered and rebuilt at the South Baker shops. No. 50's whistle was later found at the wreck site and now resides at the Prairie City Dewitt Museum. (Elvin Endecott Collection; Casey Carlson.)

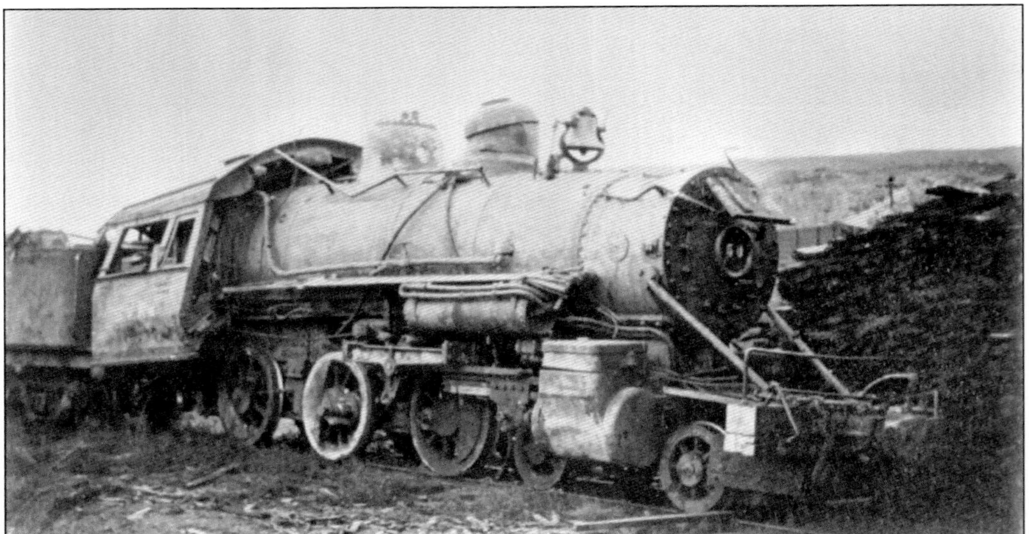

Locomotive No. 50 is shown after being recovered from the Kights Trestle wreck. Note the level of damage, and then see the following photograph after the shops have rebuilt her. (Elvin Endecott Collection; Casey Carlson.)

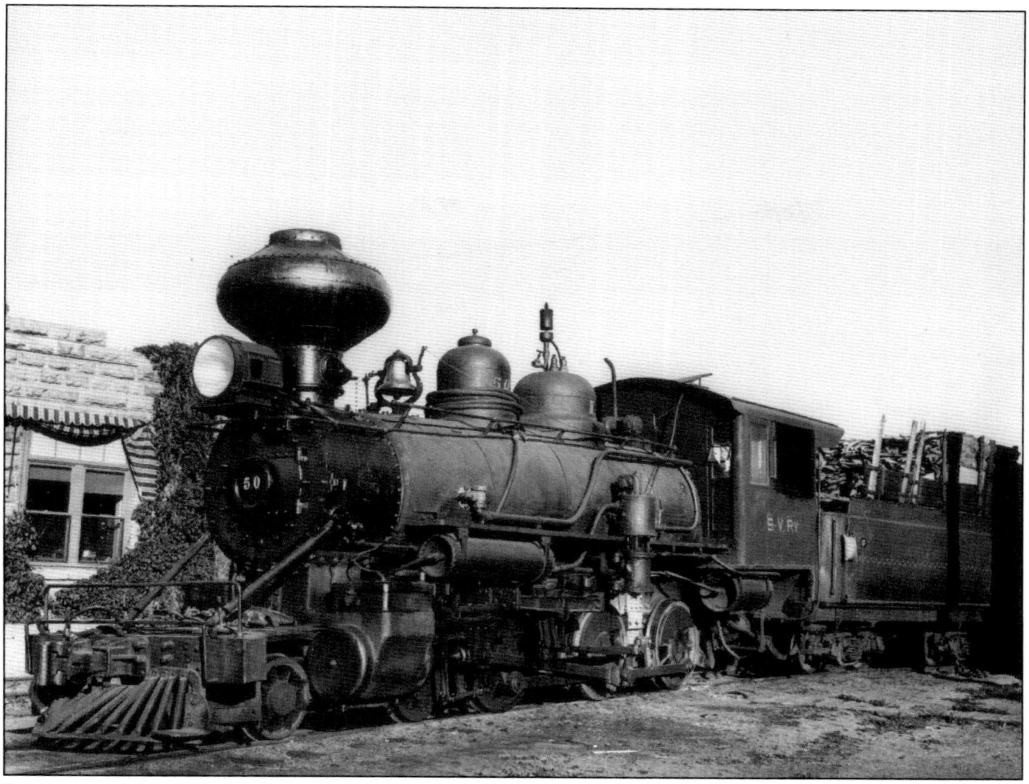

Locomotive No. 50 sits beside the Sumpter Valley Railway's company office building in South Baker with a west-bound passenger train in the mid-1930s. (Photograph by C. P. Atherton; Matt Mattioda.)

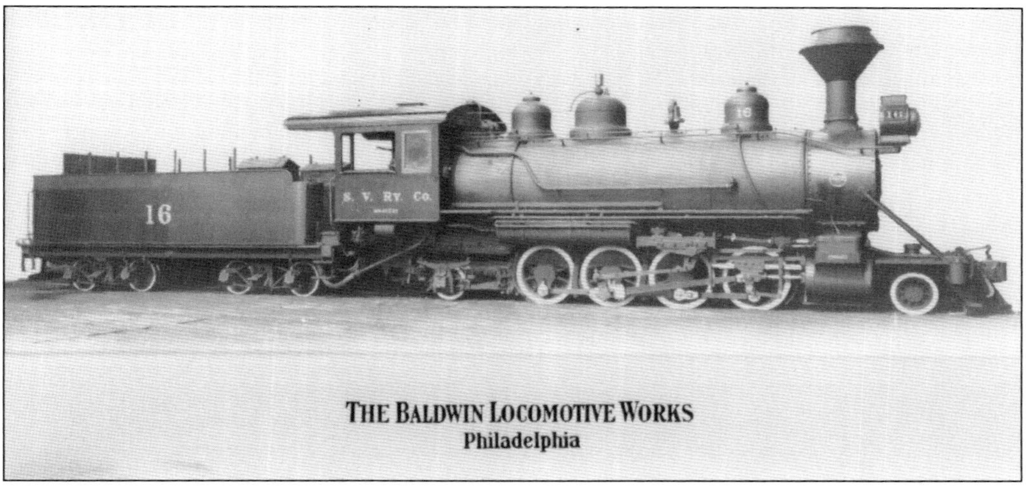

The Baldwin builder's photograph of locomotive No. 16 shows her heavy, functional lines. No. 16 was purchased in 1915 as part of a group of three Mikados (2-8-2) to update the freight motive power. (H. L. Broadbelt from original Baldwin Railroad negative; Sumpter Valley Railroad Restoration, Inc.)

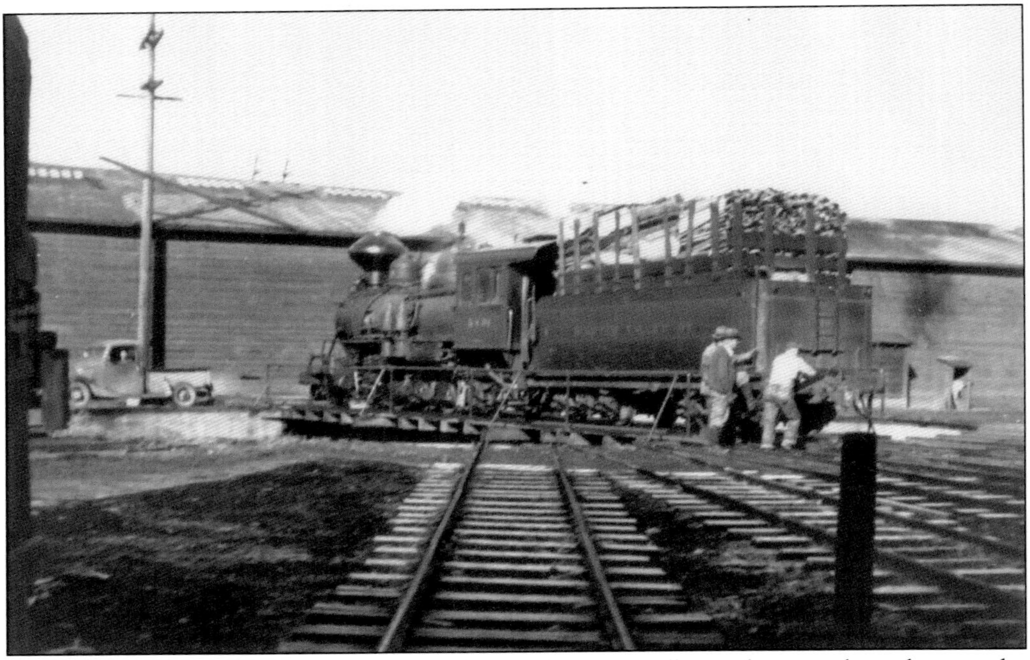

Locomotive No. 16 is being turned by hand at the Baker roundhouse for an up-bound run in the 1930s. This photograph shows the large cordwood loads for which the Sumpter Valley Railway was noted. They were the last common carrier in the United States to use wood as their primary locomotive fuel. (H. R. Griffiths Collection; Sumpter Valley Railroad Restoration, Inc.)

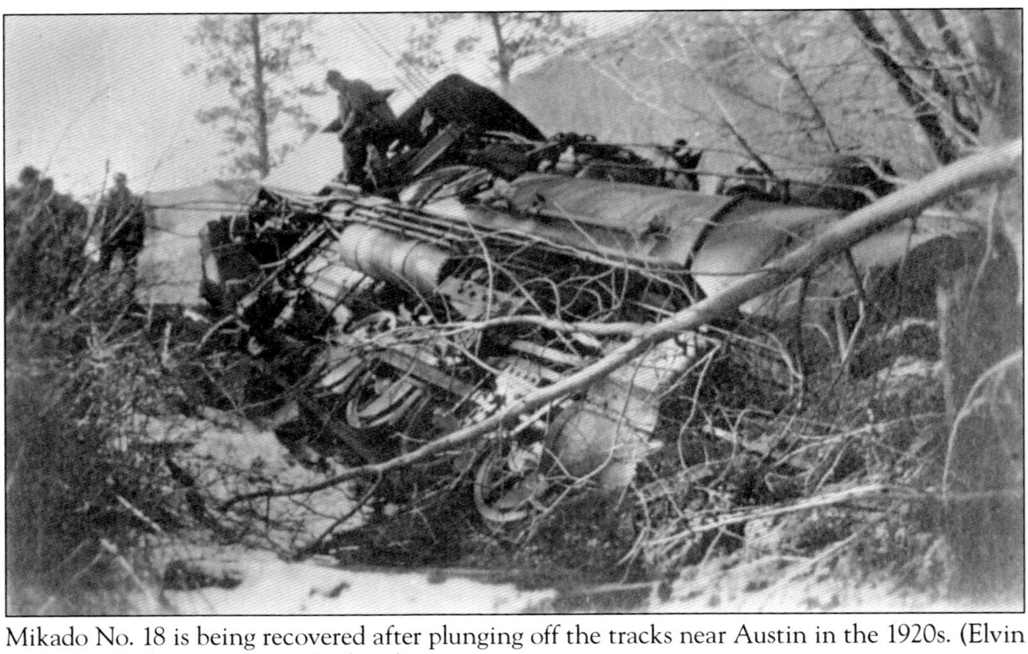

Mikado No. 18 is being recovered after plunging off the tracks near Austin in the 1920s. (Elvin Endecott Collection; Casey Carlson.)

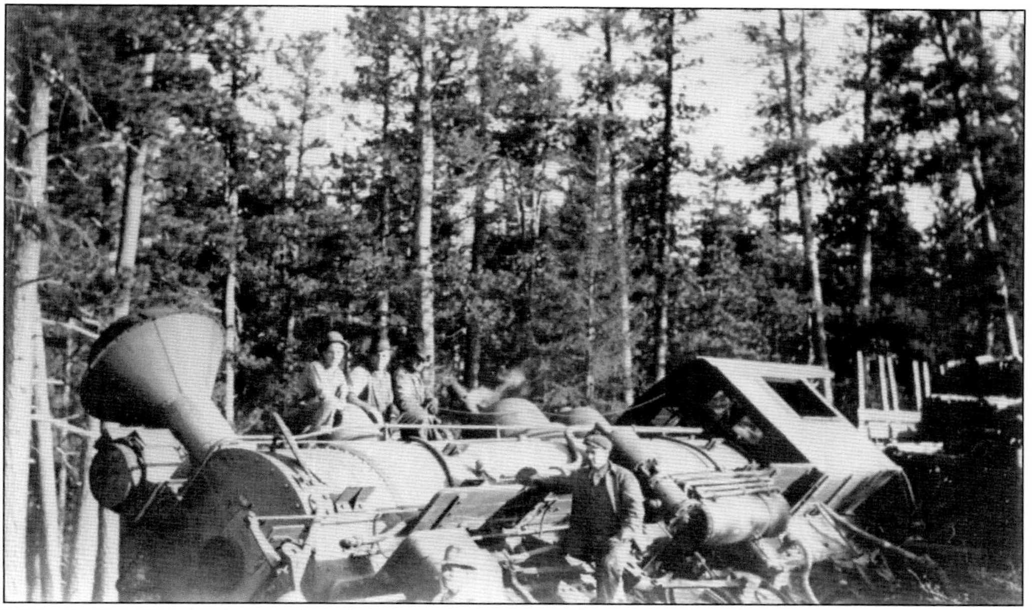

Mikado No. 17 is laid over after finding a soft spot on the rails. After the Sumpter Valley Railway purchased the Mikados, many changes were required to the roadbed and curves to allow the engines to run safely, with the issues regularly being found the hard way. (Elvin Endecott Collection; Casey Carlson.)

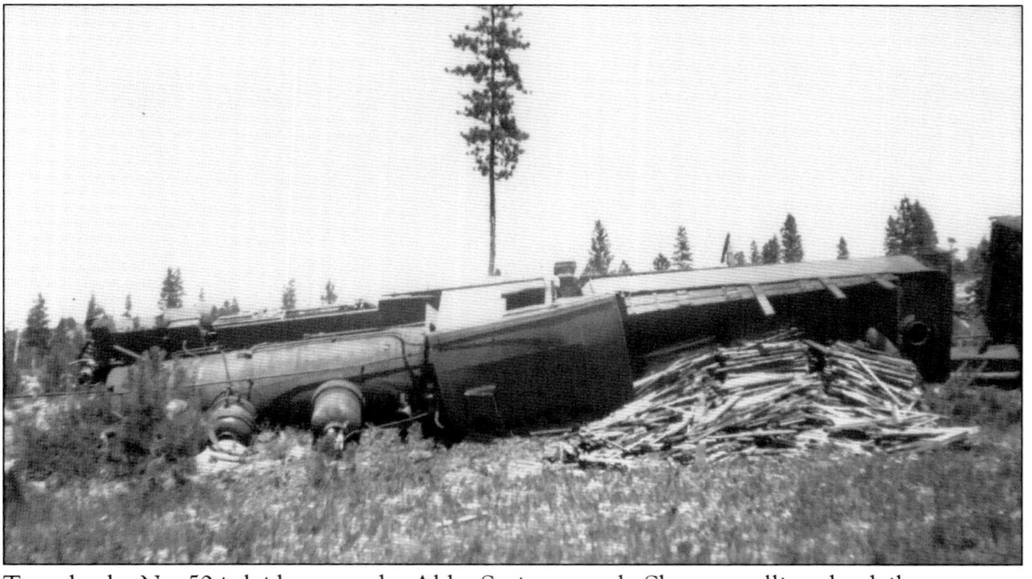

Ten-wheeler No. 50 is laid over at the Alder Springs wreck. She was pulling the daily passenger train at the time. There were no fatalities, though there were several serious injuries caused by falling seats in the cars. A rescue train took the injured to Austin by boxcar. (Elvin Endecott Collection; Casey Carlson.)

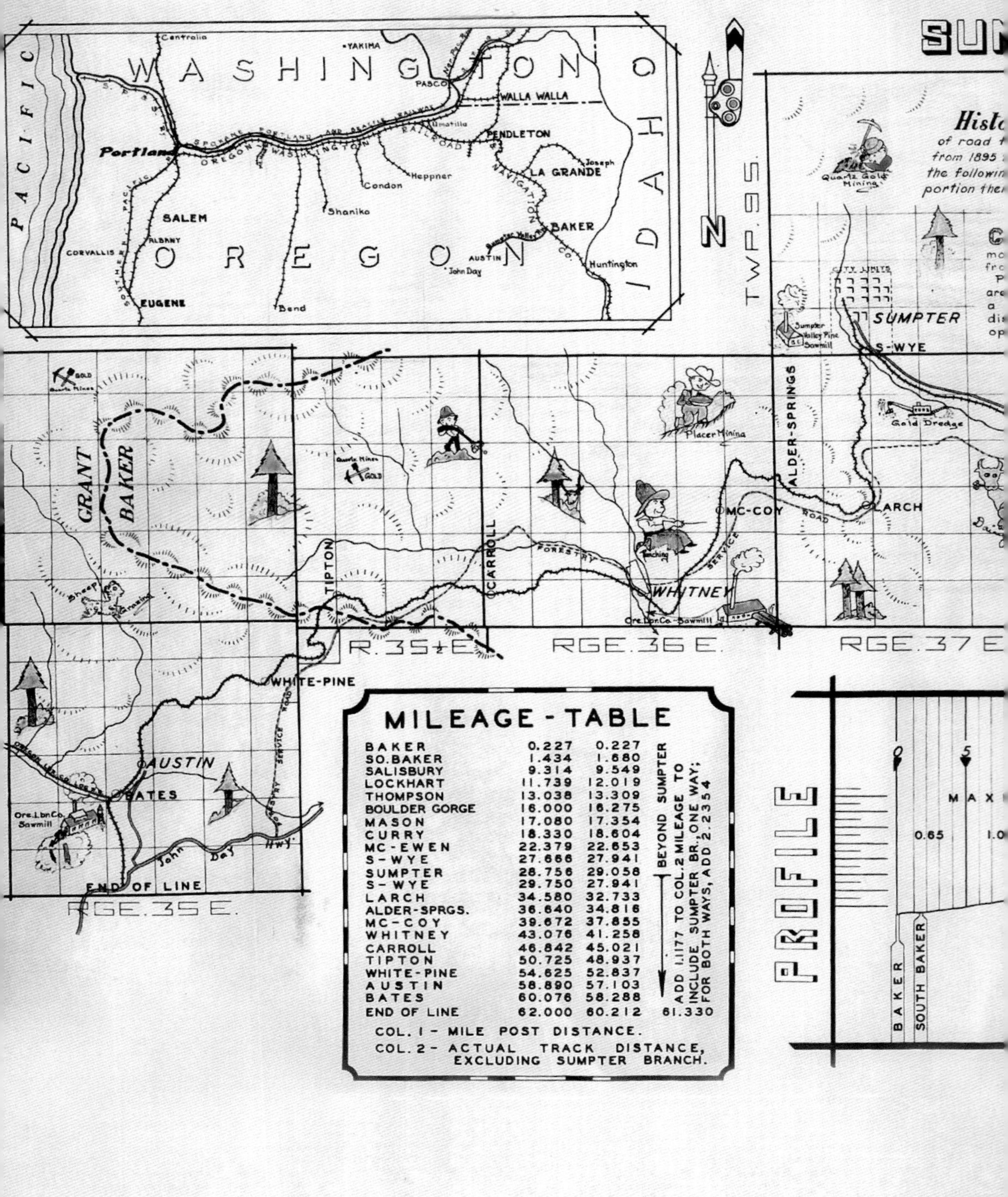

MILEAGE - TABLE

	COL. 1	COL. 2	
BAKER	0.227	0.227	
SO. BAKER	1.434	1.680	
SALISBURY	9.314	9.549	
LOCKHART	11.739	12.019	
THOMPSON	13.038	13.309	
BOULDER GORGE	16.000	16.275	
MASON	17.080	17.354	
CURRY	18.330	18.604	
MC-EWEN	22.379	22.653	
S-WYE	27.666	27.941	
SUMPTER	28.756	29.058	
S-WYE	29.750	27.941	
LARCH	34.580	32.733	
ALDER-SPRGS.	36.640	34.816	
MC-COY	39.672	37.855	
WHITNEY	43.076	41.258	
CARROLL	46.842	45.021	
TIPTON	50.725	48.937	
WHITE-PINE	54.625	52.837	
AUSTIN	58.890	57.103	
BATES	60.076	58.288	
END OF LINE	62.000	60.212	61.330

BEYOND SUMPTER — ADD 1.1177 TO COL. 2 MILEAGE TO INCLUDE SUMPTER BR. ONE WAY; FOR BOTH WAYS, ADD 2.2354

COL. 1 - MILE POST DISTANCE.

COL. 2 - ACTUAL TRACK DISTANCE, EXCLUDING SUMPTER BRANCH.

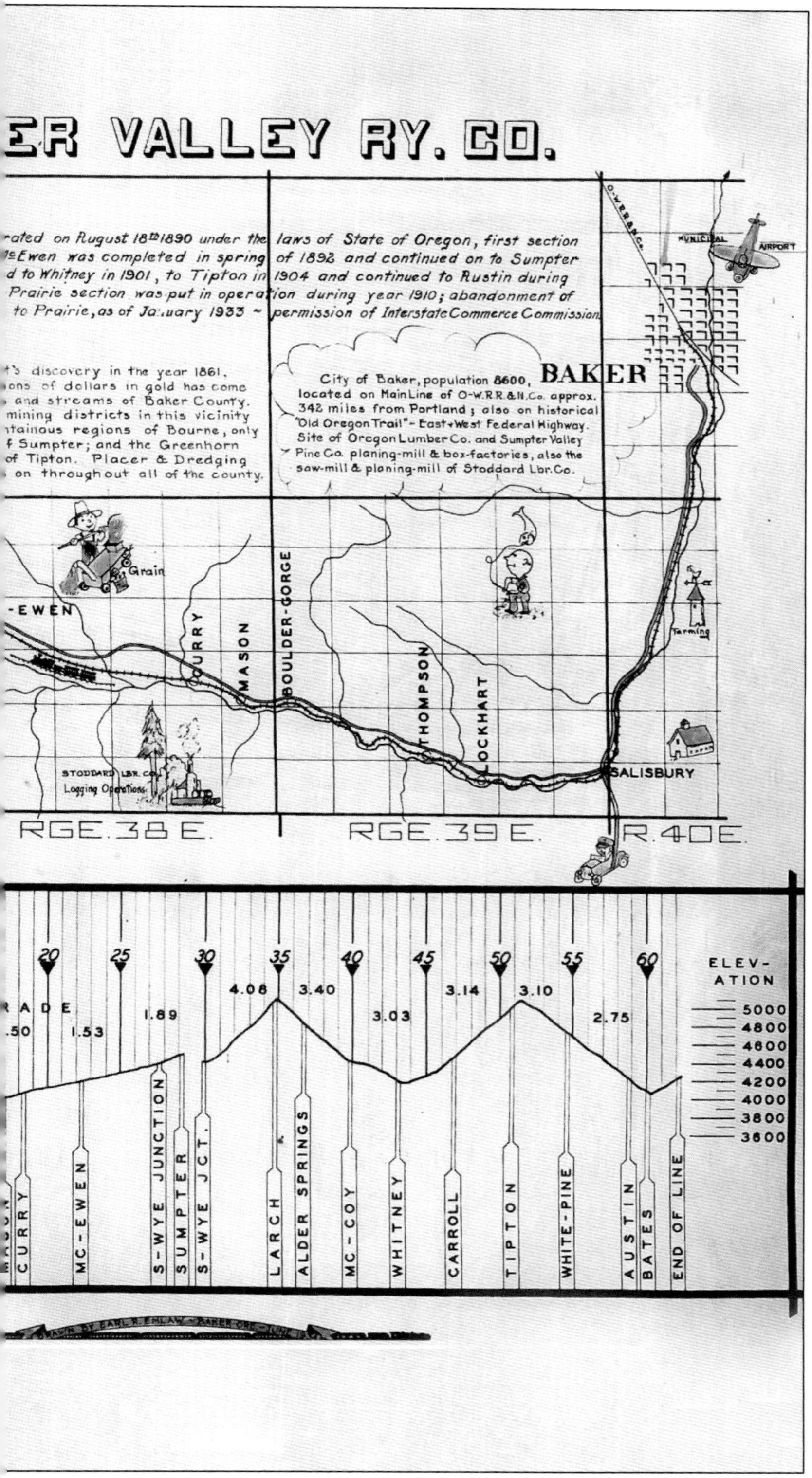

Earl Emlaw, the last superintendant of the railroad, created this tourist map of the Sumpter Valley Railway. This map ends at Bates. By the time this was drawn, the 20 miles from Bates to Prairie City had been abandoned. Even with this missing, it gives a good flavor of what riding the Sumpter Valley Railway was like. It shows the many twists, turns, and elevation changes. The line from Bates to Prairie City continued down Bridge Creek. The line then proceeded up to Dixie Summit and switchbacked down into Prairie City. (Emlaw Collection; National Railway Historical Society, Pacific Northwest Chapter.)

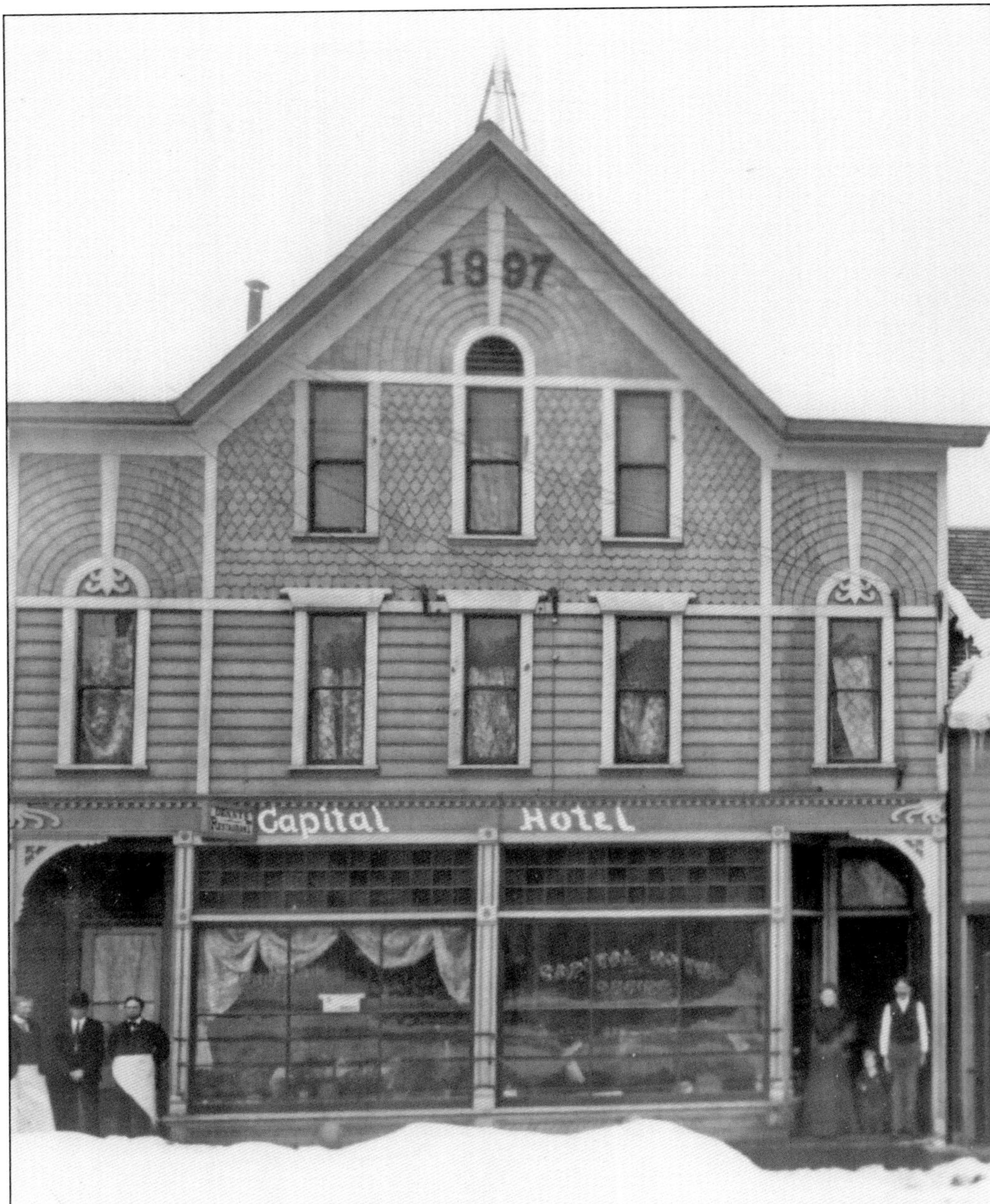

A winter picture of the Capital Hotel, located on the corner of Granite and Cracker Streets in Sumpter, was taken around 1905. On the fateful night of August 17, 1917, a fire started in the cook's quarters that led to the destruction of most of Sumpter's business district. (McCord Collection; Baker County Library, Baker City, Oregon, Image No. T88/1992.1.181.)

Five

Fires, Turtlebacks, and the End of Dreams (1917–1935)

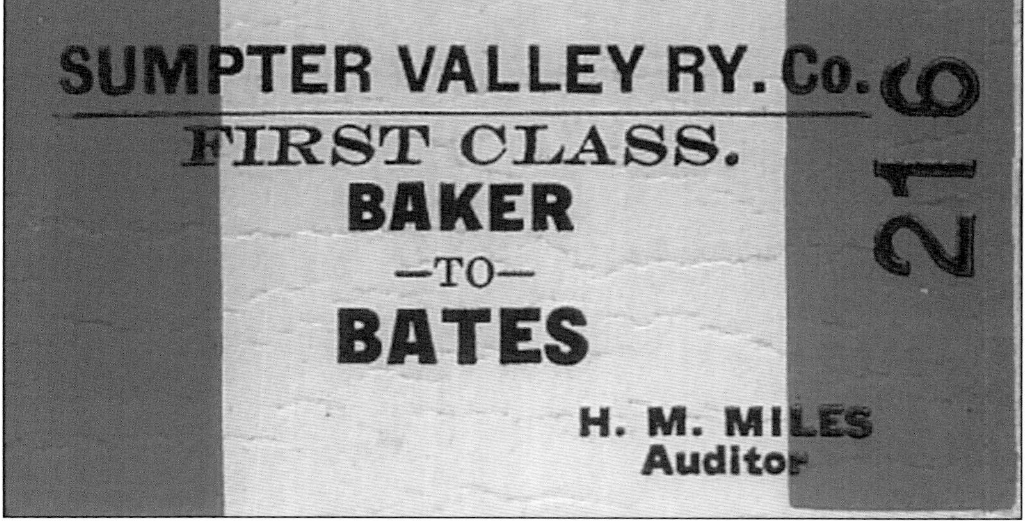

This is a copy of a 1930s original ticket to Bates. (Earl Emlaw Collection; National Railway Historical Society, Pacific Northwest Chapter.)

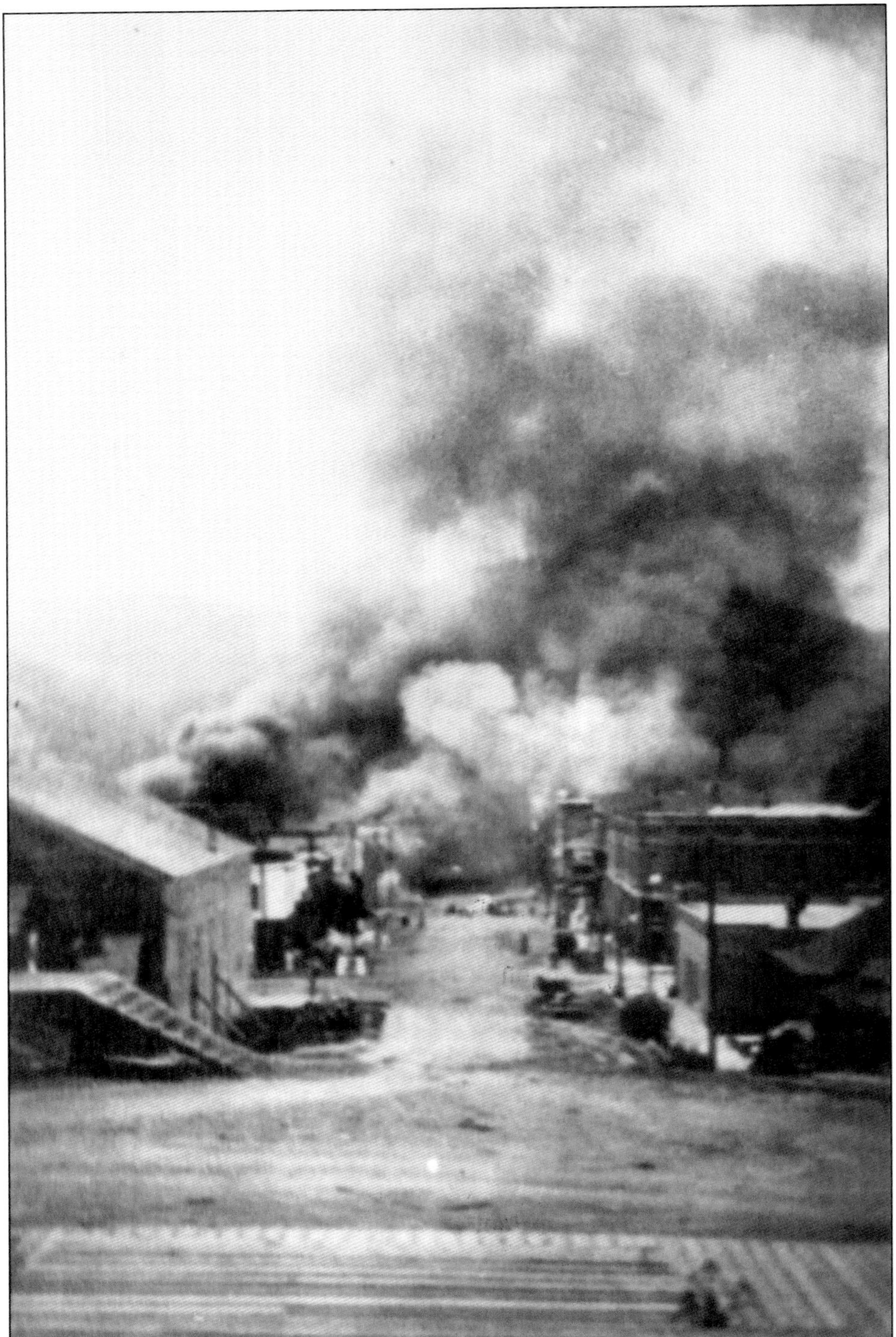

This was the scene that followed. Starting in the cook's room of the Capital Hotel, the fire soon spread, and by sunset of August 17, 1917, Sumpter's business district was nothing more than ashes. (McCord Collection; Baker County Library, Baker City, Oregon, Image No. T23.)

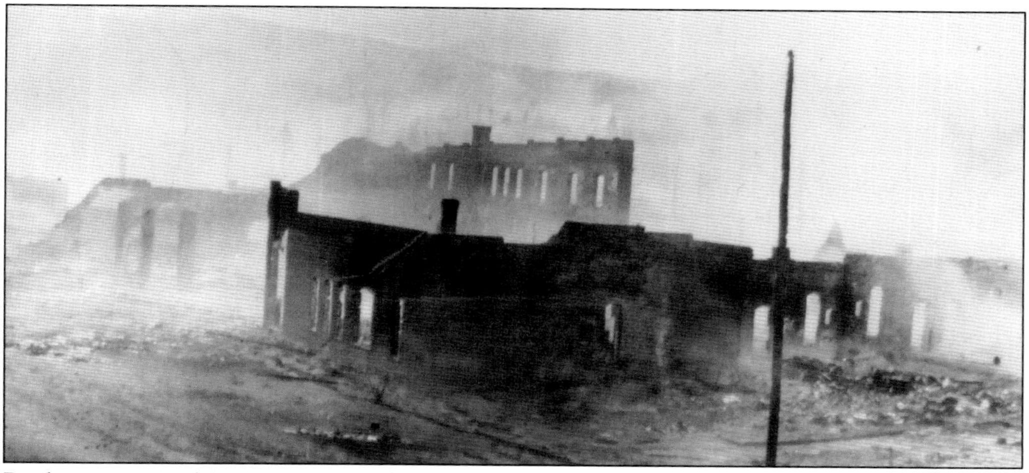

By the morning of August 18, 1917, this sight greeted the citizens of Sumpter. In the back are the ruins of the once grand Sumpter Hotel. The first National Bank Building is in front, looking west on Auburn Street. (Photograph by Carl Holmans, E. P. Culp Collection; Baker County Library, Baker City, Oregon, Image No. A9-C/1992.1.1506.)

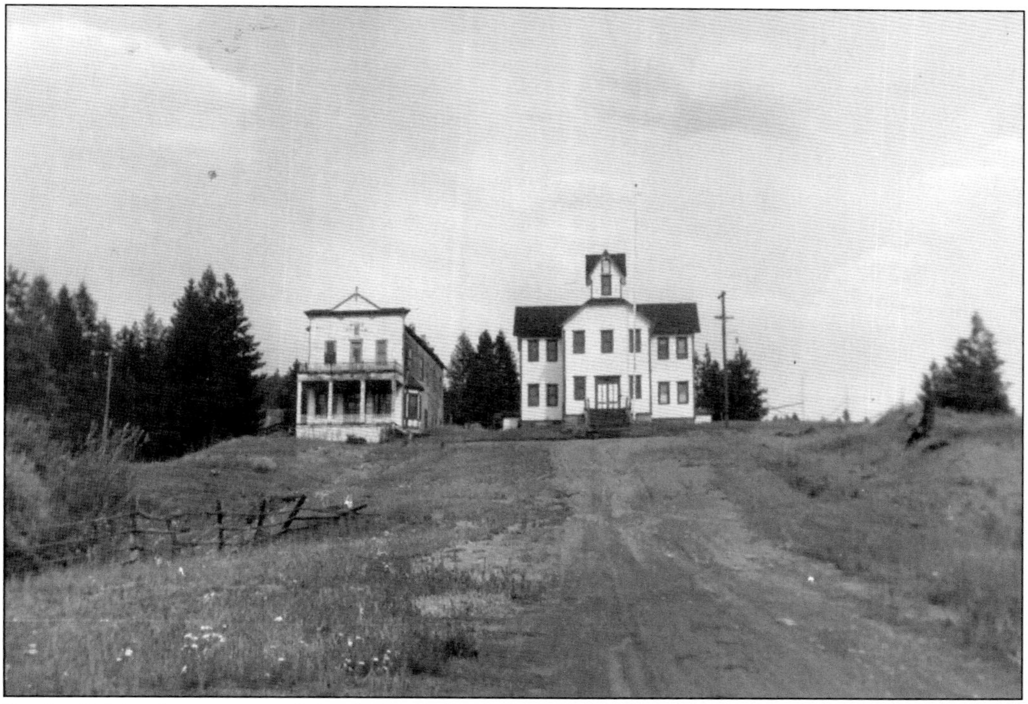

By the 1920s, the remains of the fire were long gone. Two of the survivors of the fire, the hospital and school, were lonely reminders of the glory days of Sumpter. The hospital was now the McEwen Masonic Temple; and the school, saved by a handful of its students in 1917, still taught the remaining locals. (Walla Walla Extension Service; Baker County Library, Baker City, Oregon, Image No. T84/1992.1.241.)

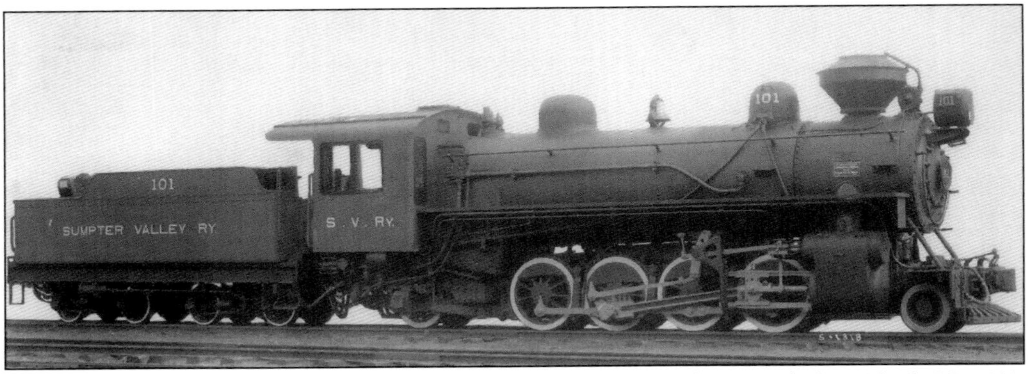

This is the ALCO (American Locomotive Company) builder's photograph for Mikado No. 101, purchased in 1920 with No. 102. They came numbered 101 and 102, but due to conflicts with logging locomotives, they were renumbered to 19 and 20. They were the last new motive power the Sumpter Valley Railway purchased before the Mallets. (H. L. Broadbelt from original Baldwin Railroad negative; Sumpter Valley Railroad Restoration, Inc.)

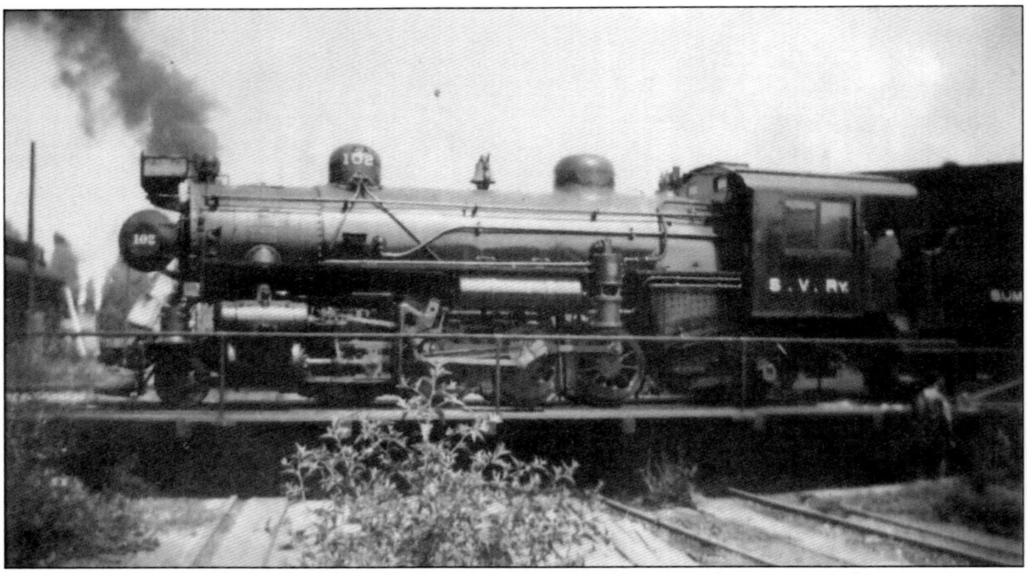

Mikado No. 20 is being put into the South Baker roundhouse after delivery from American Locomotive Company. Note the missing stack and other hardware that had been removed for shipping. (Ron Harr Collection; Sumpter Valley Railroad Restoration, Inc.)

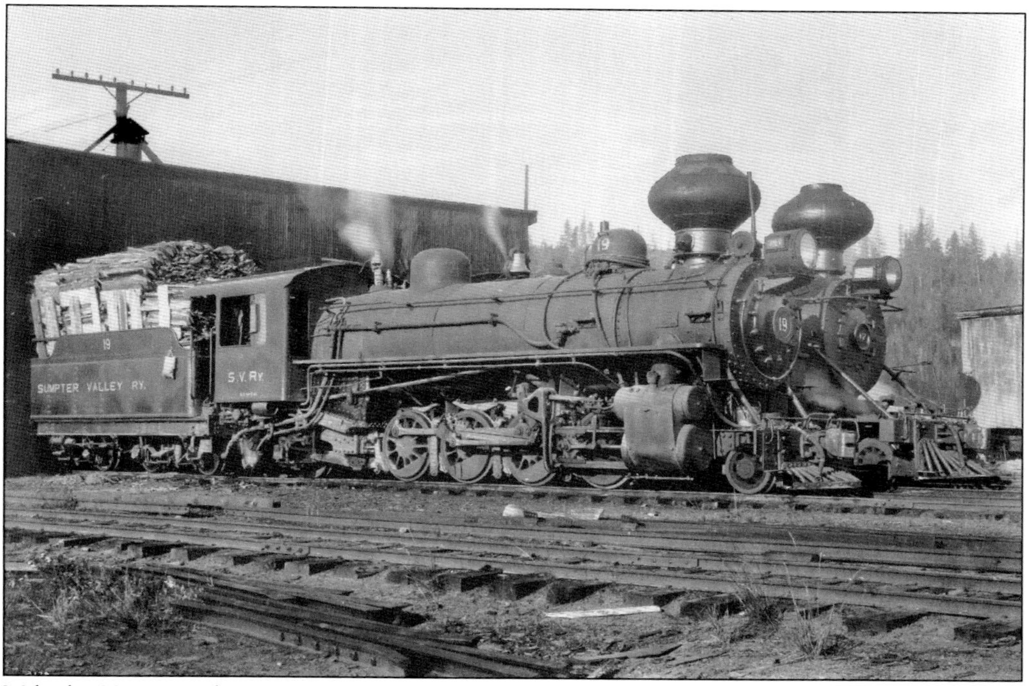

Mikados No. 19 and No. 17 simmer in front of the Austin engine house in 1938. They served as helpers over Tipton Summit. This photograph illustrates the differences between the American Locomotive Works Mikados, No. 19, and the more massive look of the Baldwin locomotives, No. 17. Note the flanger gear on No. 17's pilot deck. (Photograph by Louis McClure, Western History Collection; Denver Public Library, Call Number MCC-3179.)

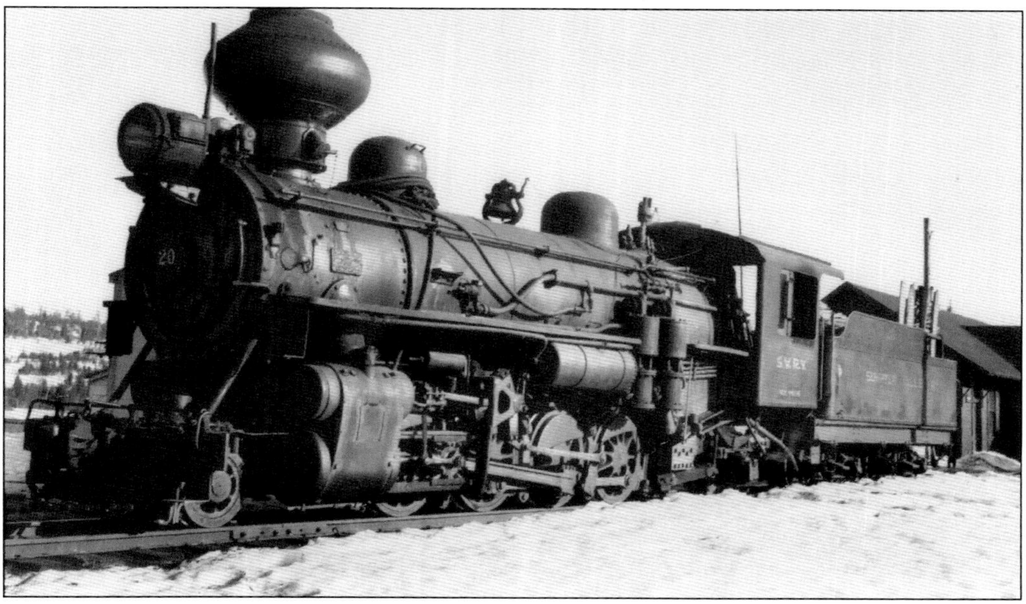

Mikado No. 19 rests at Austin after a helper run in 1939. Her crew will be loading up another eight cords of wood on the tender so she will be ready for the next run up to Tipton. (Ron Harr Collection; Sumpter Valley Railroad Restoration, Inc.)

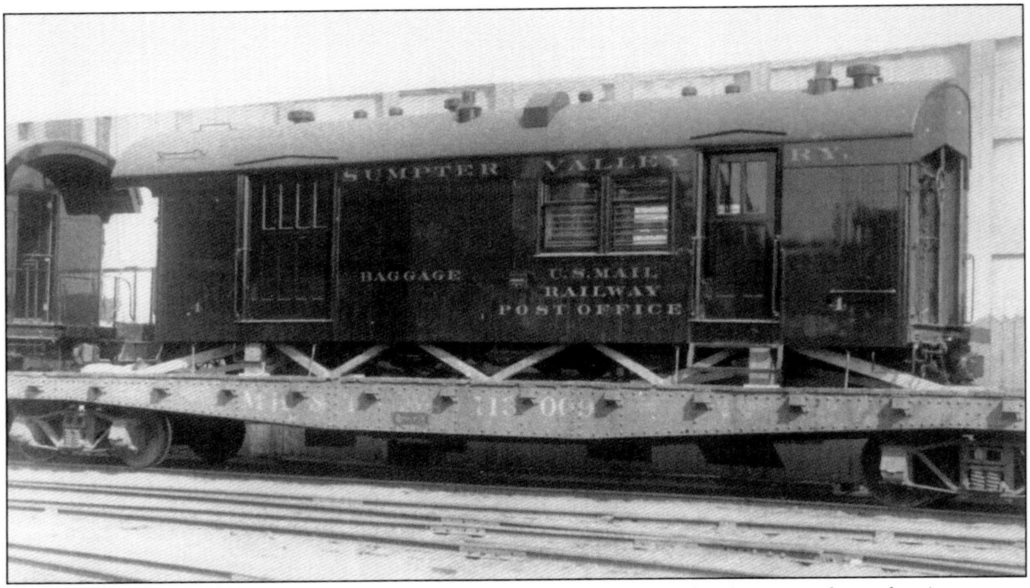

Turtleback baggage/Railway Post Office (RPO) car No. 4 is ready for shipment from the American Car and Foundry (AC&F) Plant in St. Louis, Missouri, in March 1918. The Sumpter Valley Railway cars were the last narrow-gauge passenger car orders shipped by AC&F. (AC&F Lot 8339/Negative No. 600872-A-9; Sumpter Valley Railroad Restoration, Inc.)

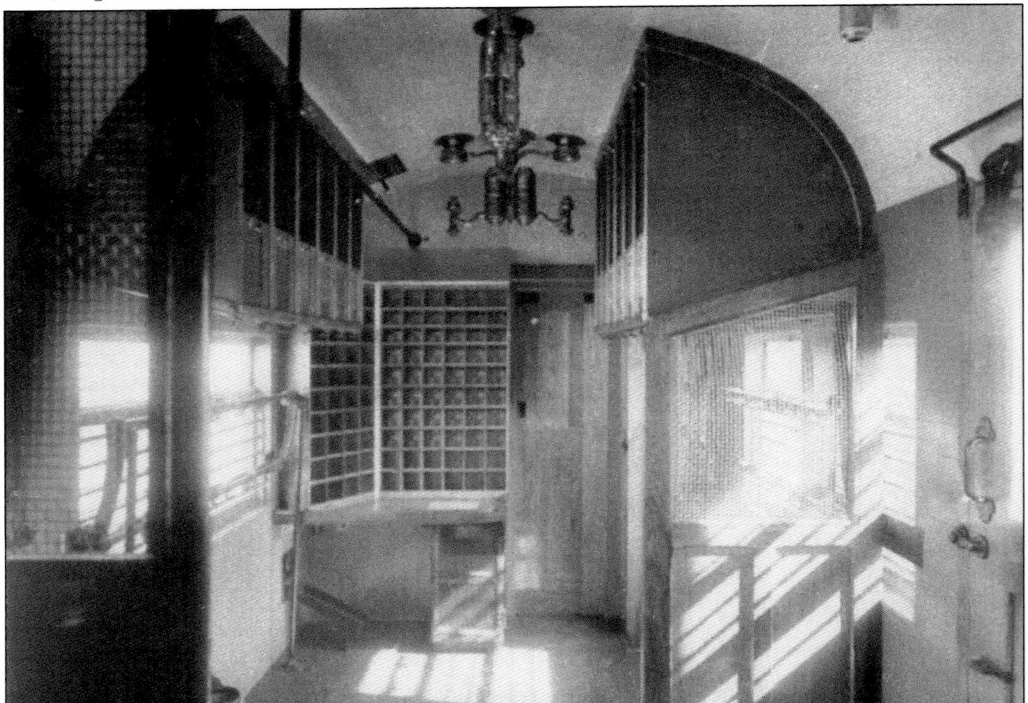

This is an interior view of RPO No. 4 looking forward. The turtleback designation refers to the curved roof, which in cross-section resembles a turtle's back. (AC&F Lot 8339/Negative No. 600872-1; Sumpter Valley Railroad Restoration, Inc.)

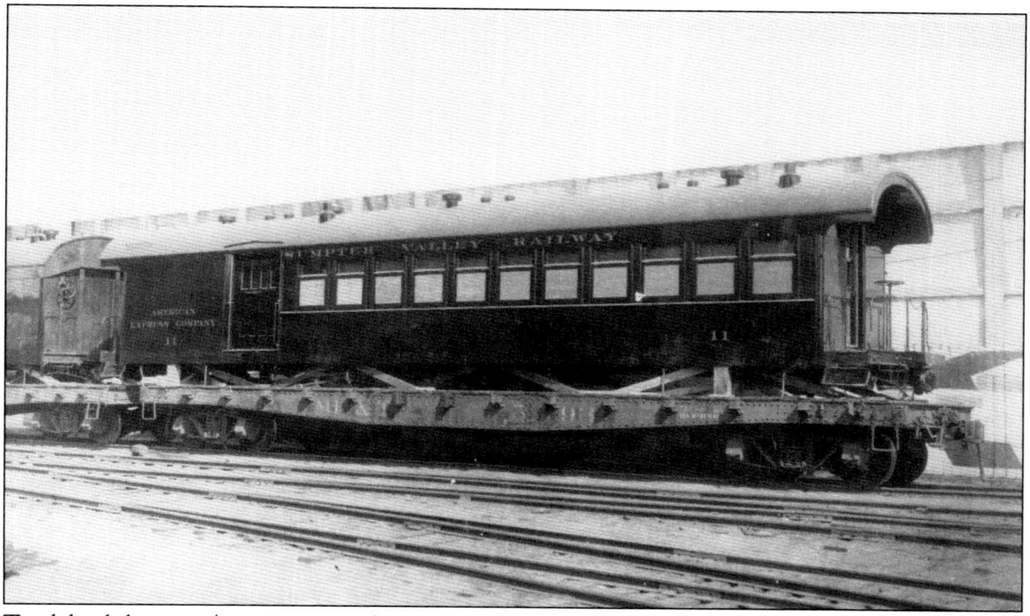

Turtleback baggage/passenger combination car (combine) No. 11 awaits shipment from AC&F. In later years, these cars had a second baggage door added and became RPO/baggage/passenger combinations. The interior is shown on page 82. (AC&F Lot 8339/Negative No. 600871-C; Sumpter Valley Railroad Restoration, Inc.)

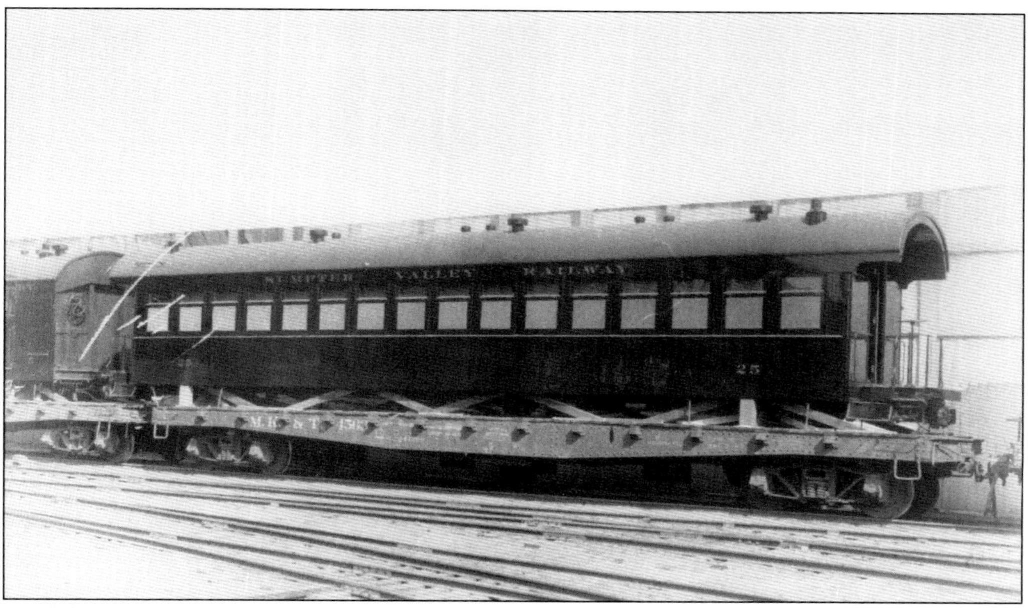

Turtleback Coach No. 25 with baggage/RPO No. 5 awaits shipment from AC&F. Both RPOs are now lost; the last one burned as it was being stored for restoration. Both sets of combine/coach cars remain in service on the White Pass and Yukon Railway. The interior is shown on page 83. (AC&F Lot 8337/Negative No. 600870-A-8; Sumpter Valley Railroad Restoration, Inc.)

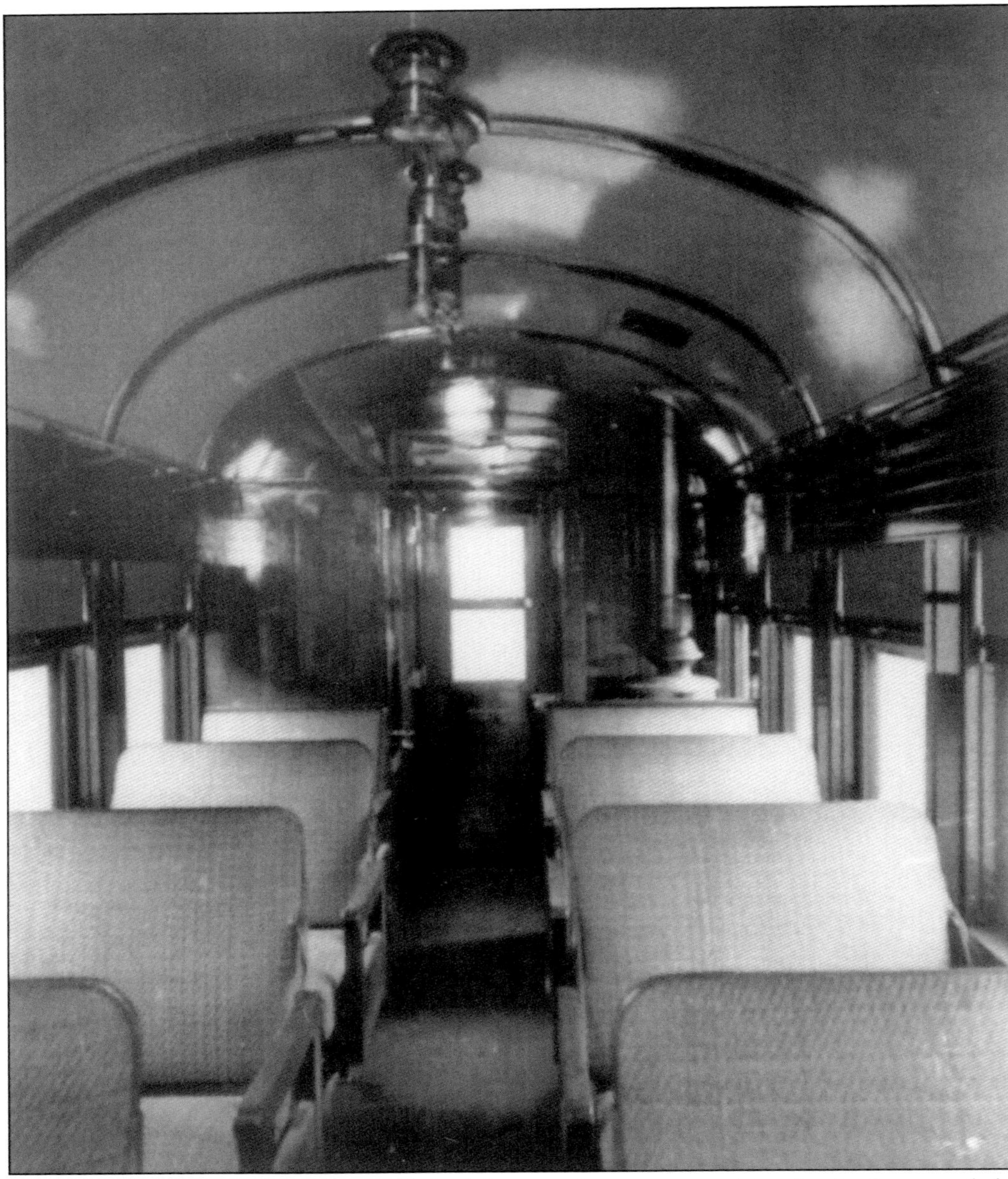

This interior photograph of the Turtleback baggage/passenger combination looks toward the baggage compartment as it is delivered. (AC&F Lot 8338/Negative No. 600871.A; Sumpter Valley Railroad Restoration, Inc.)

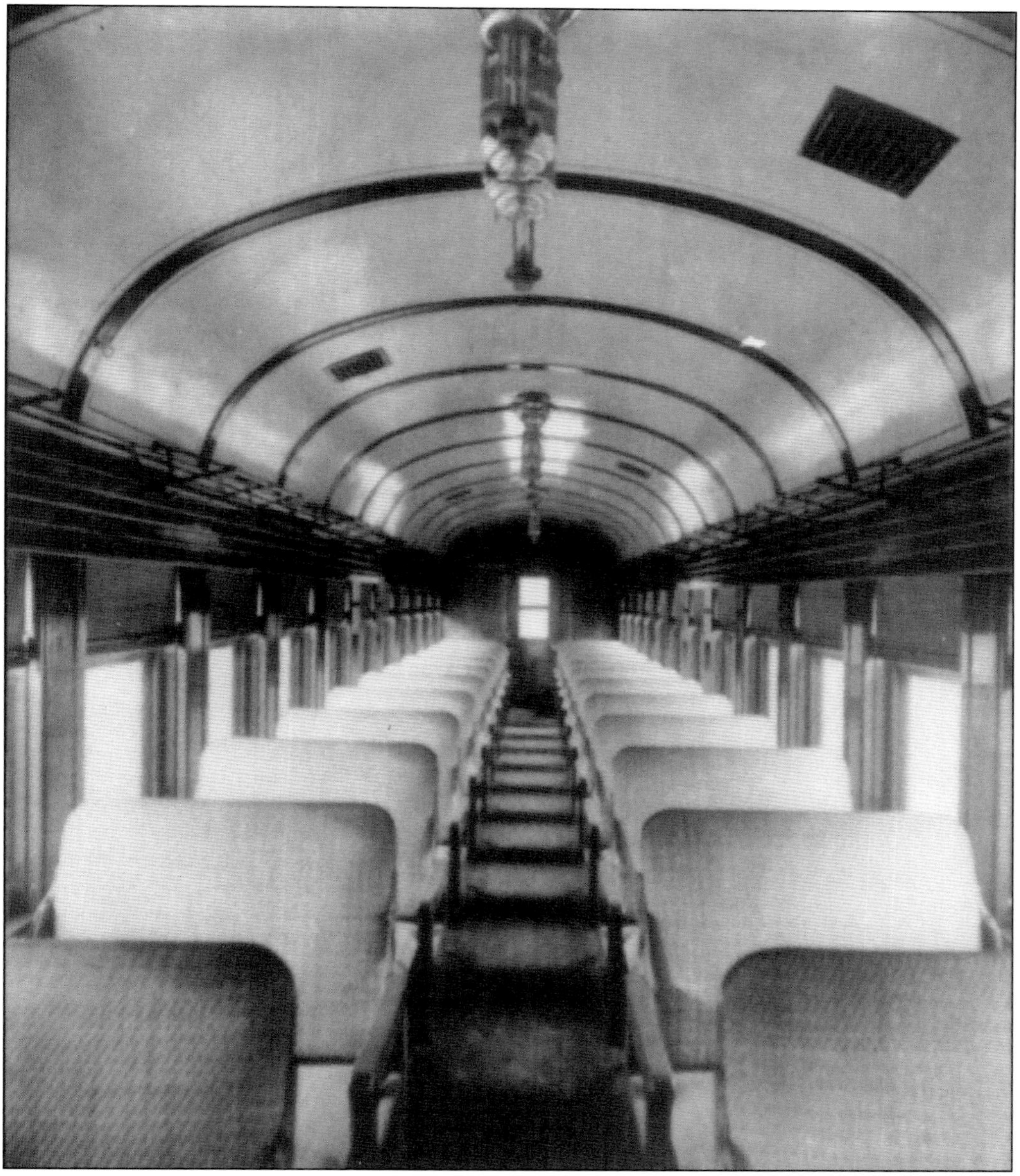

An interior photograph shows the Turtleback coach as shipped from AC&F. (AC&F Lot 8337/ Negative No. 600870-D; Sumpter Valley Railroad Restoration, Inc.)

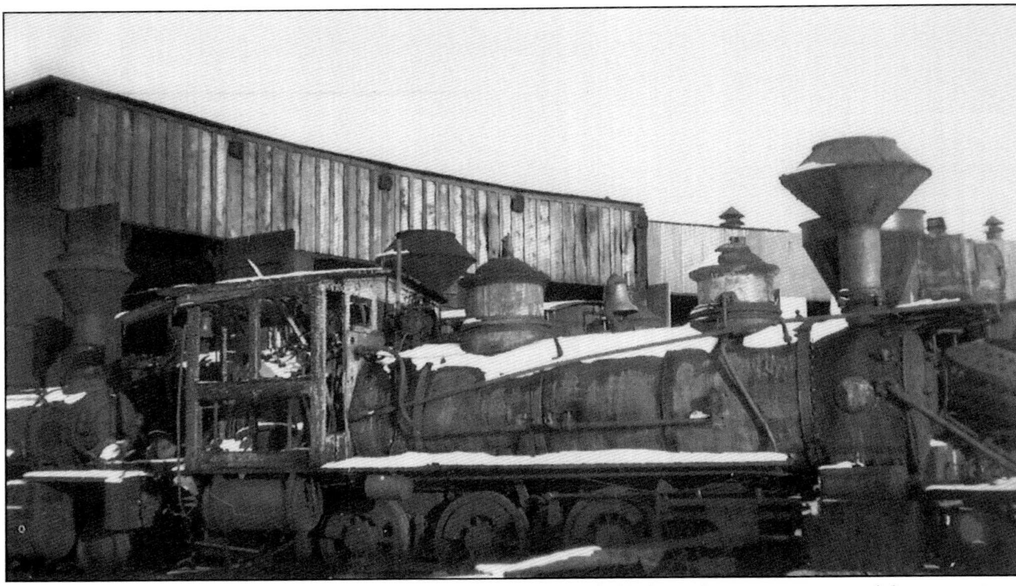

In early 1921, a fire destroyed the roundhouse in South Baker, damaging several locomotives, including the newly arrived ALCO Mikados. This image shows the rebuilt roundhouse behind a line of older locomotives awaiting repair. (Jim Grigsby Collection; Sumpter Valley Railroad Restoration, Inc.)

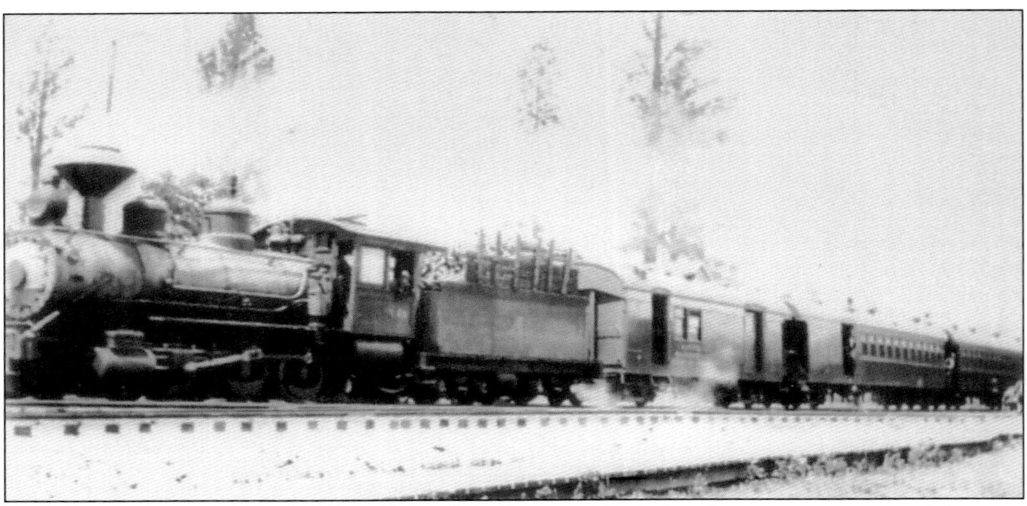

Tonopah Mogul No. 4 steams out of South Baker in 1918 with a first passenger run of the new AC&F Turtleback passenger cars. Two sets were purchased to allow them to run from opposite ends of the line each day. (Ron Harr Collection; Sumpter Valley Railroad Restoration, Inc.)

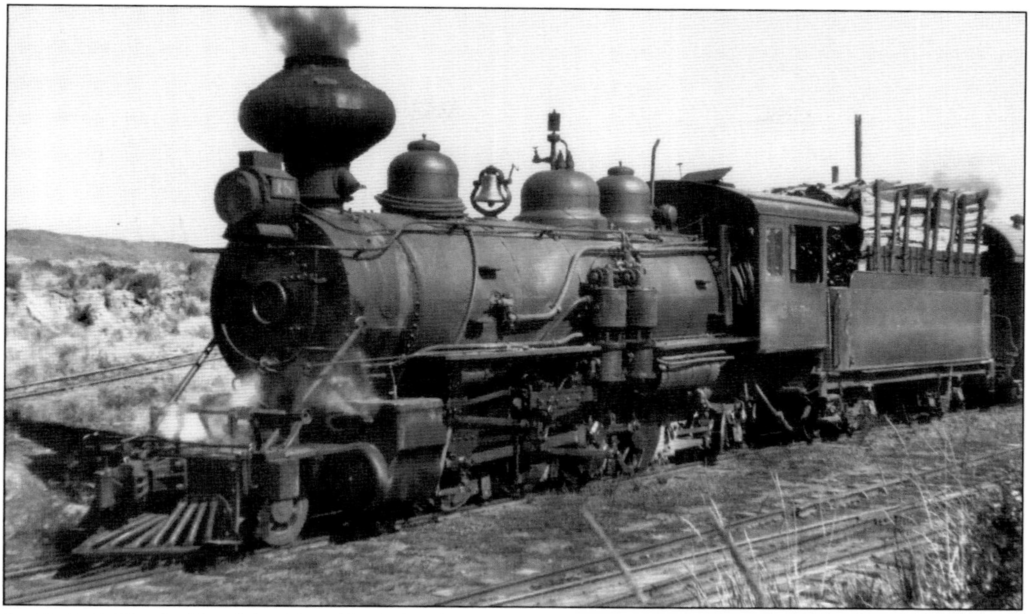

Baldwin Mikado No. 18 with a Turtleback passenger car in tow steams through the South Baker yard in the mid-1930s. (Ron Harr Collection; Sumpter Valley Railroad Restoration, Inc.)

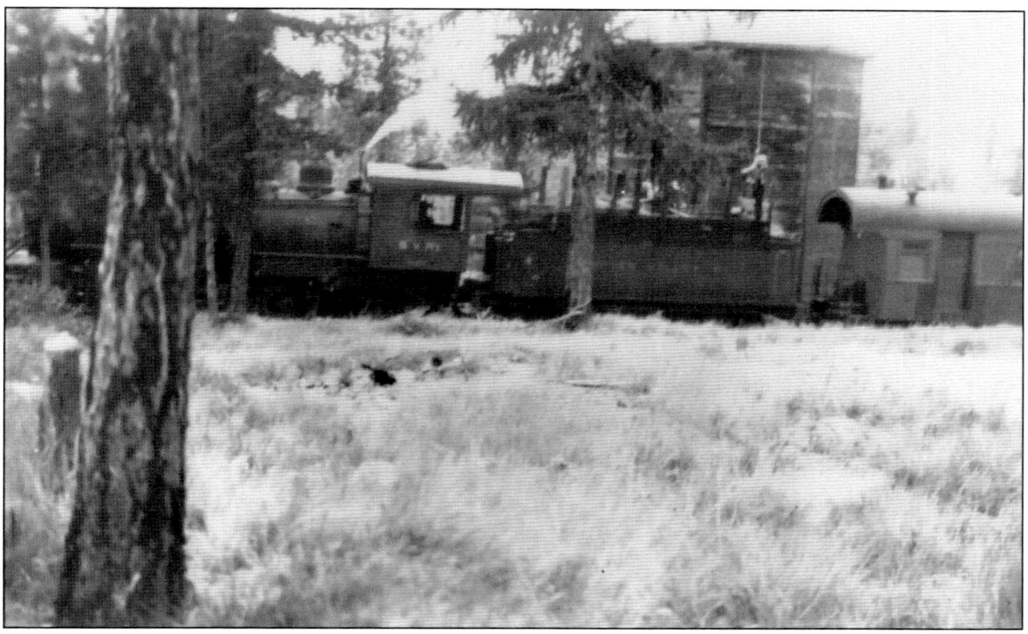

Baldwin Mikado No. 16 with an RPO/baggage/passenger car pauses in the early 1930s at the water tank in Carroll. Note the fully enclosed structure to protect the tank from freezing. (Ron Harr Collection; Sumpter Valley Railroad Restoration, Inc.)

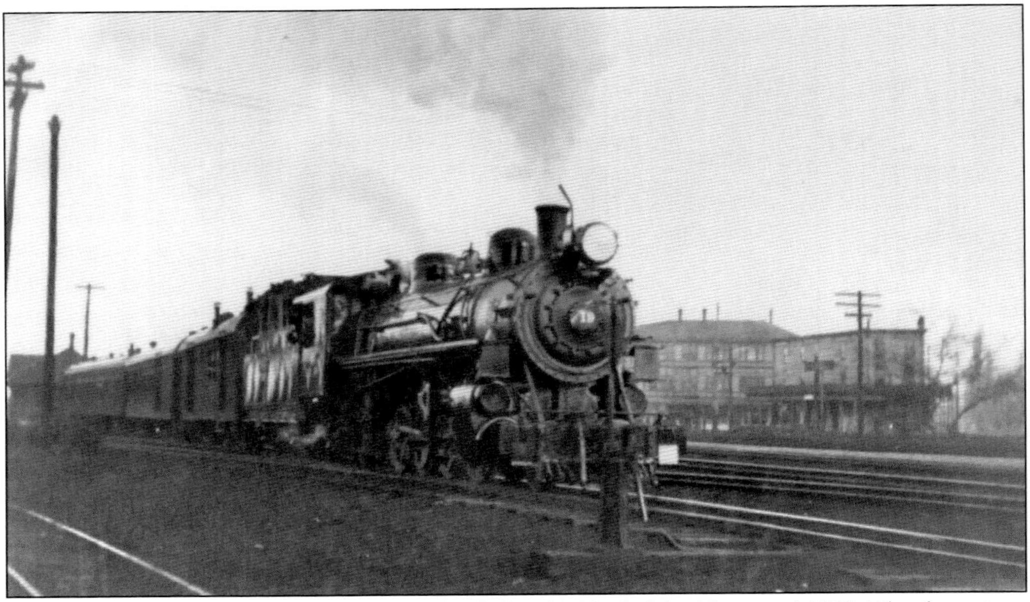

The daily passenger train is departing Baker behind Mikado No. 19 around 1922. The depot is at the left, behind the train, with the Crabill and Columbia hotels on Columbia Street located to the right. (McCord Collection; Baker County Library, Baker City, Oregon, Image No. Tr-8.)

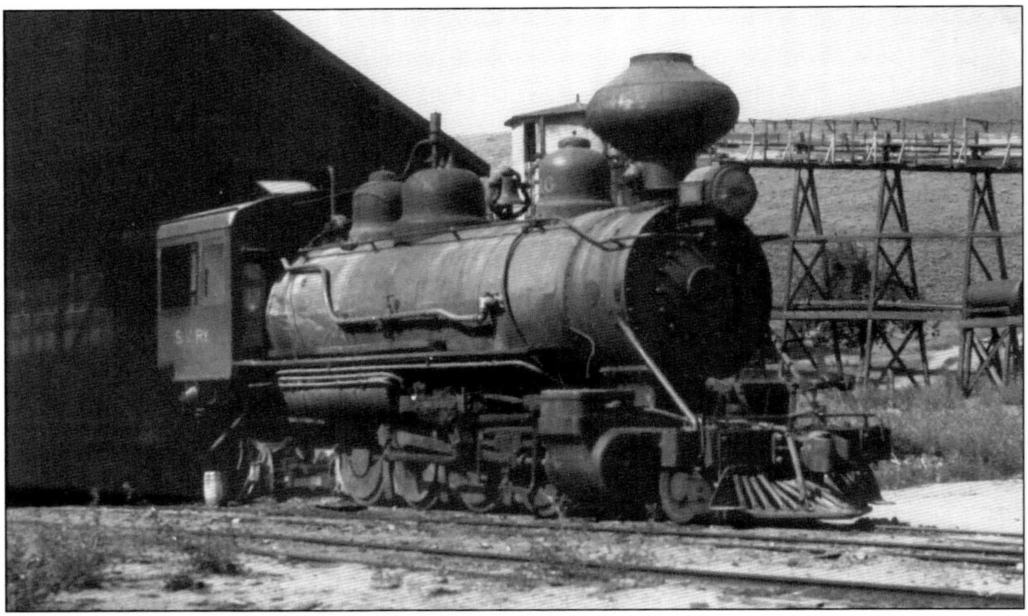

Mikado No. 16 is snoozing in the shadow of the South Baker back shops in the late 1930s. She is showing the effects of almost two decades of hard work. (Ron Harr Collection; Sumpter Valley Railroad Restoration, Inc.)

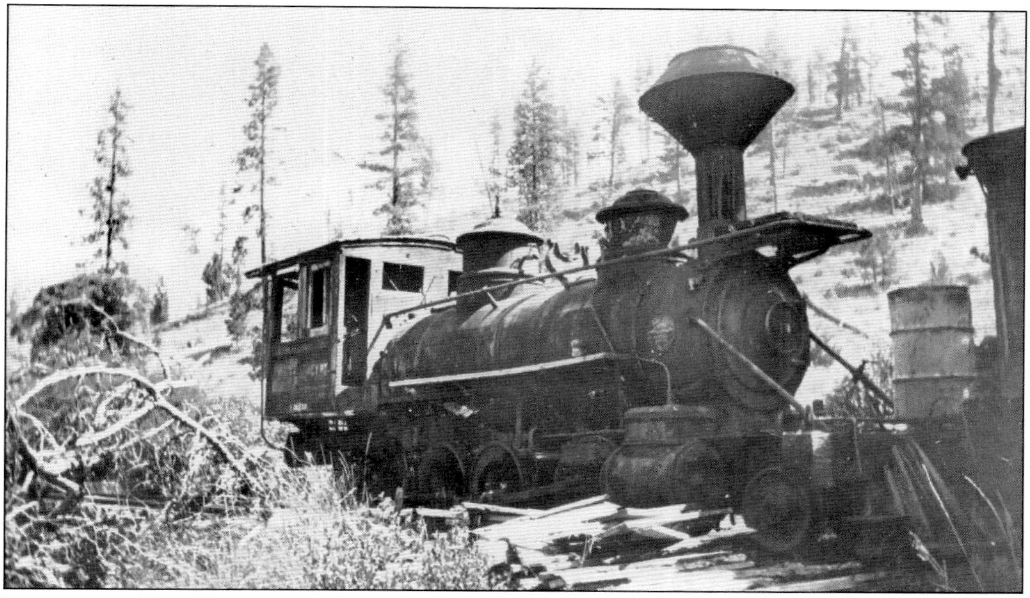

Locomotive No. 10, a consolidation built by Baldwin Locomotive Works in 1880, sits on the deadline near Bates around 1936. (Photograph by Lamar Ferguson, Brett Bane Collection.)

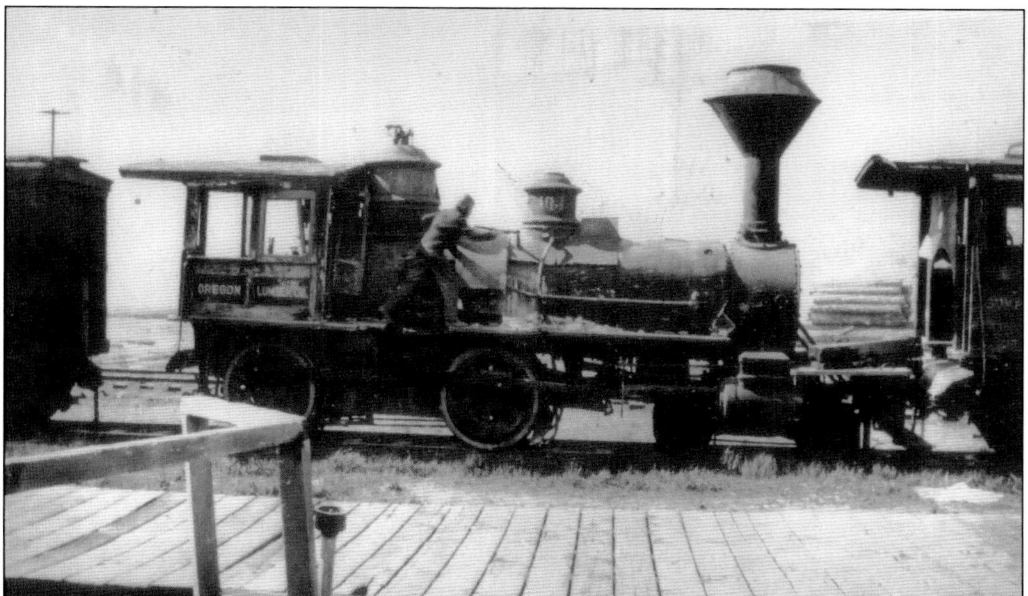

"Candelaria" was originally purchased from Carson and Colorado Railroad and is now Oregon Lumber Company No. 103. She sits forlornly on the Bates deadline, waiting her date with the cutting torch around 1936. (Ron Harr Collection; Sumpter Valley Railroad Restoration, Inc.)

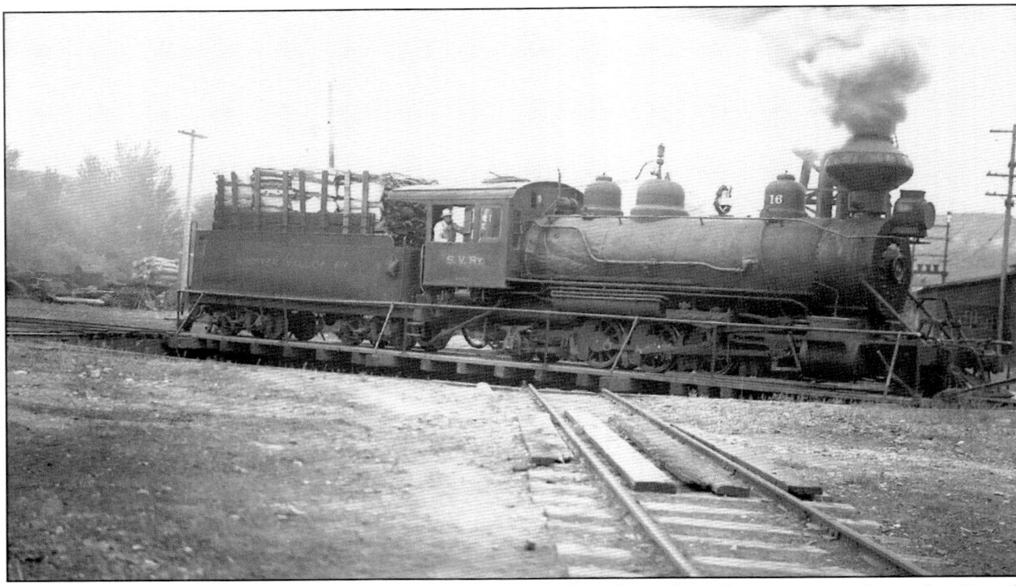

Mikado No. 16 with engineer U. S. Carpenter at the throttle is being turned on the South Baker turntable for the last passenger run to Bates on July 31, 1937. (Sumpter Valley Railroad Restoration, Inc.)

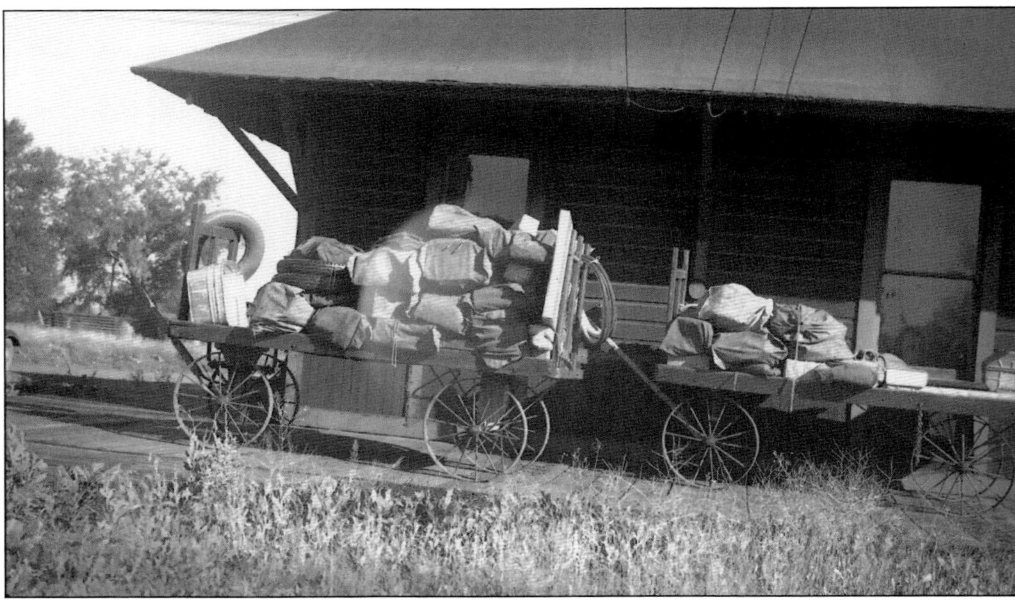

Baggage and mail are waiting at the South Baker Depot for the last passenger train to Prairie City. (Sumpter Valley Railroad Restoration, Inc.)

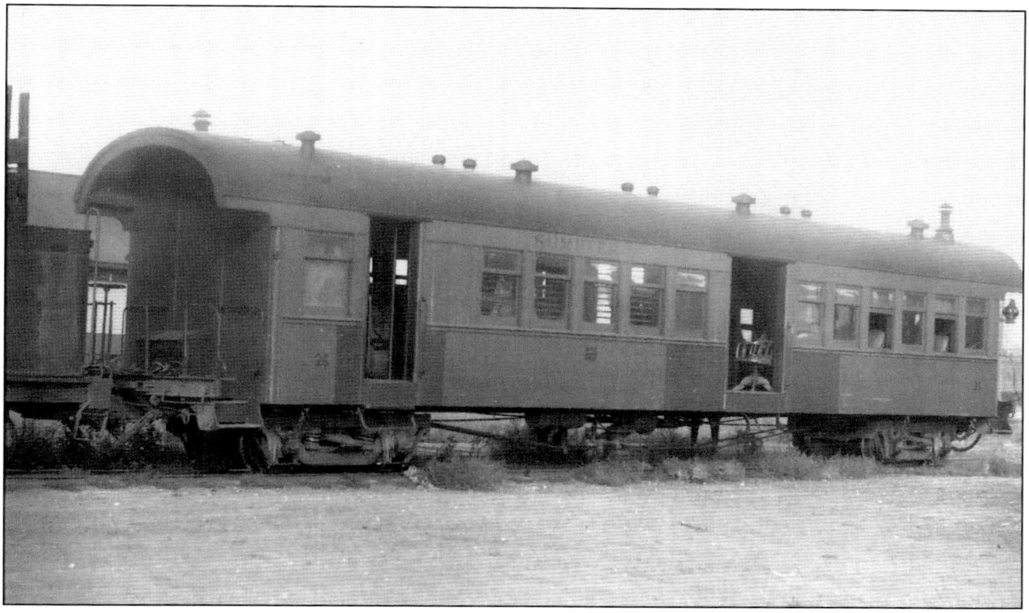

No longer as elegant as when factory fresh nearly two decades earlier, No. 26 has been modified over the years from a day coach to a combine/baggage/coach/RPO amalgamation as traffic declined. (Sumpter Valley Railroad Restoration, Inc.)

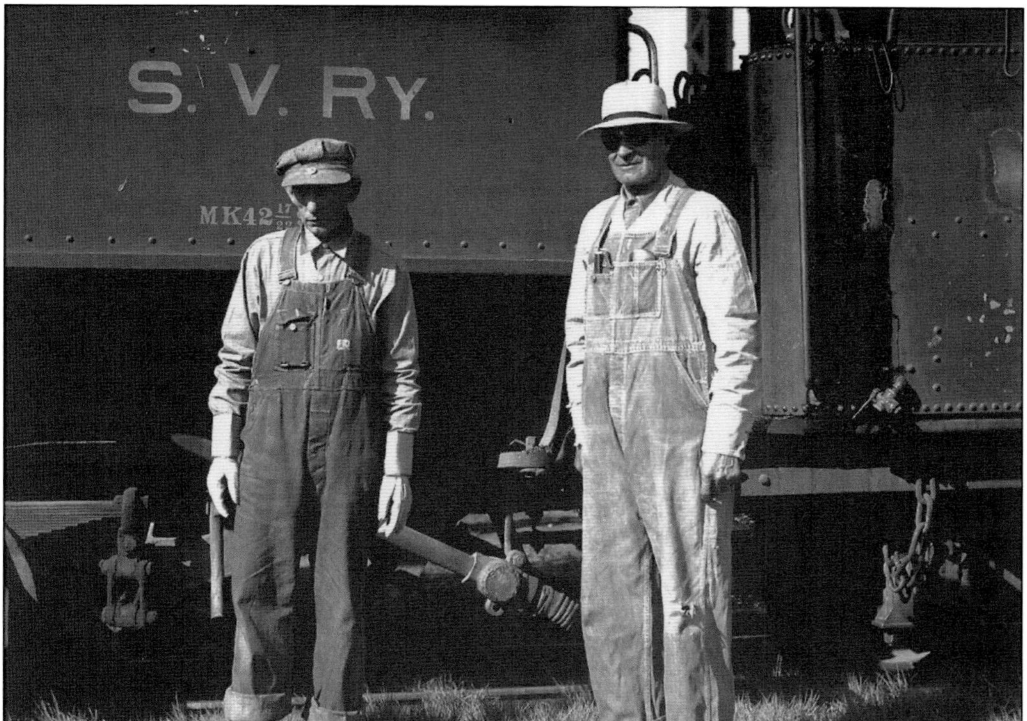

A melancholy crew, U. S. Carpenter (the engineer on the right), and his unidentified fireman (left) stand alongside No. 16 as departure time nears. (Sumpter Valley Railroad Restoration, Inc.)

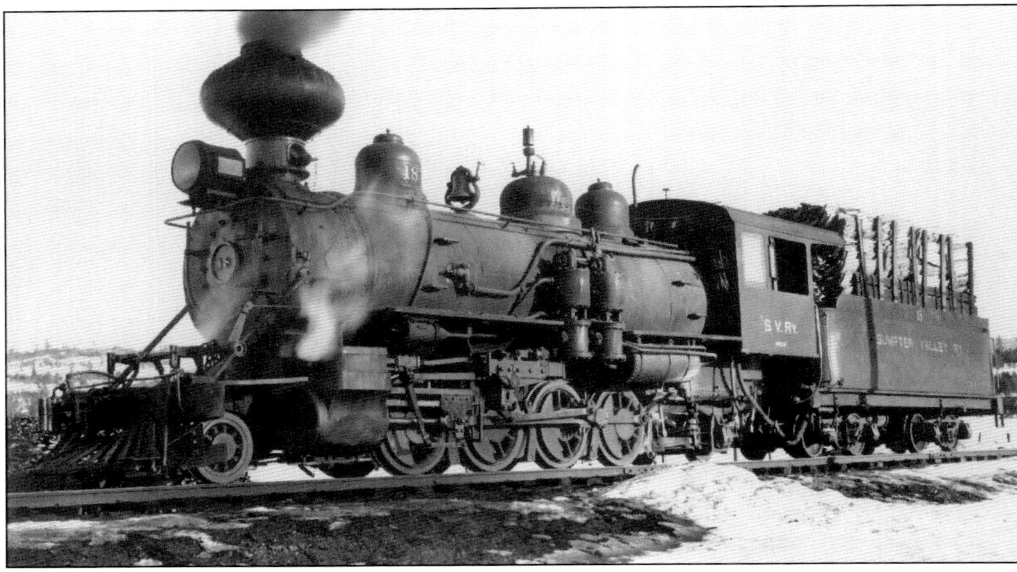

Mikado No. 18 pauses at Bates in 1939 before returning to South Baker with a lumber train. Note the full wood load that would get them halfway to South Baker, and the snow flanging ploughs are clearly visible under the pilot deck. (Photograph by Lamar Ferguson; Matt Mattioda.)

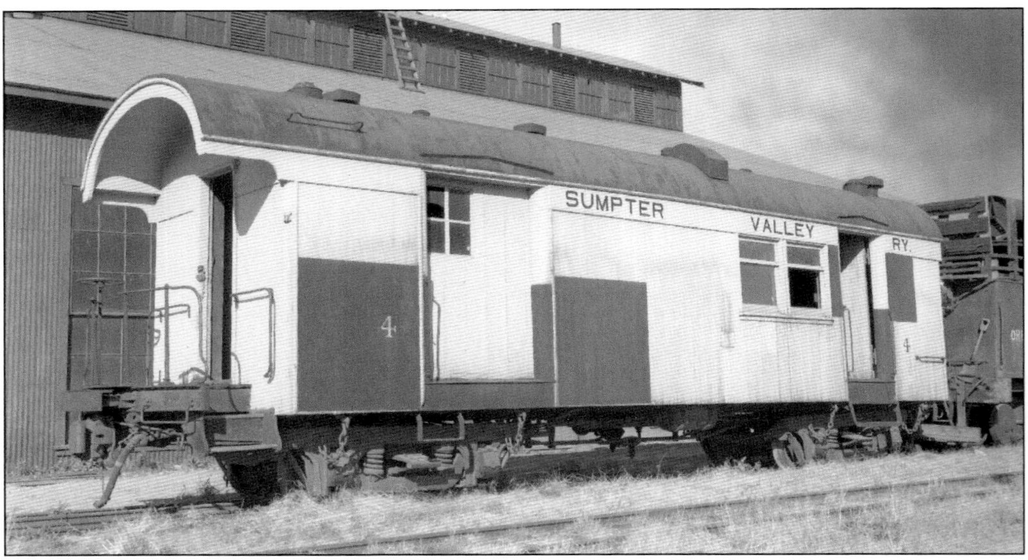

By the late 1930s, the baggage cars still remained in service, but as work train and crew cars. Car No. 4 is showing age and neglect by the time this photograph was taken in the mid-1940s. (Wittaker Collection; Matt Mattioda.)

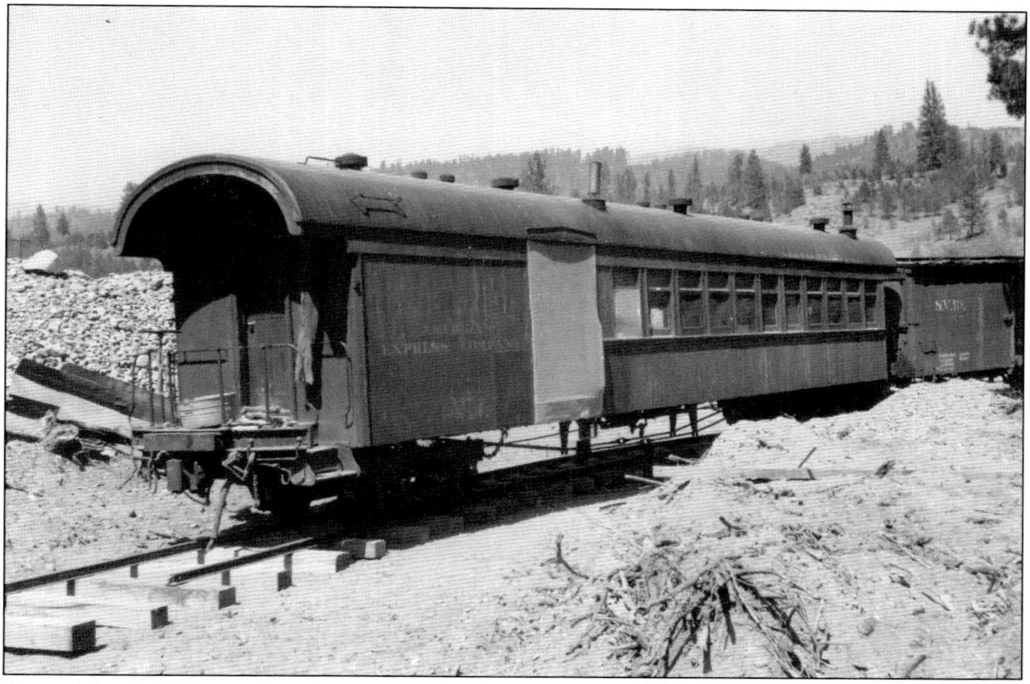

One of the AC&F combines is now serving in work train duties while S-Wye is being relocated to allow the Yuba dredge to continue to chew its way up the Sumpter Valley. Even by the late 1930s, the devastation caused by the dredge is quite evident. (Matt Mattioda.)

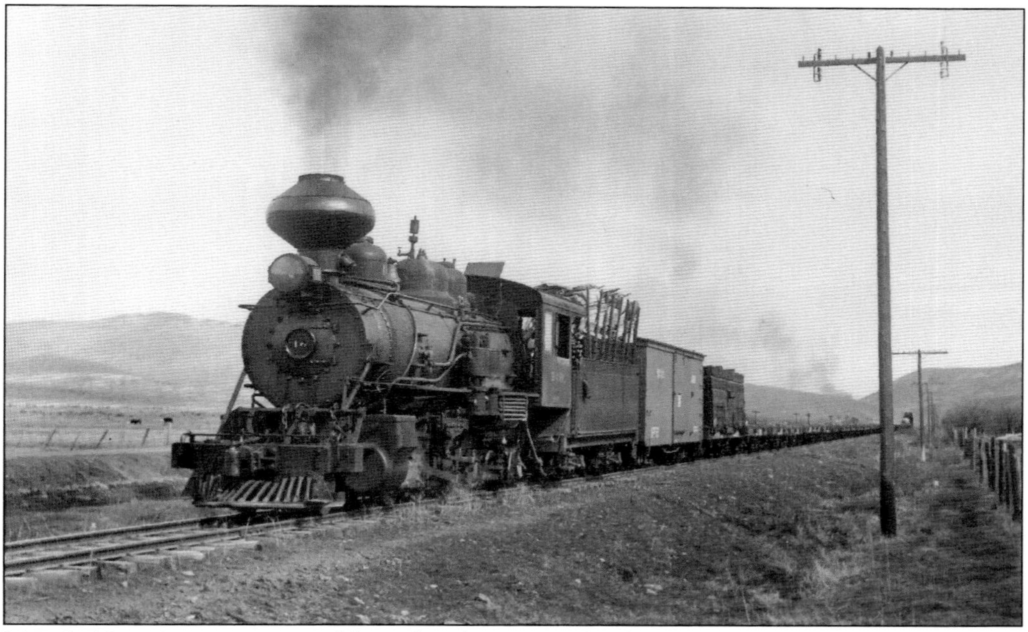

Mikado No. 16 is running southbound with a 34-car freight train to Bates through the Bowen Valley on March 30, 1939. Notice the hog fuel car right behind the boxcar. The Oregon Lumber Company used the mill tailings and sawdust from the sawmills to power the planing mill. (H. R. Griffiths Collection; National Railway Historical Society, Pacific Northwest Chapter.)

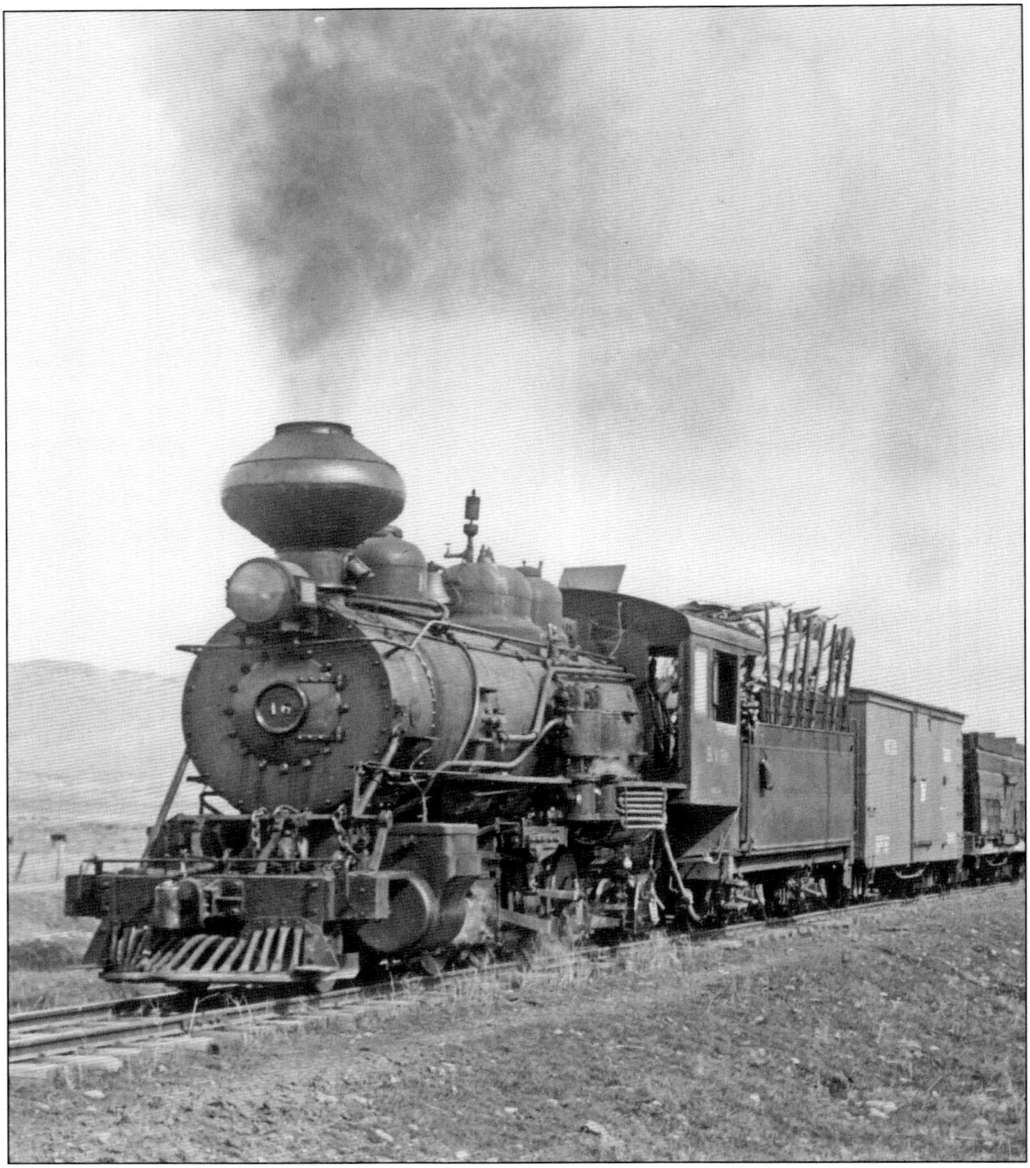

Mikado No. 16 highballs a mixed train across the Bowen Valley between Lockhart and Salisbury. The Elkhorns rise in the background, giving a premonition of the challenging grades ahead. (H. R. Griffiths Collection; Sumpter Valley Railroad Restoration, Inc.)

Six

Retreat to Bates and Back to Logging (1935–1941)

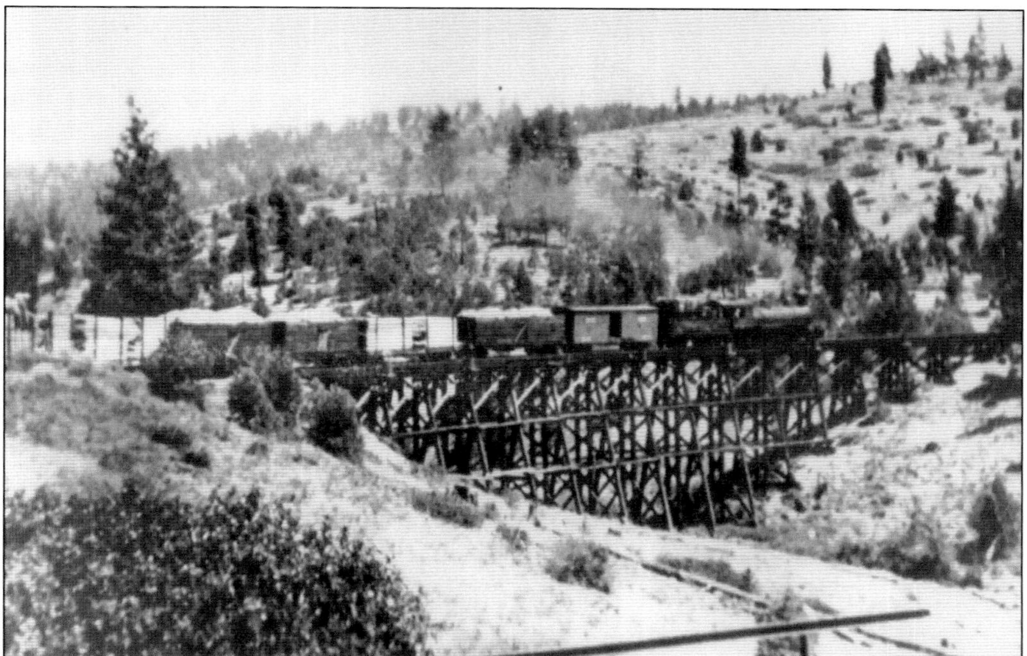

An unidentified Baldwin Mikado leads a mixed freight over the Alder Springs trestle about 1936. Note the mix of hog fuel and rough-cut lumber loads. (McCord Collection; Baker County Library, Baker City, Oregon, Image No. Tr-2.)

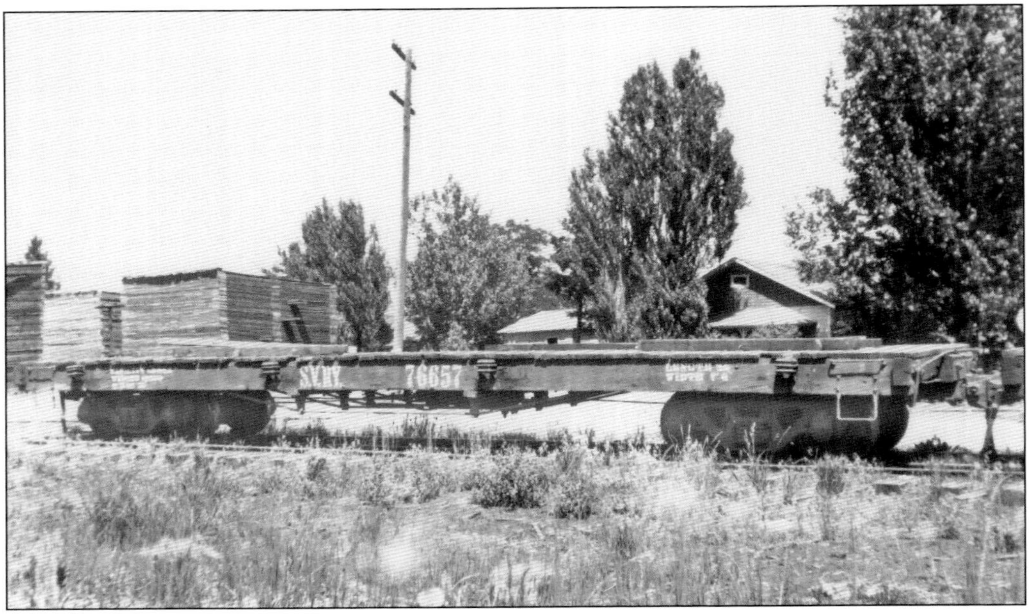

The standard Sumpter Valley Railway flatcar was the workhorse of the railroad. The cars were wood framed; were 36 feet long, 7 feet, 6 inches wide, and truss rodded; and had a tare weight of 17,600 pounds, with a capacity of 60,000 pounds. (Chandler Collection, courtesy of John E. Lewis; Sumpter Valley Railroad Restoration, Inc.)

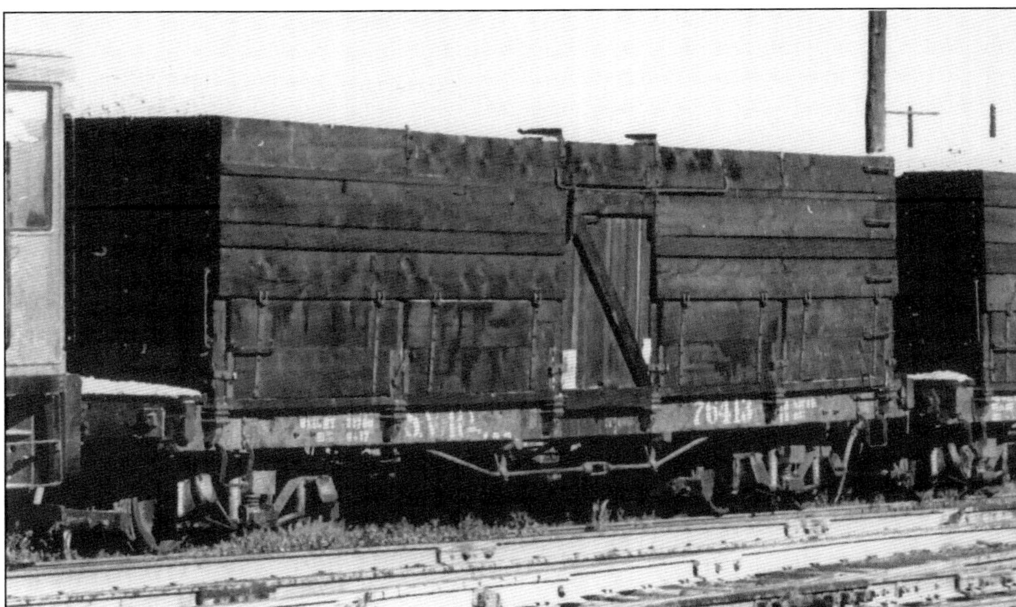

This is a basic sawdust or hog fuel car built by the Sumpter Valley Railway. These cars, based on a flatcar, were braced with rail at the top and had side flaps that opened for emptying. The doors provided access to sweep them out. (Ron Harr Collection; Sumpter Valley Railroad Restoration, Inc.)

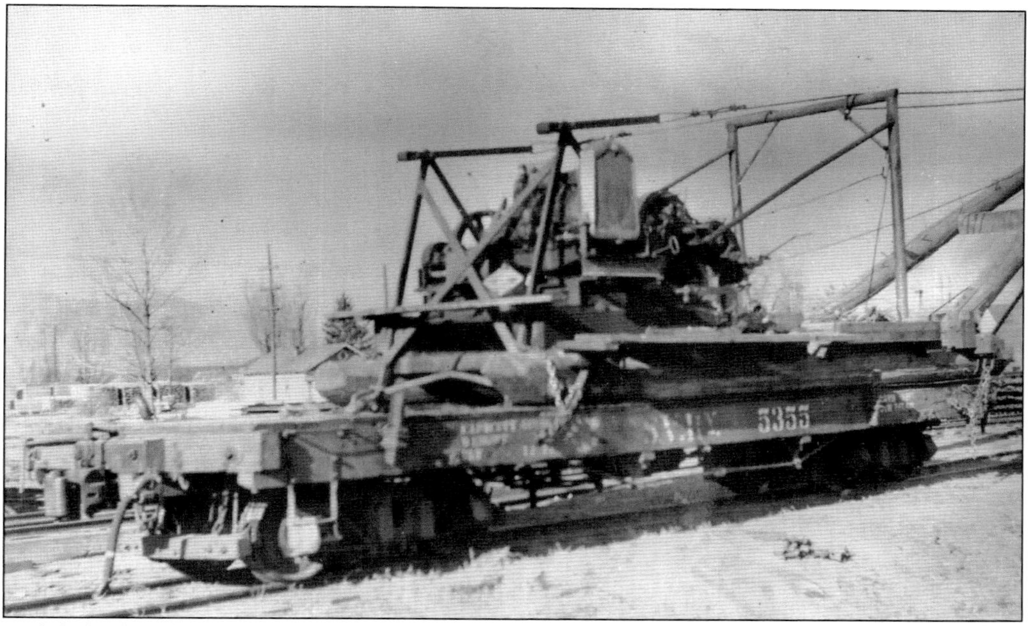

A slide-back A-frame log loader on an older series flatcar was powered by a Ford Model A engine. These loaders were the power that loaded the logs after horses left the woods in the mid-1920s. (Matthew Mattioda; Sumpter Valley Railroad Restoration, Inc.)

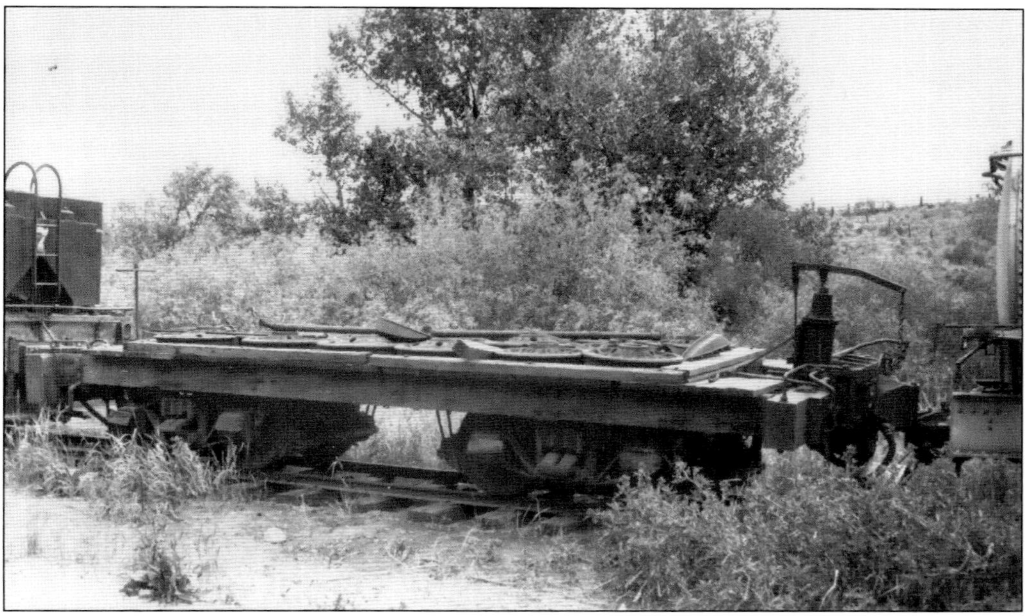

This idler car was built from the tender of the second locomotive No. 2. The adjustable coupler assembly is salvaged from an earlier switch engine. Note the freight car wheels and other scrap piled on the deck to provide stability for the car. (Chandler Collection, courtesy of John E. Lewis; Sumpter Valley Railroad Restoration, Inc.)

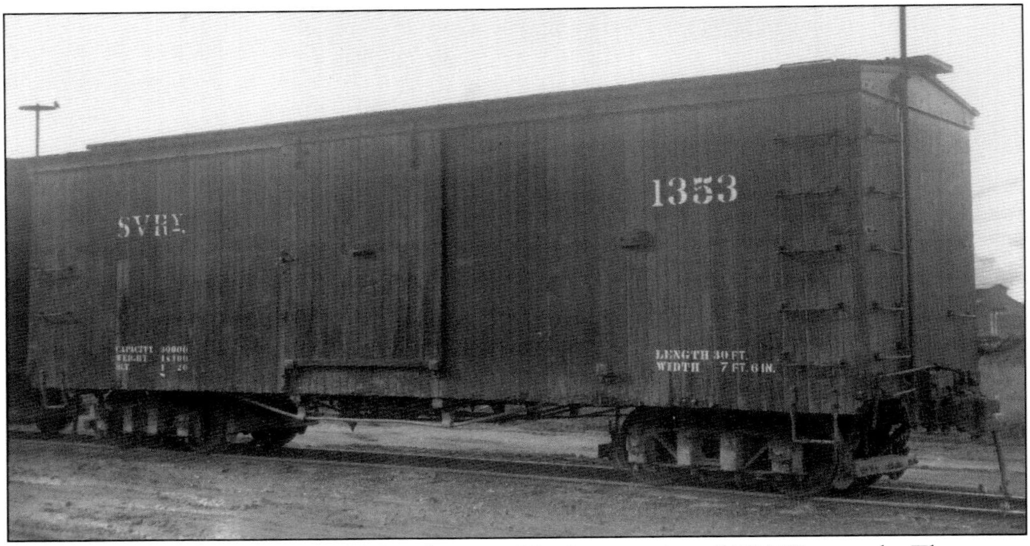

The early series boxcars were 30 feet long and had a capacity of 30,000 pounds. They were equipped with Archbar trucks that had a lighter duty rating than the later Vulcan steel trucks used on 1600-series cars. (Chandler Collection, courtesy of John E. Lewis; Sumpter Valley Railroad Restoration, Inc.)

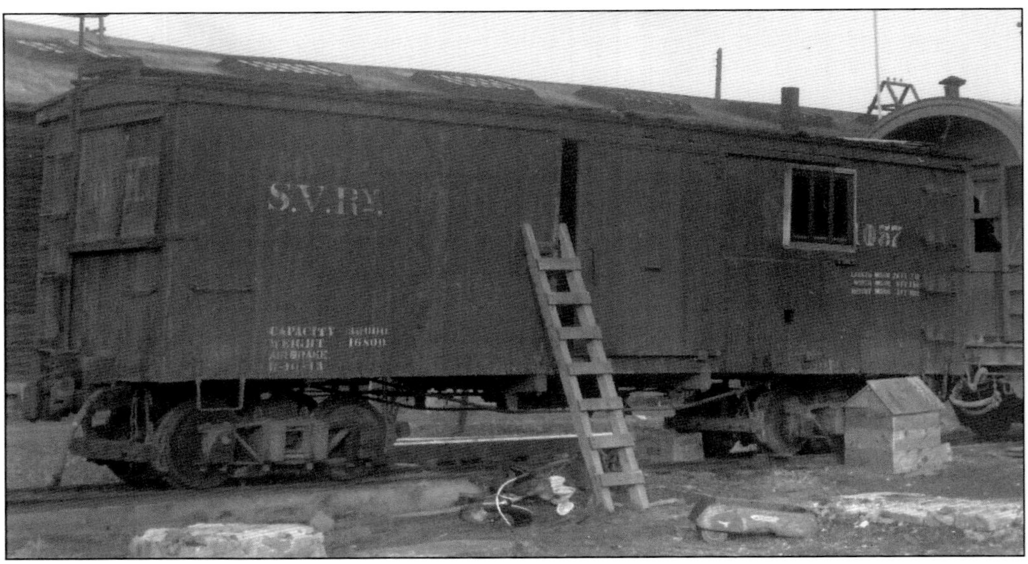

An early series boxcar was converted to a crew car for the bridge and building (B&B) gang. Most of the early equipment found its way either into B&B duty or was converted for camp and storage use by the railroad and loggers. (Chandler Collection, courtesy of John E. Lewis; Sumpter Valley Railroad Restoration, Inc.)

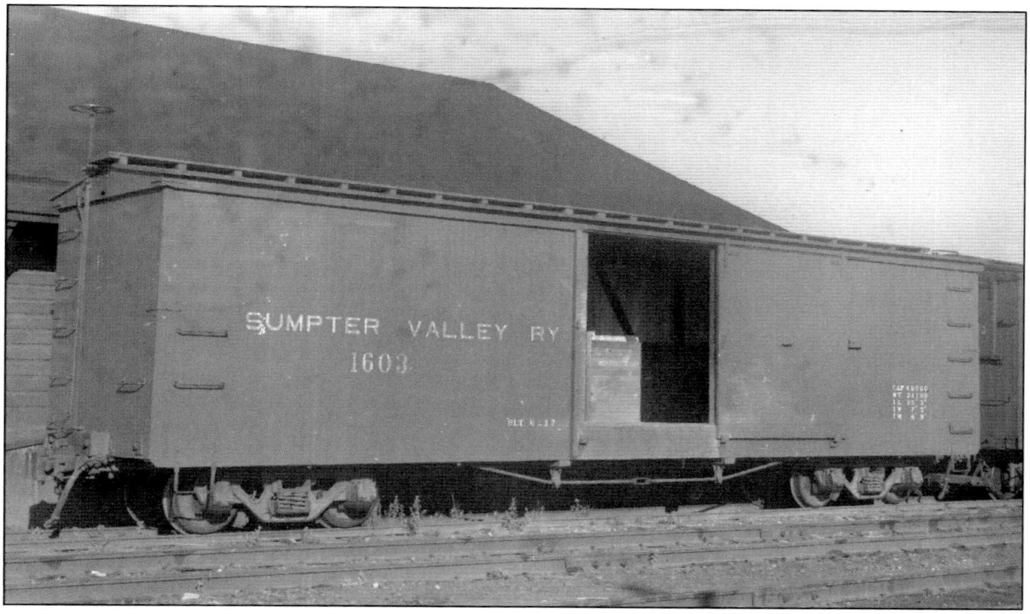

Built in 1917 by the South Baker shops, these boxcars served through the end of the Sumpter Valley Railway and beyond to South America. At 35 feet, 6 inches long and with a capacity of 60,000 pounds, they were an improvement on the earlier generation cars, using the stronger Vulcan trucks and heavier frames. (Chandler Collection, courtesy of John E. Lewis; Sumpter Valley Railroad Restoration, Inc.)

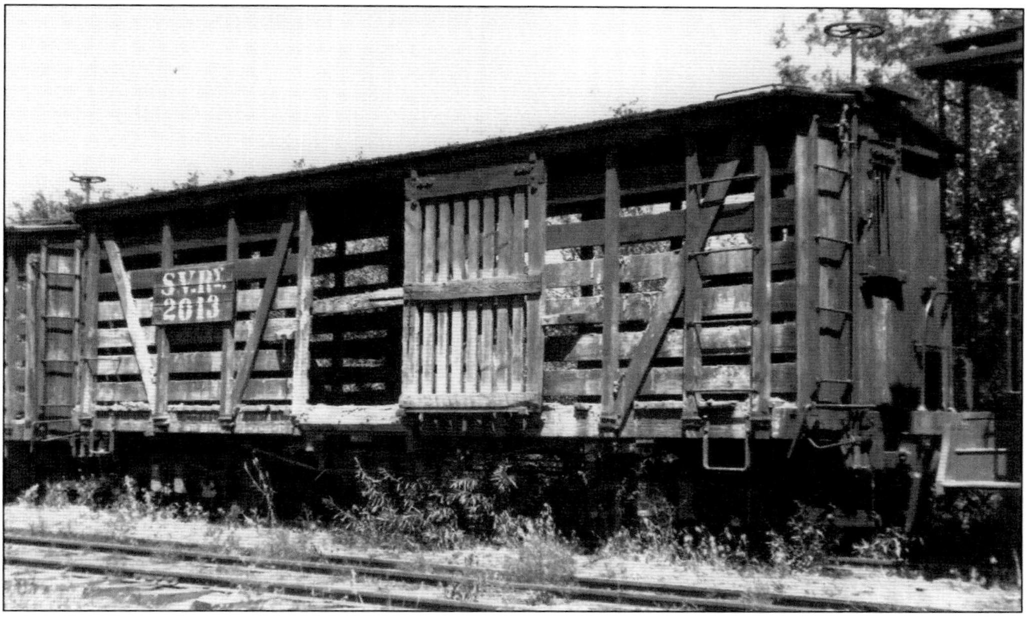

Originally built in the 1890s, these stockcars were among the smallest used by any railroad. They are 28 feet long and have a low head height. (Chandler Collection, courtesy of John E. Lewis; Sumpter Valley Railroad Restoration, Inc.)

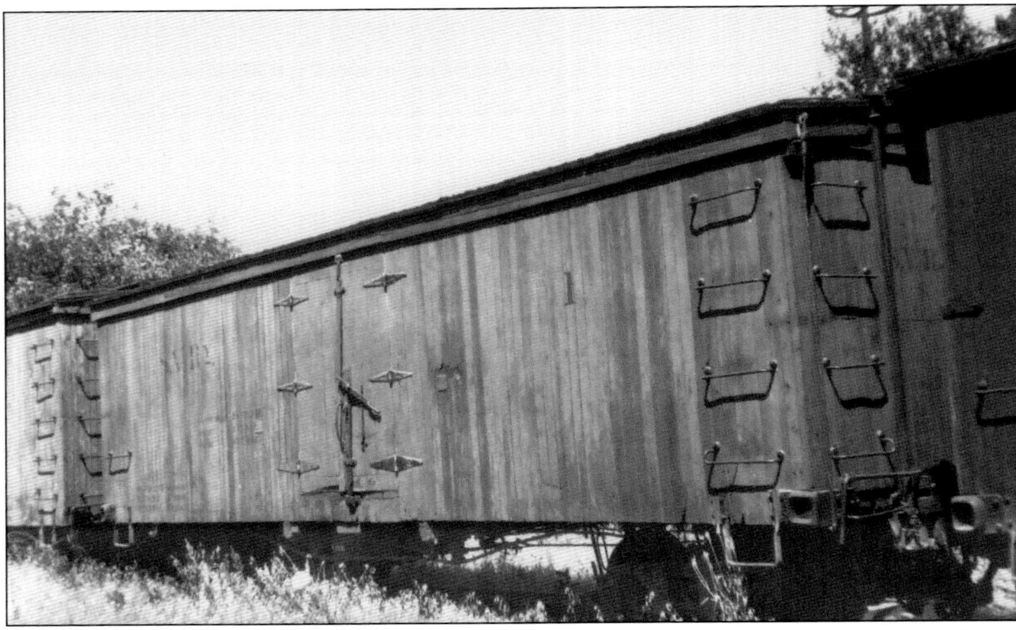

The 27-foot insulated boxcars started out life as regular boxcars and were rebuilt around 1900 into refrigerator cars using kits. The railroad discovered that the ice wasn't needed for the short trip to Prairie City, and they were converted to insulated cars for the remainder of their careers. In the early years, they were painted similar to the classic Tiffany refrigerators. (Chandler Collection, courtesy of John E. Lewis; Sumpter Valley Railroad Restoration, Inc.)

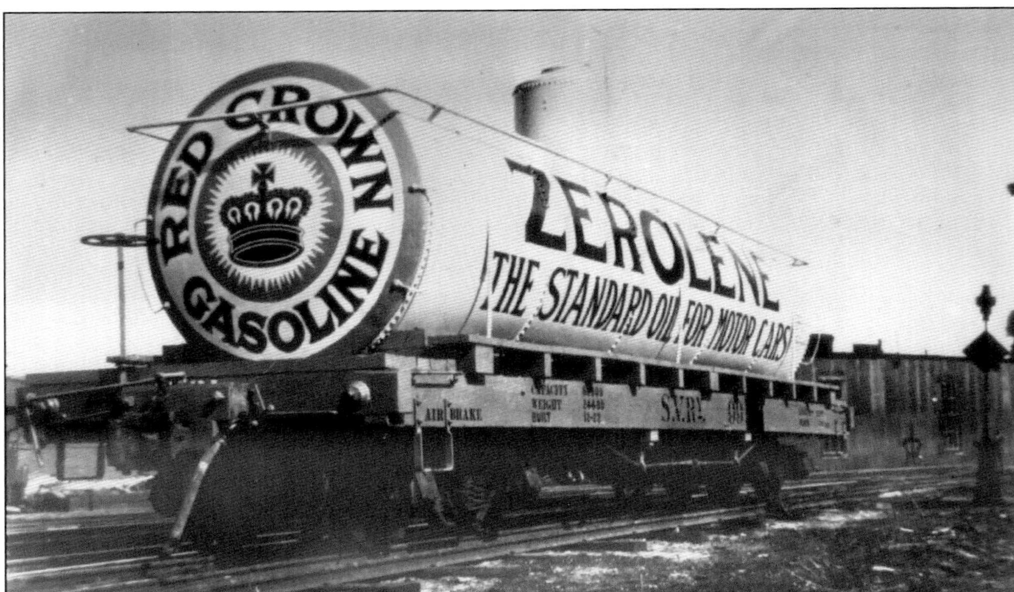

The most colorful car on the railroad was the Zerolene tank car. It consisted of a standard-gauge tank attached to a narrow-gauge flatcar frame. It was painted with a silver background and black, red, and blue logo and trim. (Chandler Collection, courtesy of John E. Lewis; Sumpter Valley Railroad Restoration, Inc.)

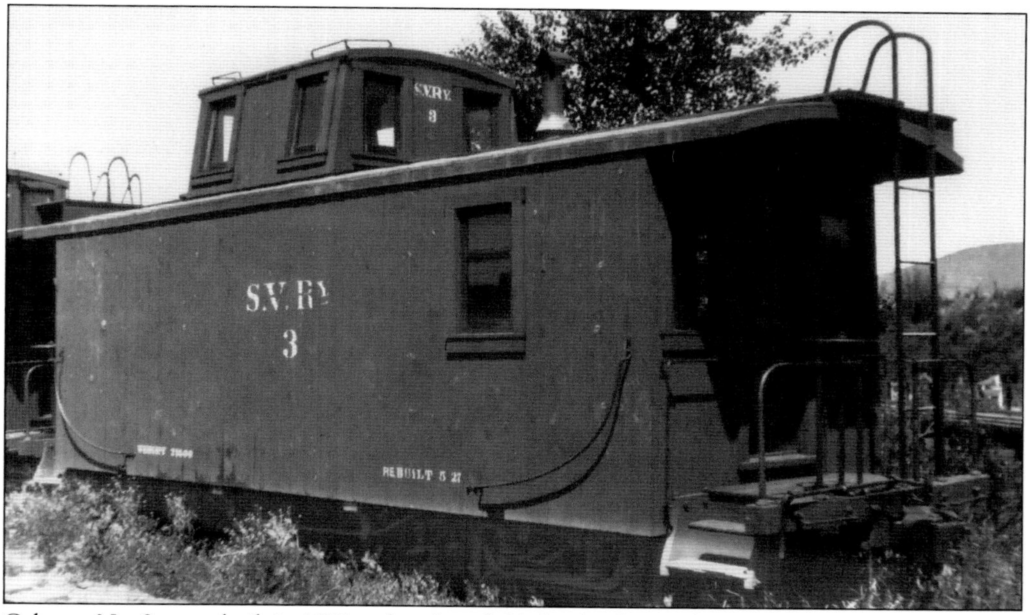

Caboose No. 3 was rebuilt in 1927 and is identifiable by the slope-side cupola. (Chandler Collection, courtesy of John E. Lewis; Sumpter Valley Railroad Restoration, Inc.)

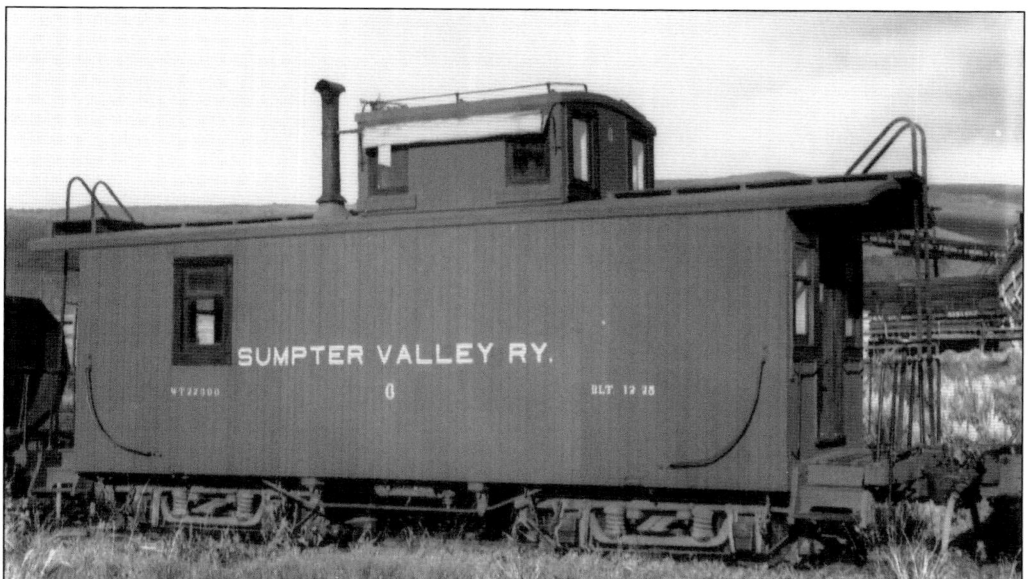

Rebuilt in 1925, caboose No. 6 received a square cupola but retained a similar layout to the other cabooses on the road. (Ron Harr Collection; Sumpter Valley Railroad Restoration, Inc.)

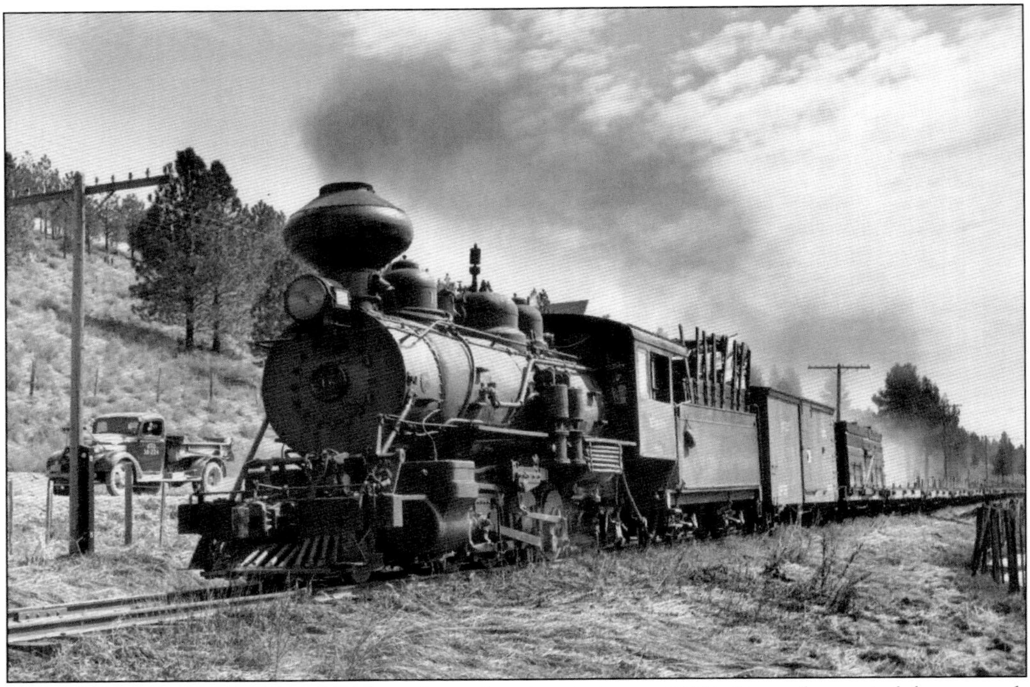

Mikado No. 16 near Lockhart heads up-bound to Austin in the 1930s. Note the period dump truck on the left and the water/food bag hanging on the side of the tender. (H. R. Griffiths Collection; Sumpter Valley Railroad Restoration, Inc.)

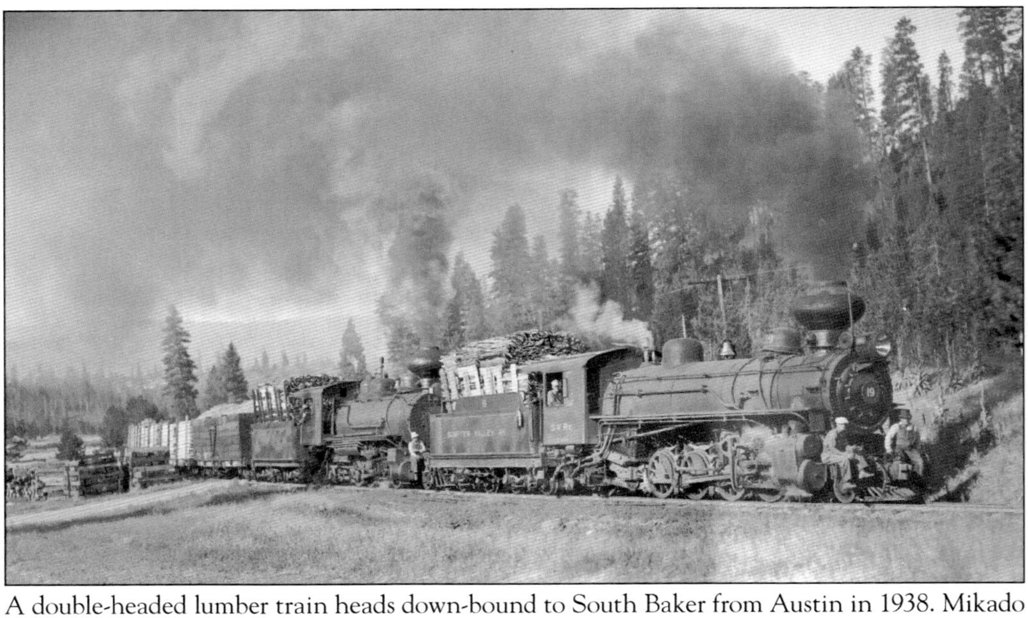

A double-headed lumber train heads down-bound to South Baker from Austin in 1938. Mikado No. 19 is in the lead with a Baldwin Mikado following. (Otto Perry Collection, OP-16208, Western History Collection; Denver Public Library.)

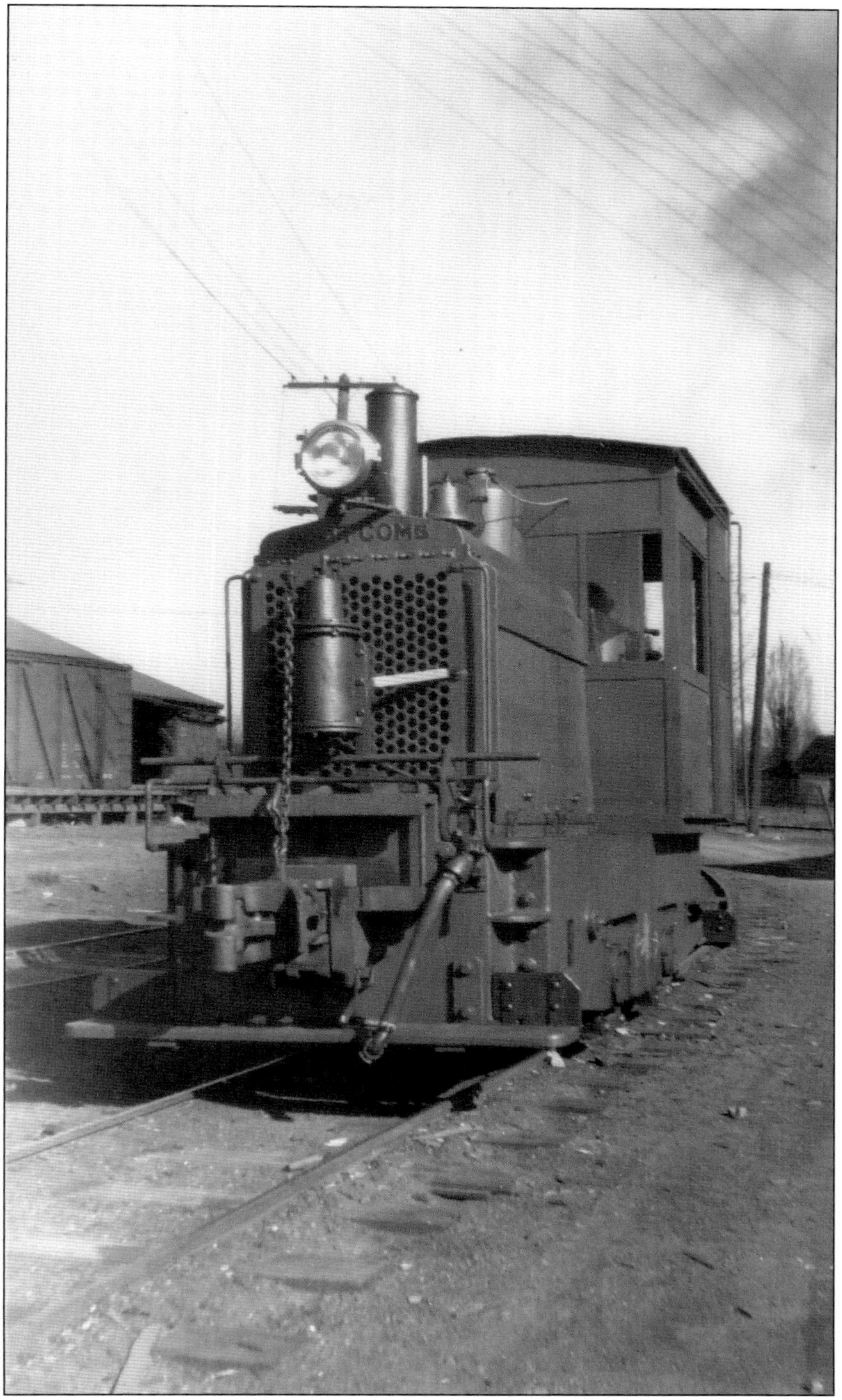

The Whitcomb gas-mechanical switcher idles in the South Baker yards in the early 1930s. Note the unusual dual-gauge coupler mechanism. A system similar to this had been in use on various yard locomotives since around 1900. (Ron Harr Collection; Sumpter Valley Railroad Restoration, Inc.)

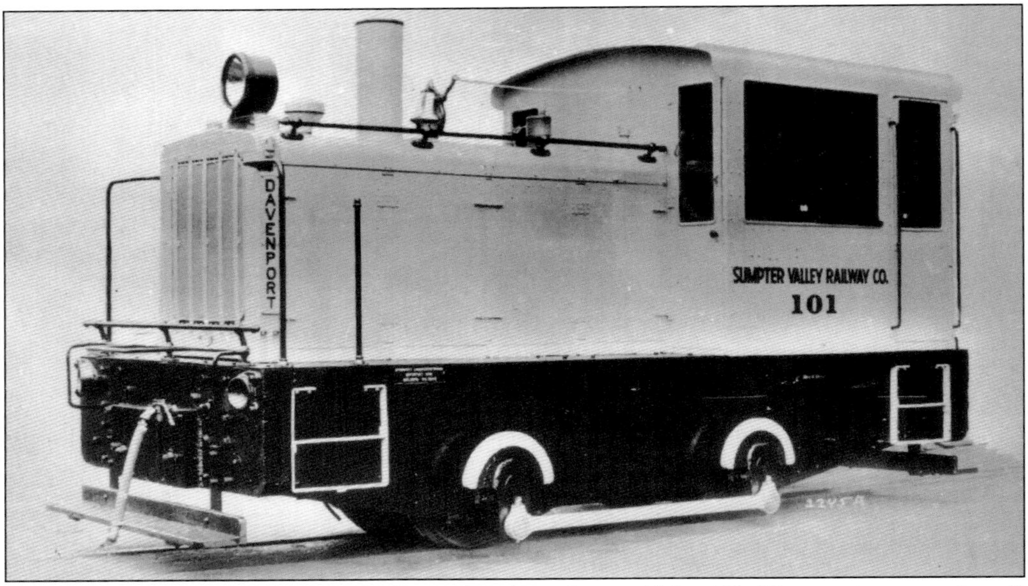

A Davenport builder's photograph shows diesel mechanical No. 101. This engine served until the very end of the Sumpter Valley Railway. It migrated to the Denver and Rio Grande Western in Durango, Colorado, and is now being restored by the Colorado Railroad Museum. (Ron Harr Collection; Sumpter Valley Railroad Restoration, Inc.)

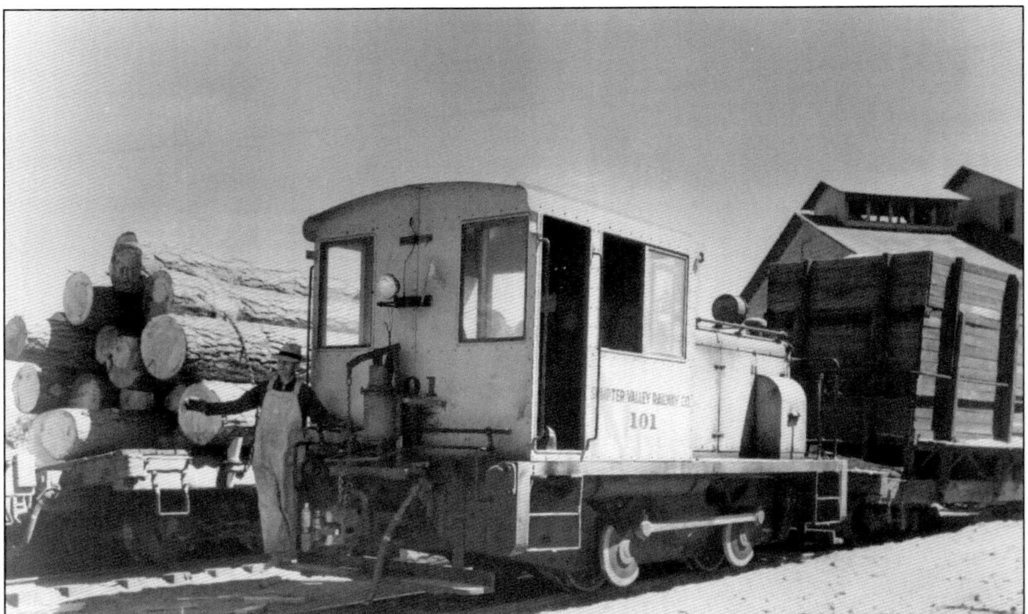

Sumpter Valley Railway No. 101 is shown switching at the Stoddard Mill in the 1940s. Once again, the dual-gauge coupler mechanism is visible. (Chandler Collection, courtesy of J. E. Lewis; Sumpter Valley Railroad Restoration, Inc.)

Home-Made Gasoline Motor Car for Auxiliary Service

The Sumpter Valley Railway, Baker, Ore., recently built in its shops a gasoline motor car for auxiliary service on its narrow-gage line. A 45-hp. White motor truck engine was used and the body was built to seat twenty-seven passengers. A light four-wheel pilot truck was set under the head end and a single pair of large diameter wheels to which power was transmitted served as the rear truck. The car was designed to make an average speed of 20 m.p.h. and operated over grades up to 4 per cent. Excellent service is reported for the thirty days during which the motor was in use. At the end of that time it was completely demolished in a head-on collision.

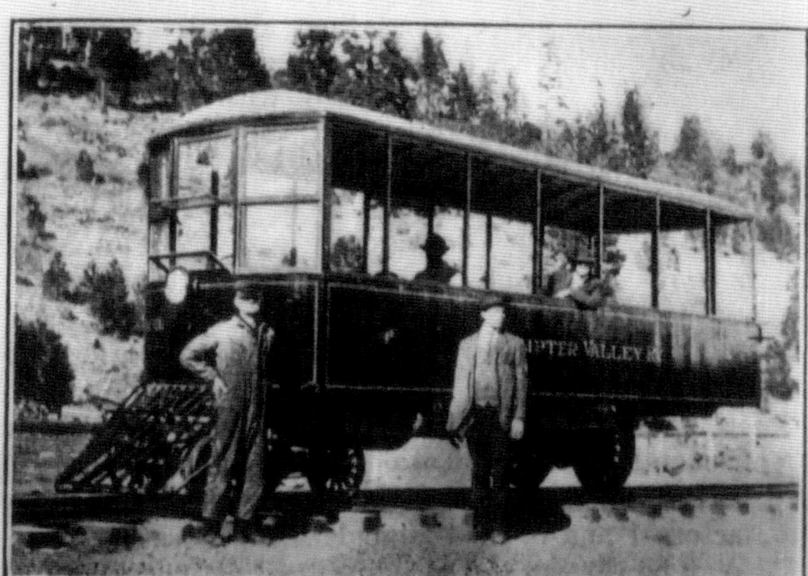

GASOLINE MOTOR CAR ON NARROW-GAGE ROAD OF SUMPTER VALLEY RAILWAY

A clipping from a late-1917 copy of the *Electric Railway Journal* gives the brief history of the Sumpter Valley Railway motorcar. (D. L. Stearns Collection through Ron Harr; Sumpter Valley Railroad Restoration, Inc.)

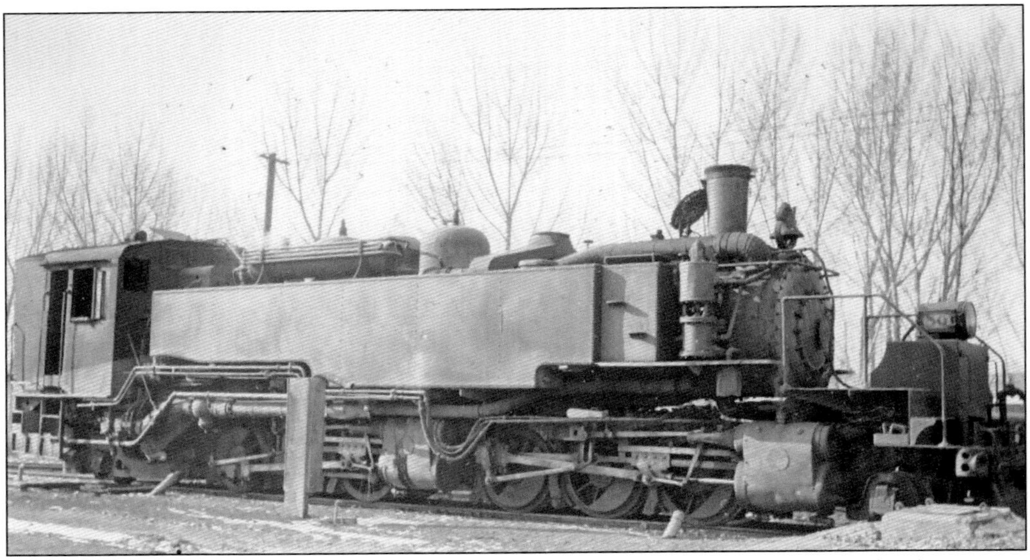

Uintah No. 50 rests near Mack, Colorado, in 1939. The Uintah Railroad had ceased rail transport of Gilsonite, and the engine awaited a call to her new home. (Bret Bane Collection.)

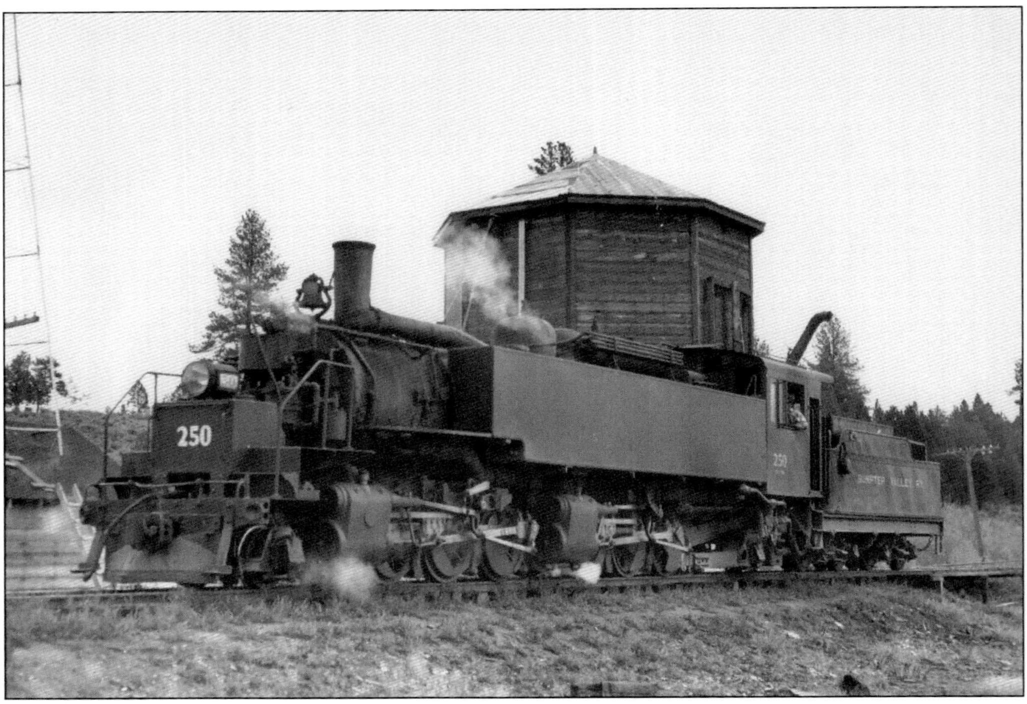

Uintah No. 50, one year later in Whitney, is pictured as SVRy No. 250. Note the saddle tanks are still installed, even though she has been renumbered. The tanks were later removed to improved visibility for the crew. (H. R. Griffiths Collection; National Railway Historical Society, Pacific Northwest Chapter.)

Seven

The Mallet Swan Song (1941–1946)

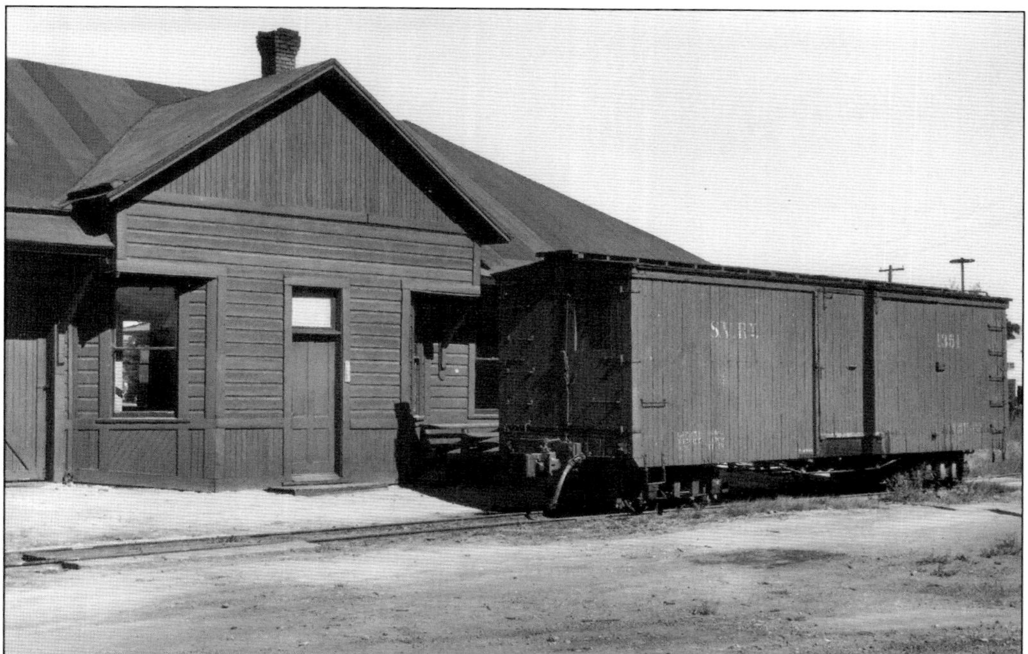

The South Baker Depot is quiet in August 1946. The weathered boxcar seems to echo the fact that the end of the railroad was near. Between 1941 and 1946, the Uintah Mallets (2-6-6-2) were the swan song of the Sumpter Valley Railway. By the end of 1946, the curtain had closed, but what a finale the Mallets provided. (H. R. Griffiths Collection; National Railway Historical Society, Pacific Northwest Chapter.)

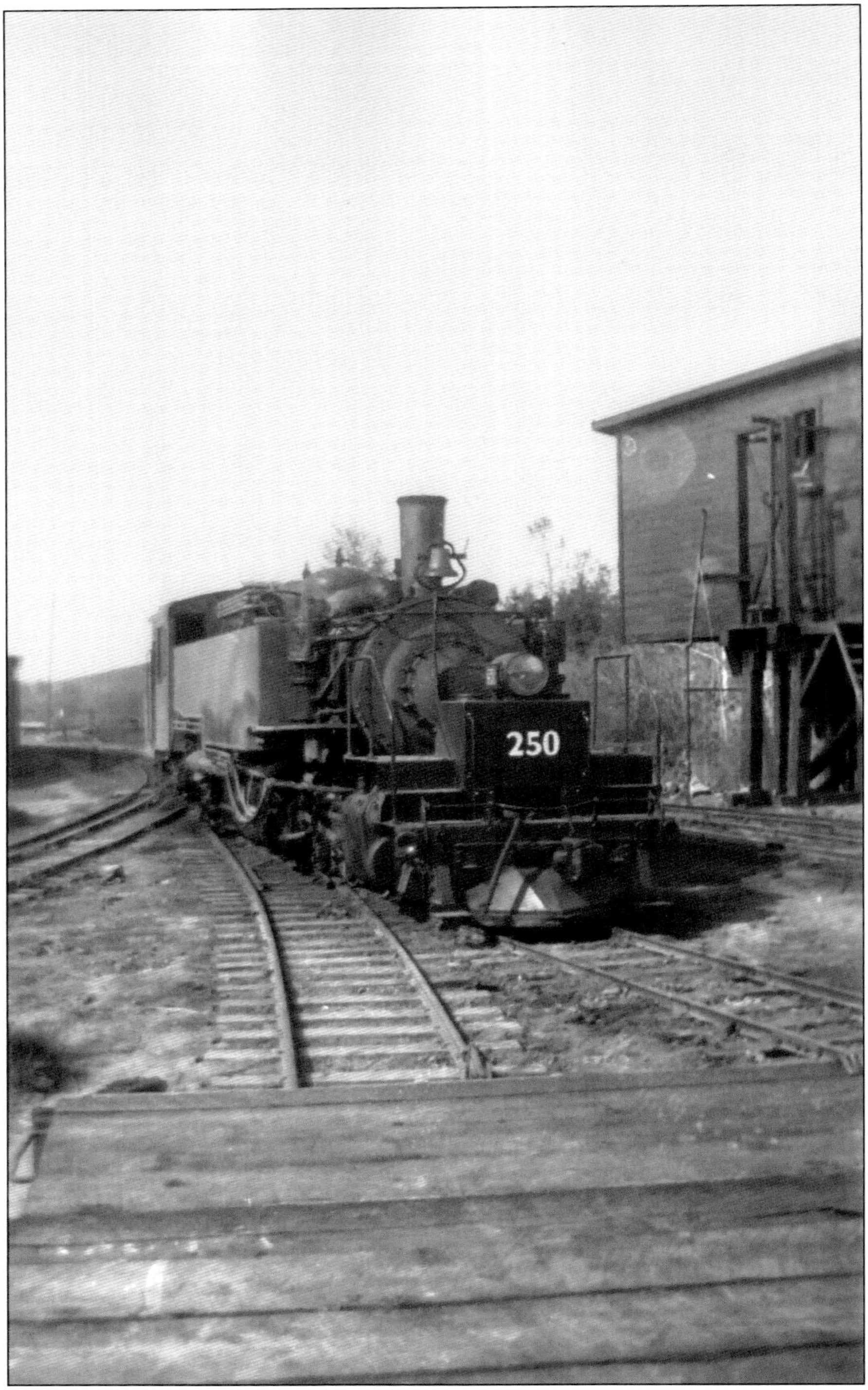

Sumpter Valley Railway Locomotive No. 250 runs by the oil tank in South Baker in late 1940. She is shown with her saddle tanks intact. (H. R. Griffiths Collection; National Railway Historical Society, Pacific Northwest Chapter.)

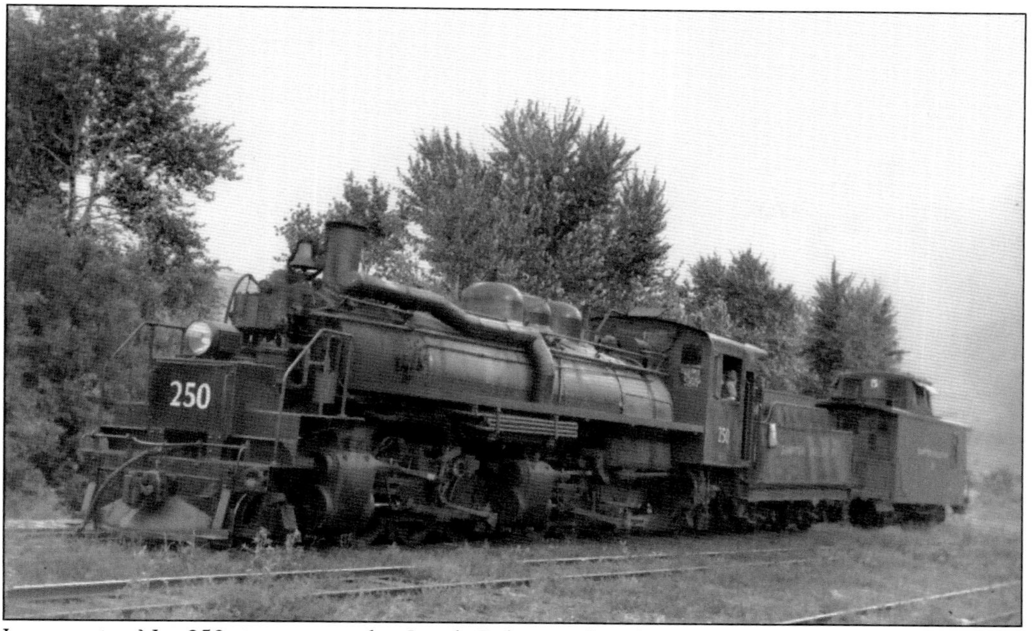

Locomotive No. 250 simmers in the South Baker yard with caboose No. 5 in the early 1940s. The saddle tanks have been replaced at this time with thick rail walkways to compensate for the weight of the tanks. (Shekell Collection; Sumpter Valley Railroad Restoration, Inc.)

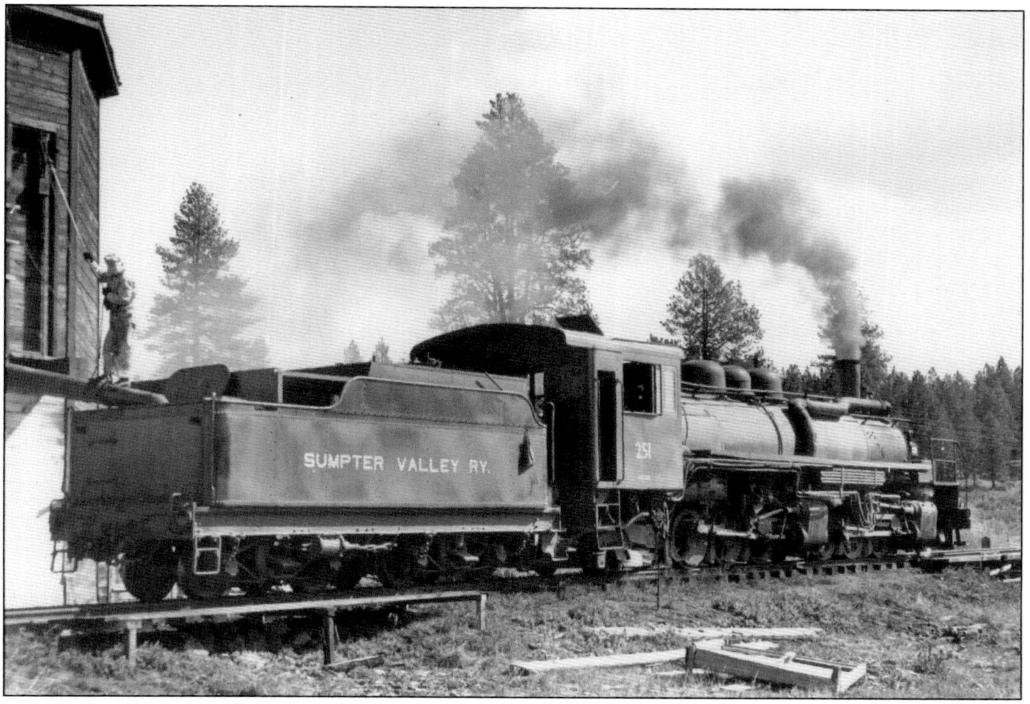

SVRy No. 251 in Whitney takes on water in August 1940. (H. R. Griffiths Collection; National Railway Historical Society, Pacific Northwest Chapter.)

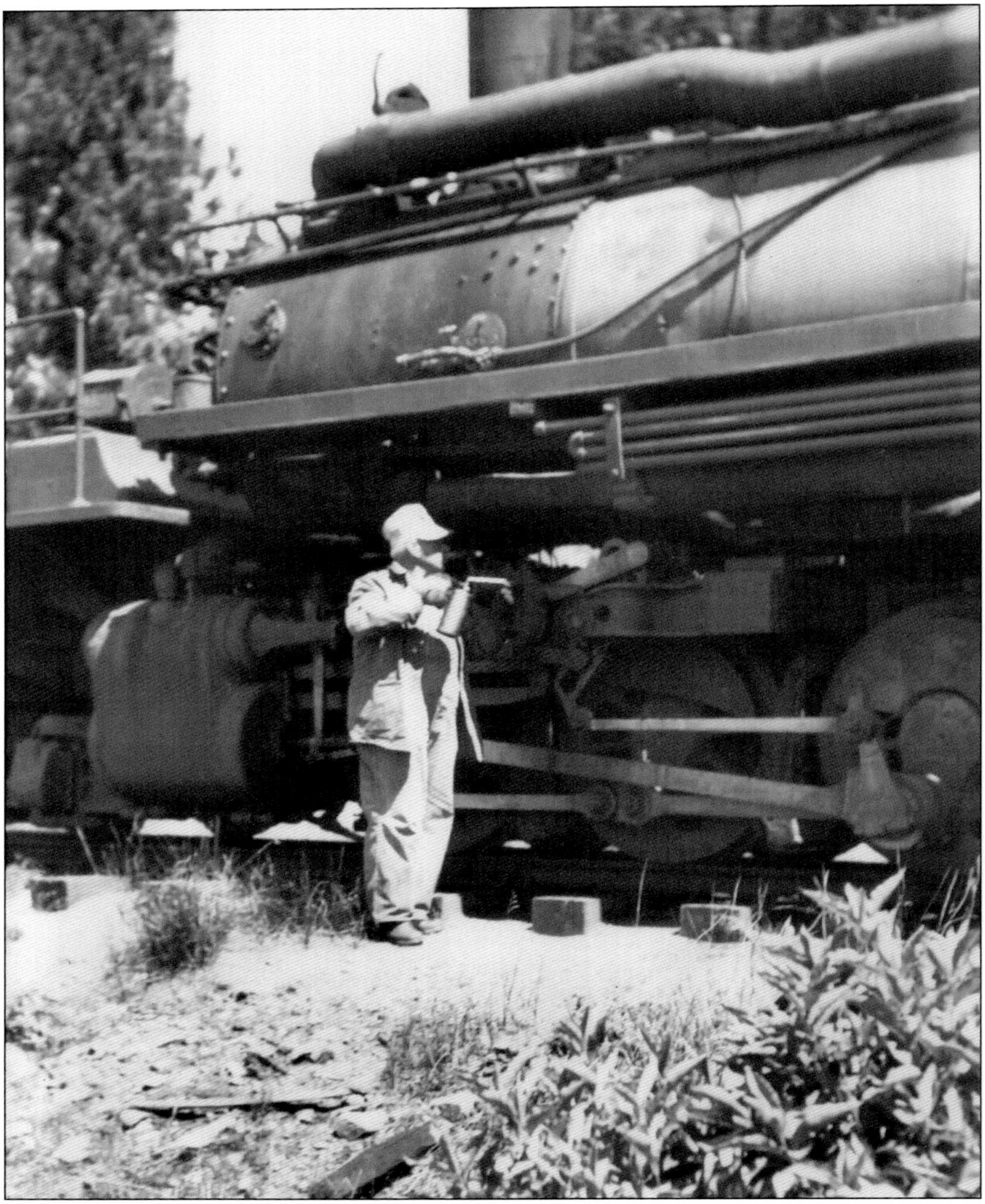

Engineer Chris Karp oils around a Mallet while taking a break at S-Wye. Here is a good view of the extra-thick boiler walks that were used as extra traction weight as well as the size of the locomotives. (H. R. Griffiths Collection; Sumpter Valley Railroad Restoration, Inc.)

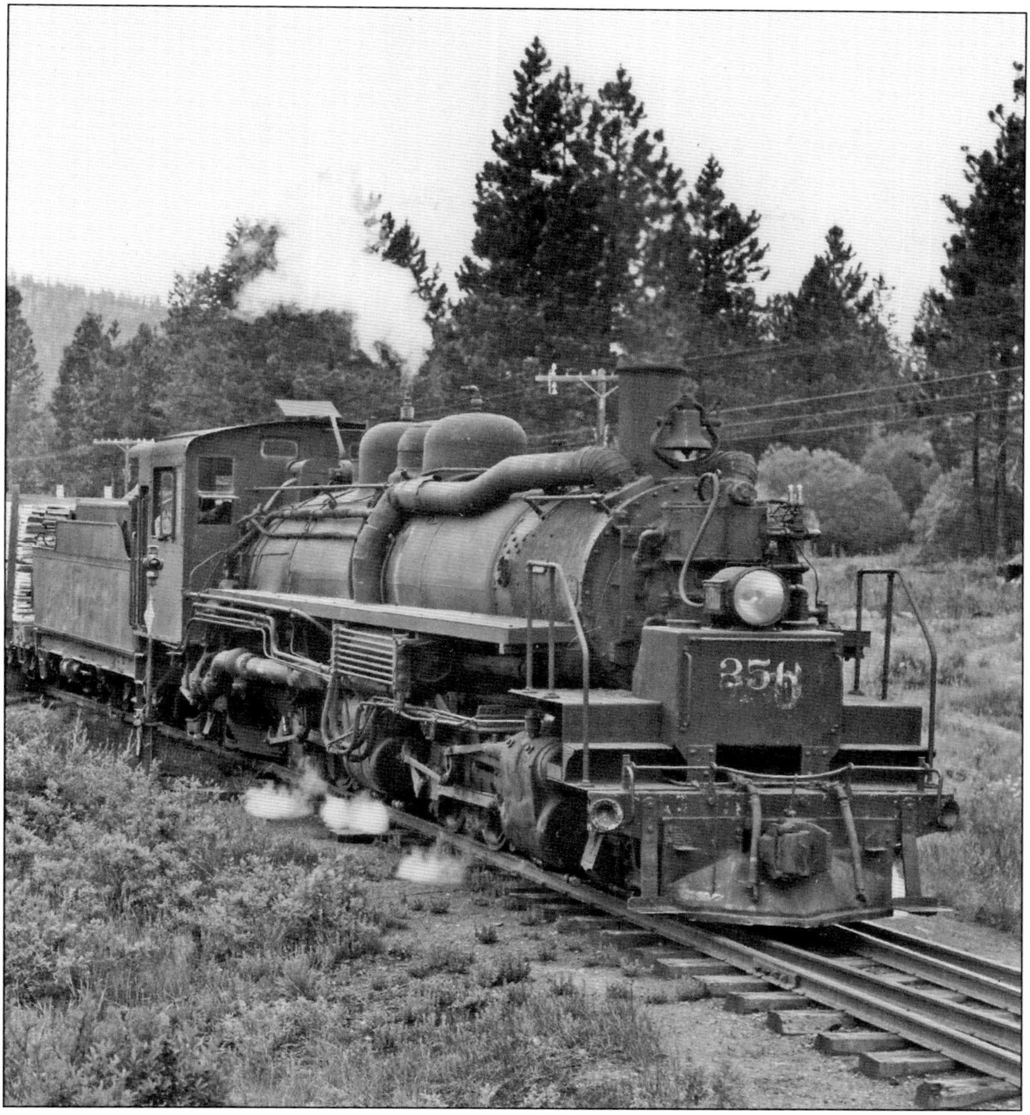

Mallet No. 250, at S-Wye, heads down-bound to South Baker in the mid-1940s. (H. R. Griffiths Collection; National Railway Historical Society, Pacific Northwest Chapter.)

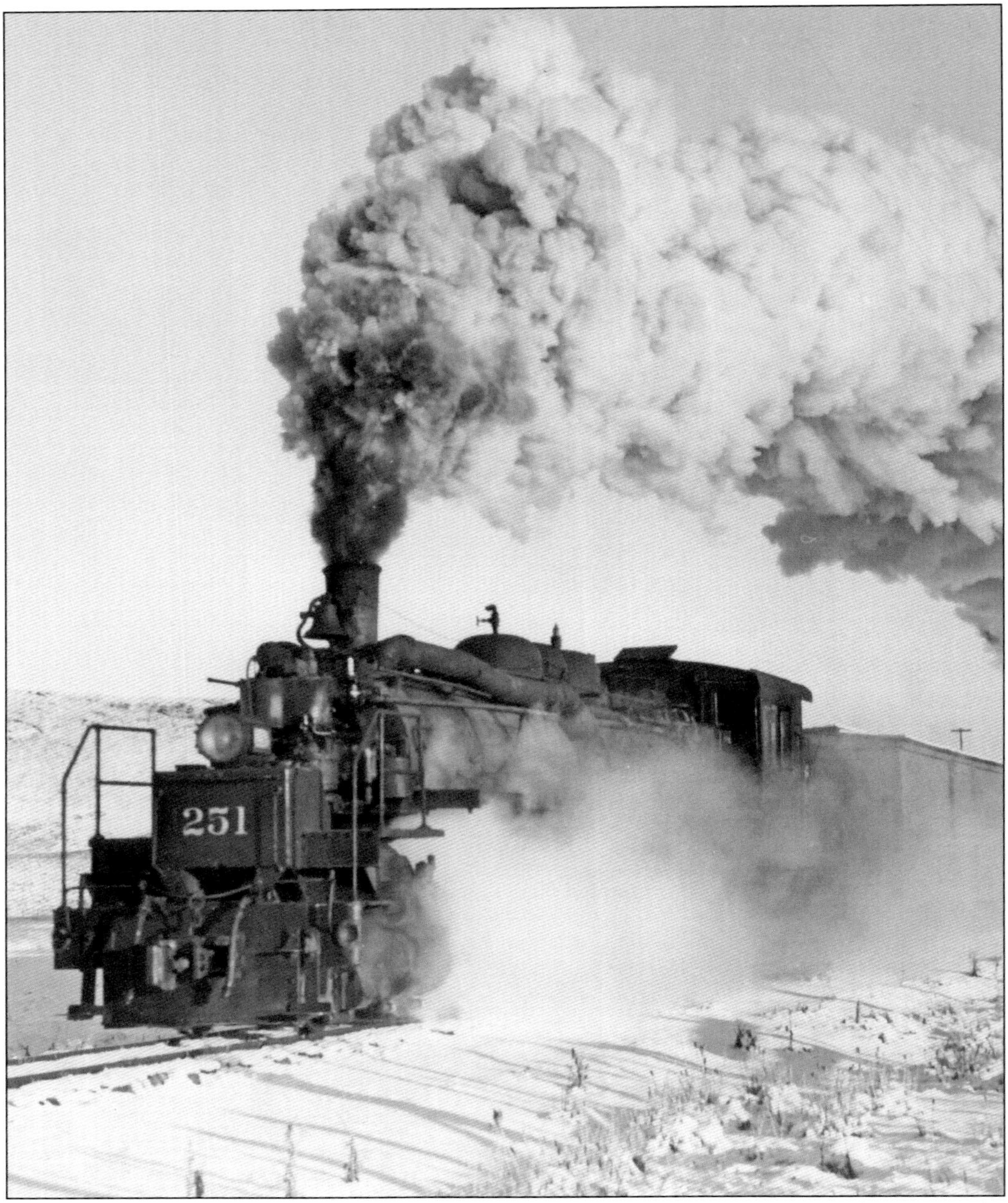

Mallet No. 251 roars across Bowen Valley, headed up-bound to Bates in the early 1940s. The steam and mist provide a dramatic frame for the locomotive. (H. R. Griffiths Collection; National Railway Historical Society, Pacific Northwest Chapter.)

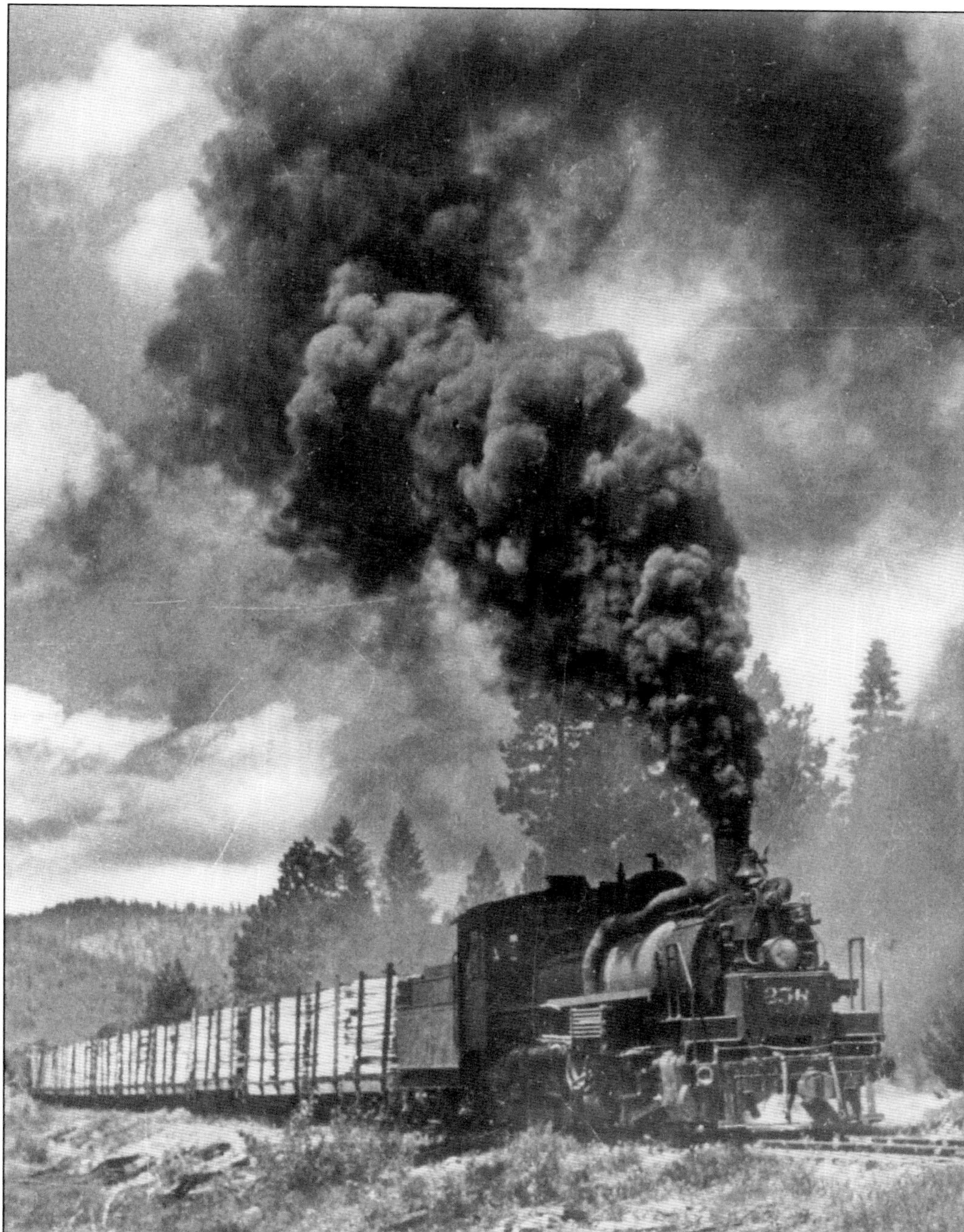

Mallet No. 250 runs down-bound from Bates with a full lumber train in the mid-1940s. The engineer most likely was creating the smoke plume for the benefit of Henry Griffiths, a well-known photographer, as most railroads frowned upon wasting oil to make smoke. (H. R. Griffiths Collection; National Railway Historical Society, Pacific Northwest Chapter.)

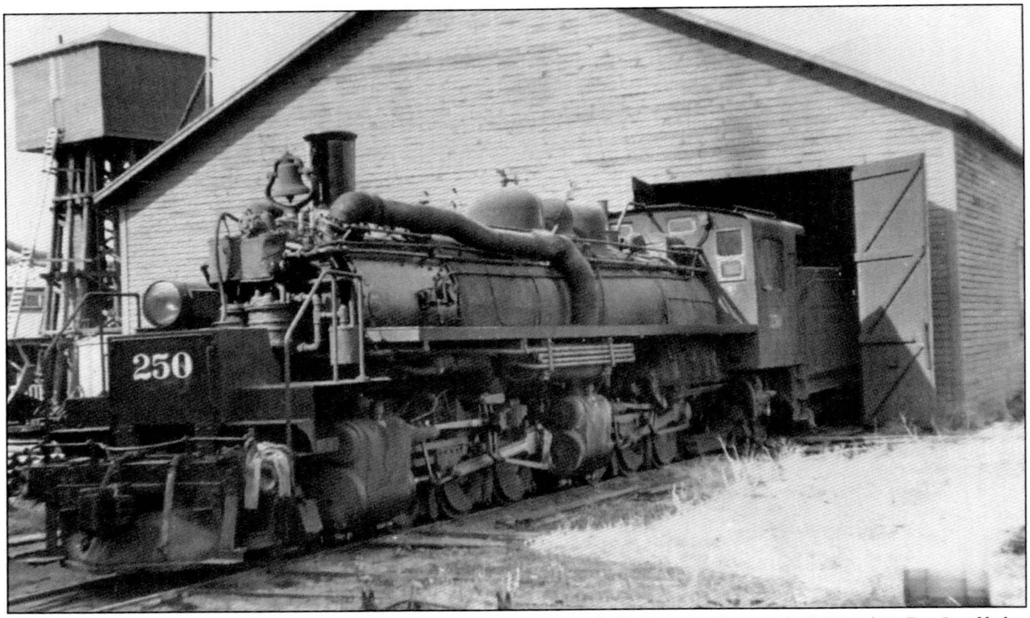

Mallet No. 250 is parked outside the mallet house in South Baker in the mid-1940s. (H. R. Griffiths Collection; National Railway Historical Society, Pacific Northwest Chapter.)

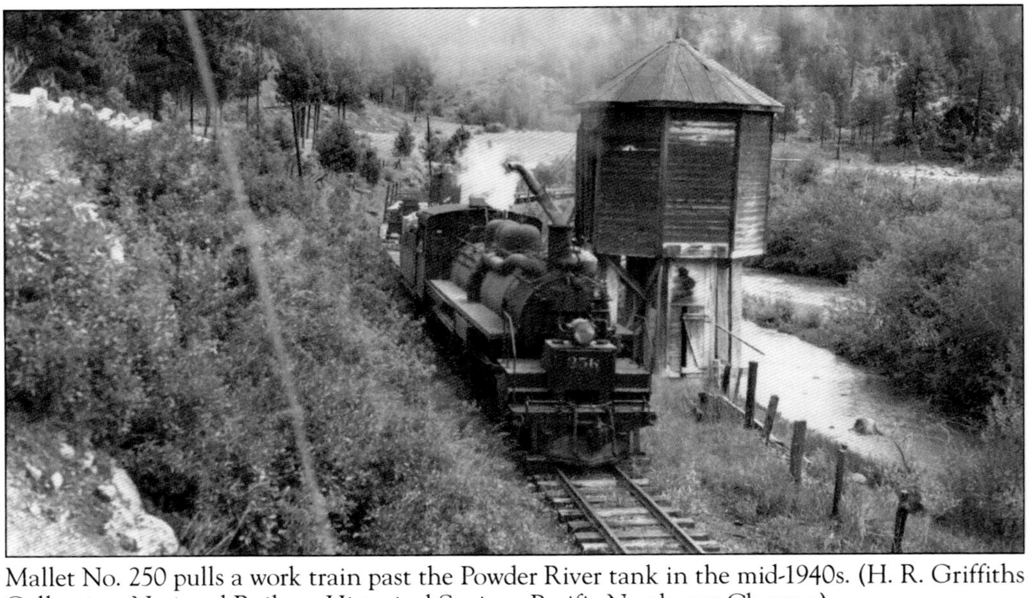

Mallet No. 250 pulls a work train past the Powder River tank in the mid-1940s. (H. R. Griffiths Collection; National Railway Historical Society, Pacific Northwest Chapter.)

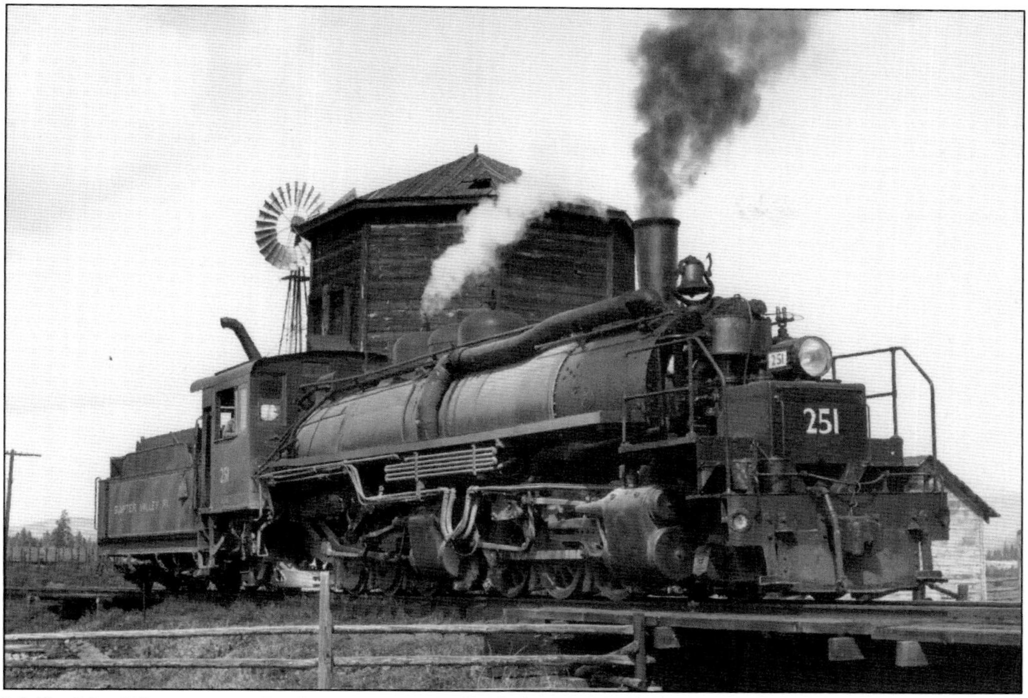

Mallet No. 251 pauses at the Austin water tank while running light. Note the windmill used to pump water for the tank. (H. R. Griffiths Collection; Sumpter Valley Railroad Restoration, Inc.)

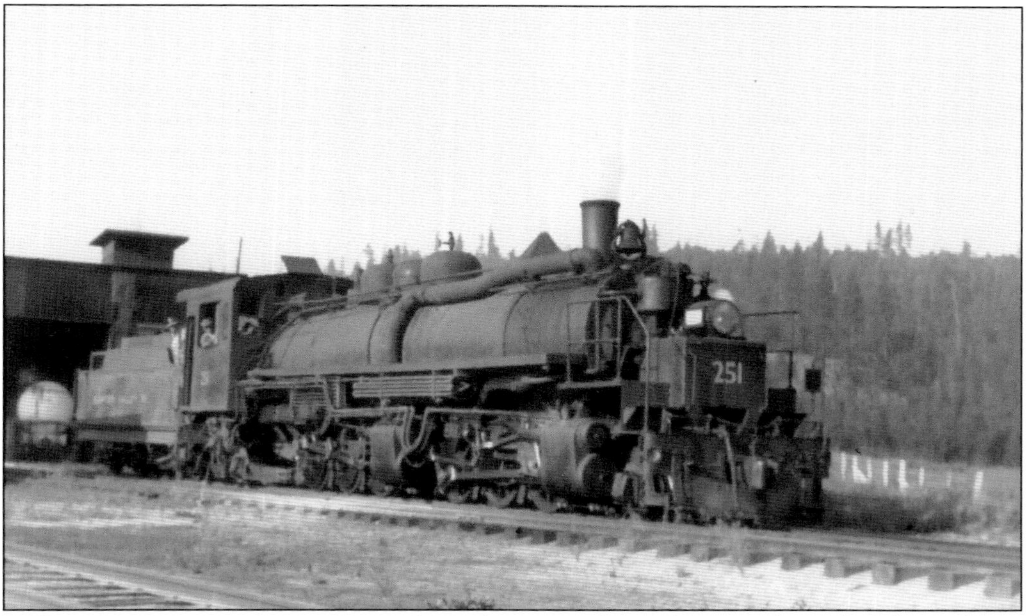

Mallet No. 251 simmers at Austin in the early 1940s. The tank car used to refuel the Mallet is located in the engine house stall behind the locomotive. (Shekell Collection; Sumpter Valley Railroad Restoration, Inc.)

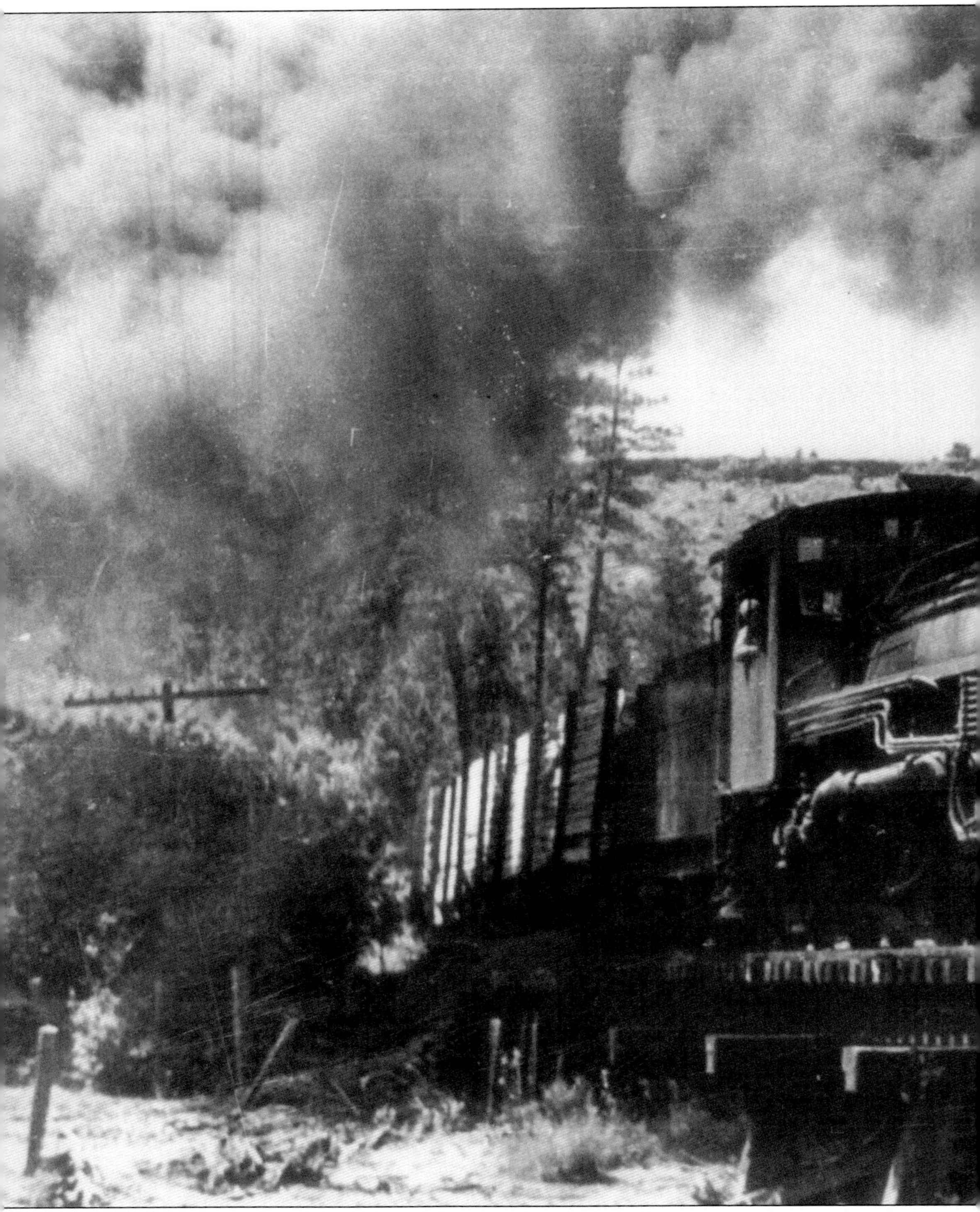

Mallet No. 250 blasts over the Powder River between Salisbury and Lockhart with a down-bound lumber train. Note the lack of hog fuel cars, as the South Baker planing mill had been

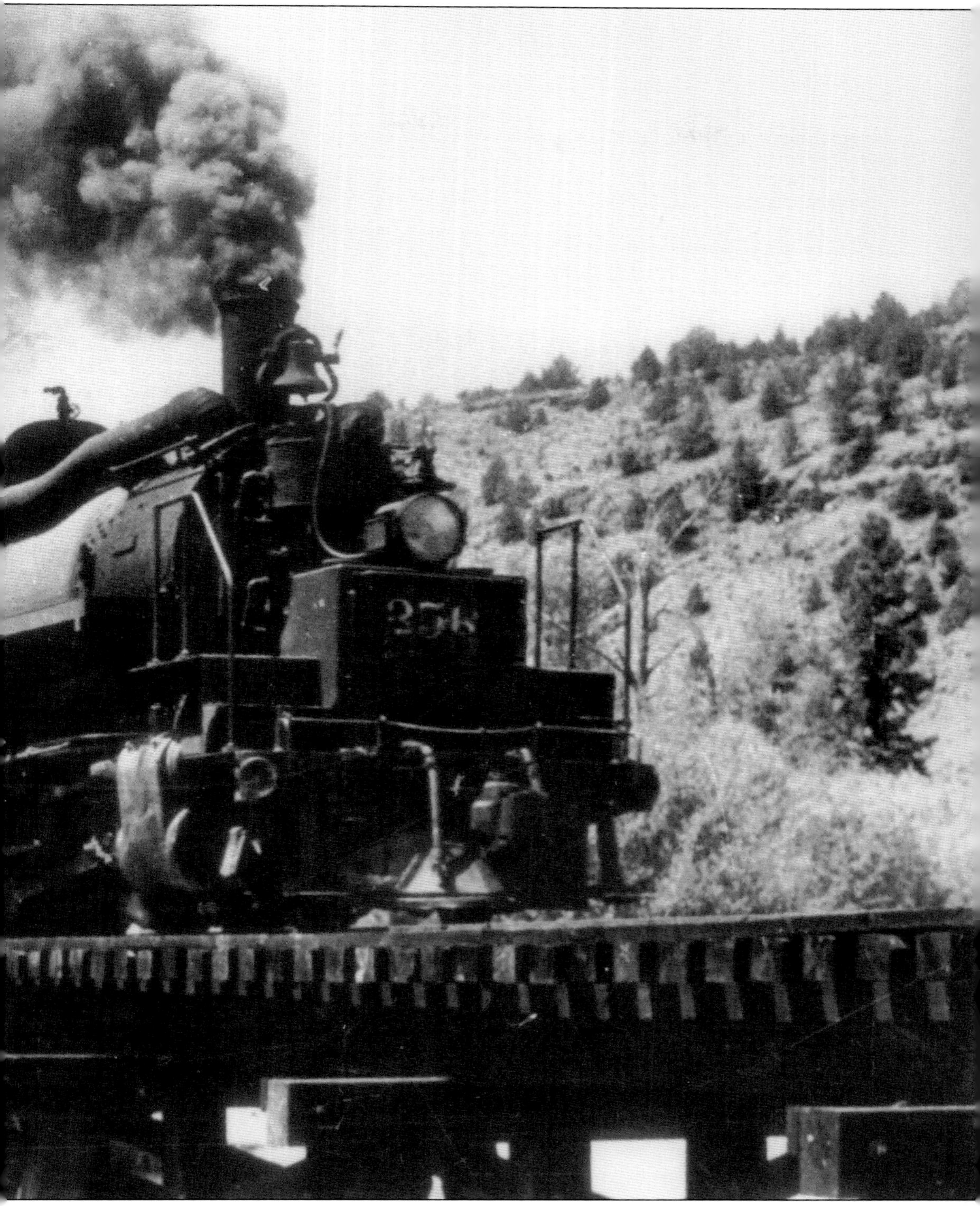

converted to electric power in the early 1940s. (H. R. Griffiths Collection; Sumpter Valley Railroad Restoration, Inc.)

NOTICE TO THE GENERAL PUBLIC

Howell H. Howard, Pres., Sumpter Valley Railway Company, 200 South Michigan Ave., Chicago, Illinois, December 18, 1961, advises and informs that effective Sunday, February 18, 1962 at 12:01 a.m., pursuant to order of the Inter-State Commerce Commission, Docket MC 106-931, permission has been granted for abandonment and termination of all Motor Carrier Operations of the Sumpter Valley Railway Company.

The end is here. The final notice of abandonment was posted in the *Oregonian*. This brought to an end a colorful and influential part of Oregon history. The closure of the South Baker planing mill within a few years closed the final chapter of the Sumpter Valley Railway. (Earl Emlaw Collection; National Railway Historical Society, Pacific Northwest Chapter.)

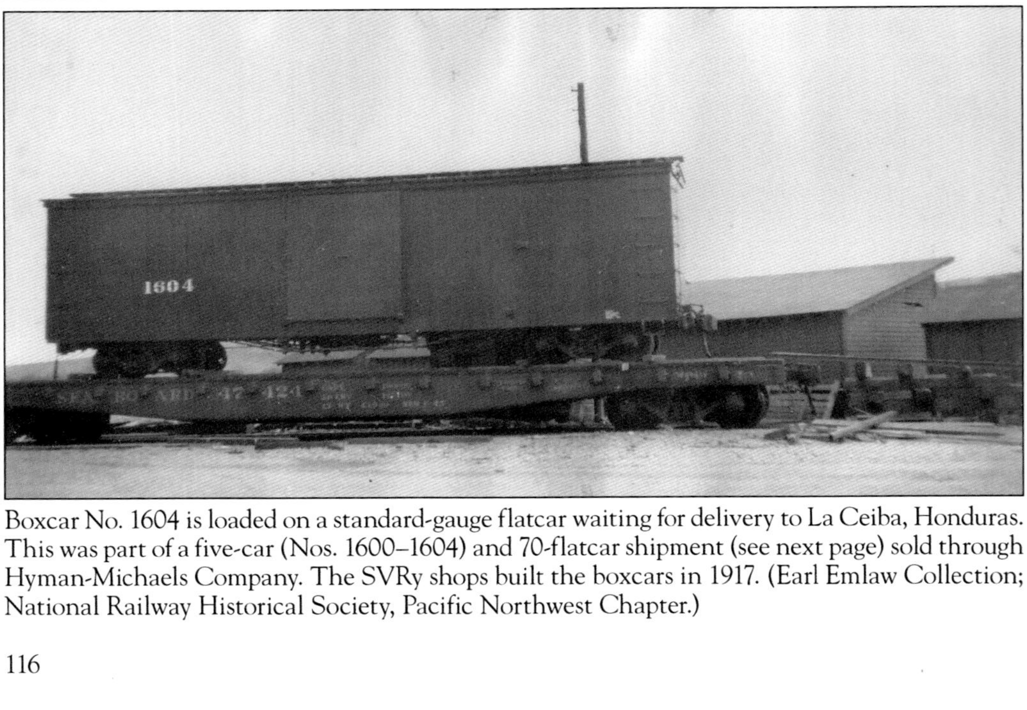

Boxcar No. 1604 is loaded on a standard-gauge flatcar waiting for delivery to La Ceiba, Honduras. This was part of a five-car (Nos. 1600–1604) and 70-flatcar shipment (see next page) sold through Hyman-Michaels Company. The SVRy shops built the boxcars in 1917. (Earl Emlaw Collection; National Railway Historical Society, Pacific Northwest Chapter.)

Eight

The Long Death (1946–1962)

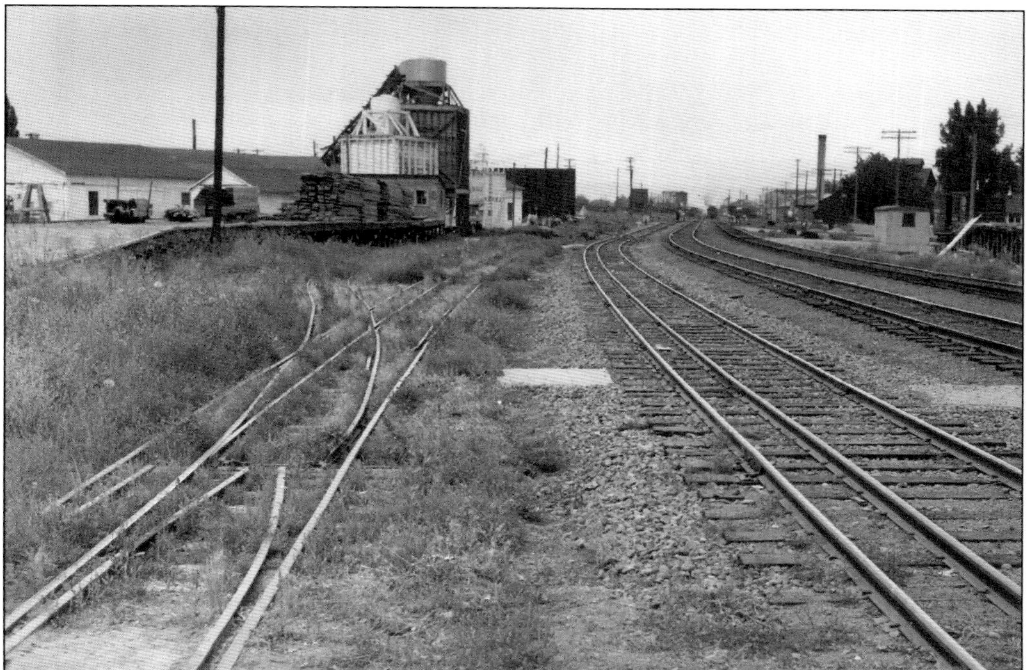

It is August 14, 1946. All is quiet in the South Baker yard. Soon only the grumble of the switchers at the mill will break the silence as diesel trucks take over the lumber hauling duties from Bates. (H. R. Griffiths Collection; National Railway Historical Society, Pacific Northwest Chapter.)

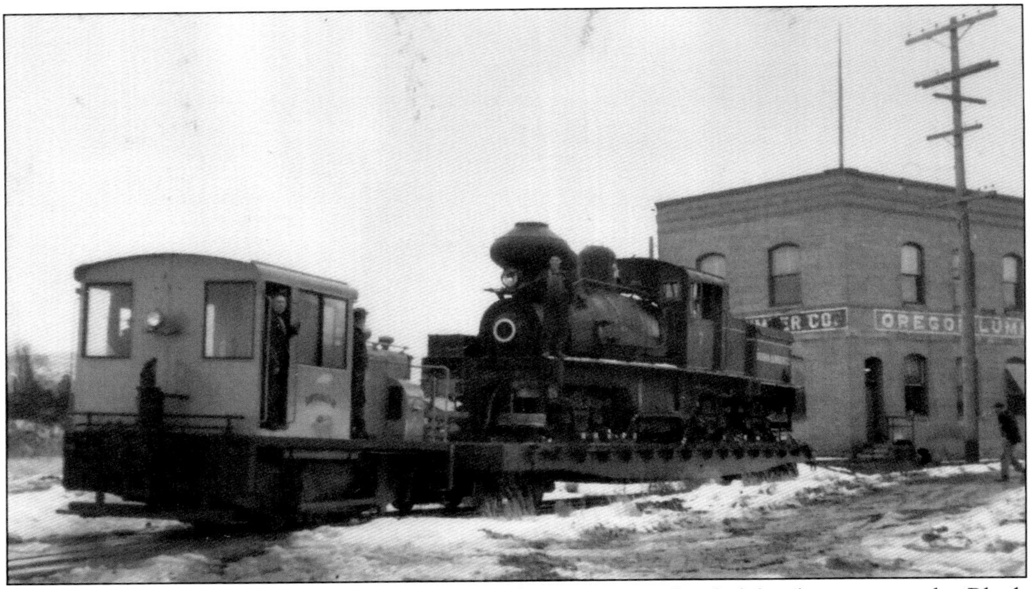

Shay No. 7, the last Oregon Lumber Company locomotive, is loaded for shipment to the Black Hills Central in February 1962. Built in 1929 for New Mexico Lumber Company and purchased by OLC in 1937, this engine is still in existence in an Indiana museum. (Earl Emlaw Collection; National Railway Historical Society, Pacific Northwest Chapter.)

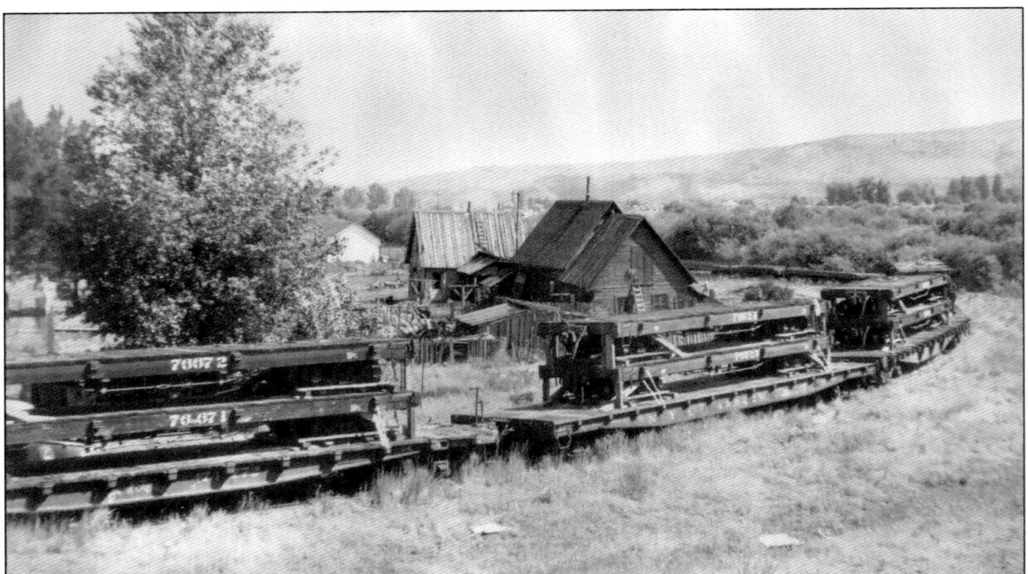

Flat cars of the 76600 class wait on the South Baker wye track, readied for shipment to La Ceiba, Honduras. This was a small portion of the 70 flatcars that were shipped in 1947. (Earl Emlaw Collection; National Railway Historical Society, Pacific Northwest Chapter.)

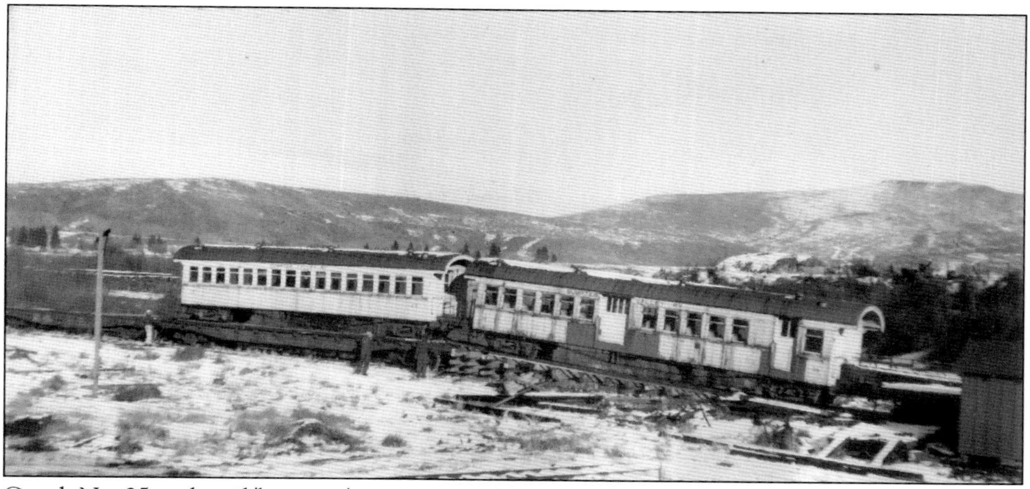

Coach No. 25 and mail/baggage/passenger car No. 26 are being loaded onto flatcars for shipment via barge to the White Pass and Yukon Railway in Skagway, Alaska. Originally purchased in 1918, they were retired from active passenger duty on August 1, 1937. (Earl Emlaw Collection; National Railway Historical Society, Pacific Northwest Chapter.)

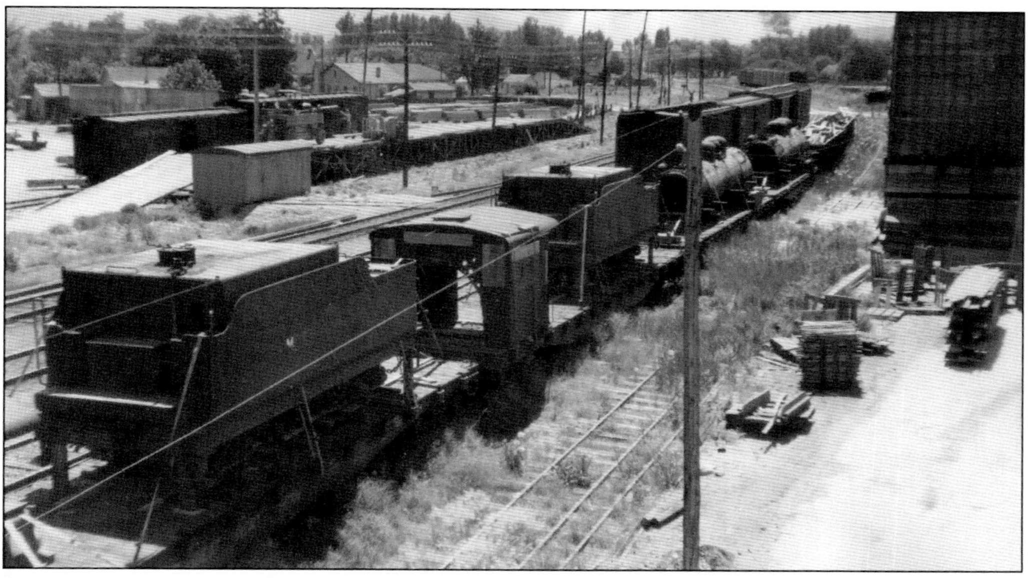

Locomotive No. 250 and No. 251 on a siding in South Baker in 1947 wait for their journey to the United Fruit Company in Anquiatu, Guatemala. The engines labored on there for another decade before being scrapped in the 1960s. (Earl Emlaw Collection; National Railway Historical Society, Pacific Northwest Chapter.)

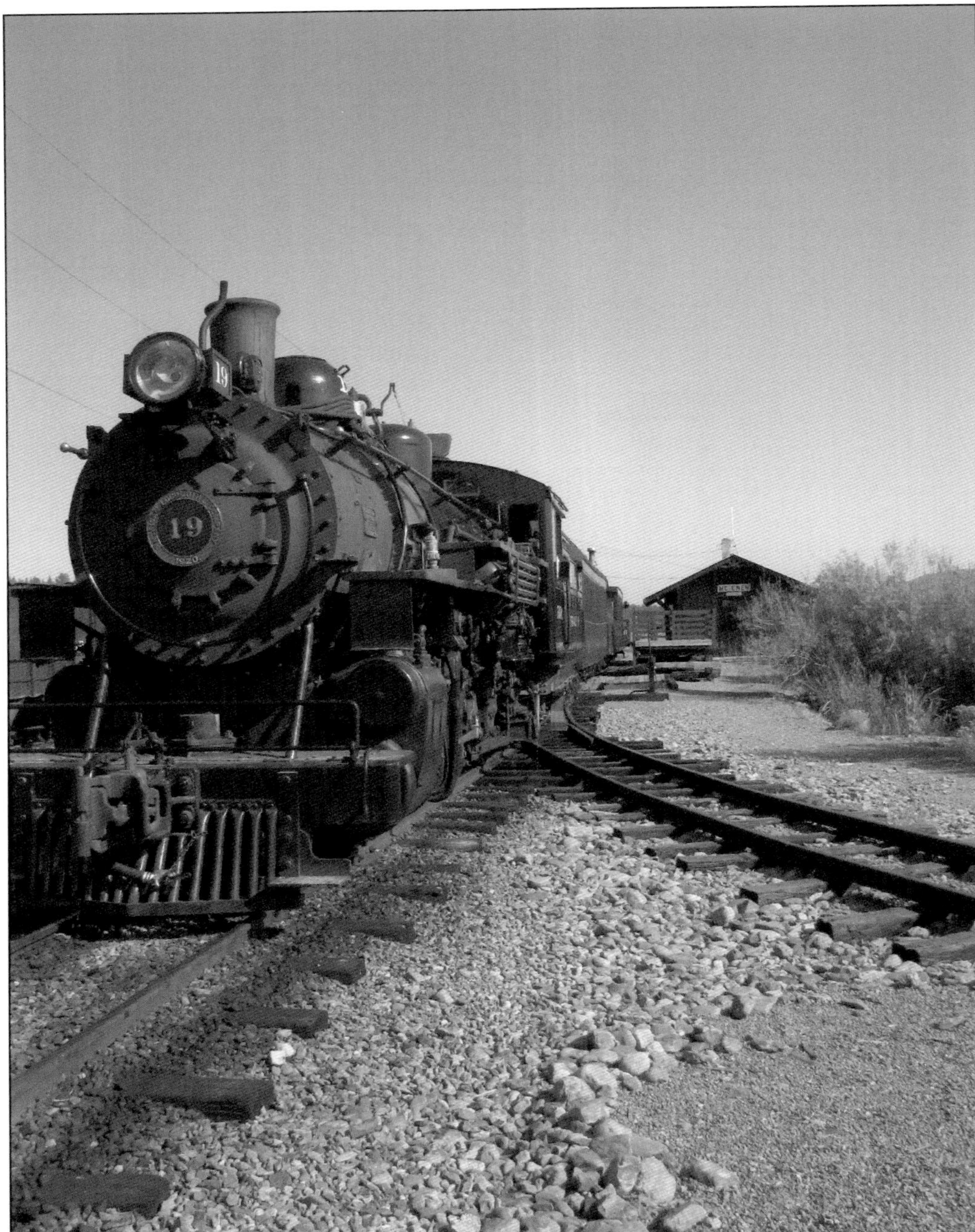

Locomotive No. 19 simmers in front of the McEwen Depot in September 2008. In a few moments, with a blast of the whistle and the ringing of the bell, she will be off to Sumpter with another passenger consist. (Alfred Mullett Collection.)

Nine

Rebirth of the Sumpter Valley Railroad (1971–Present)

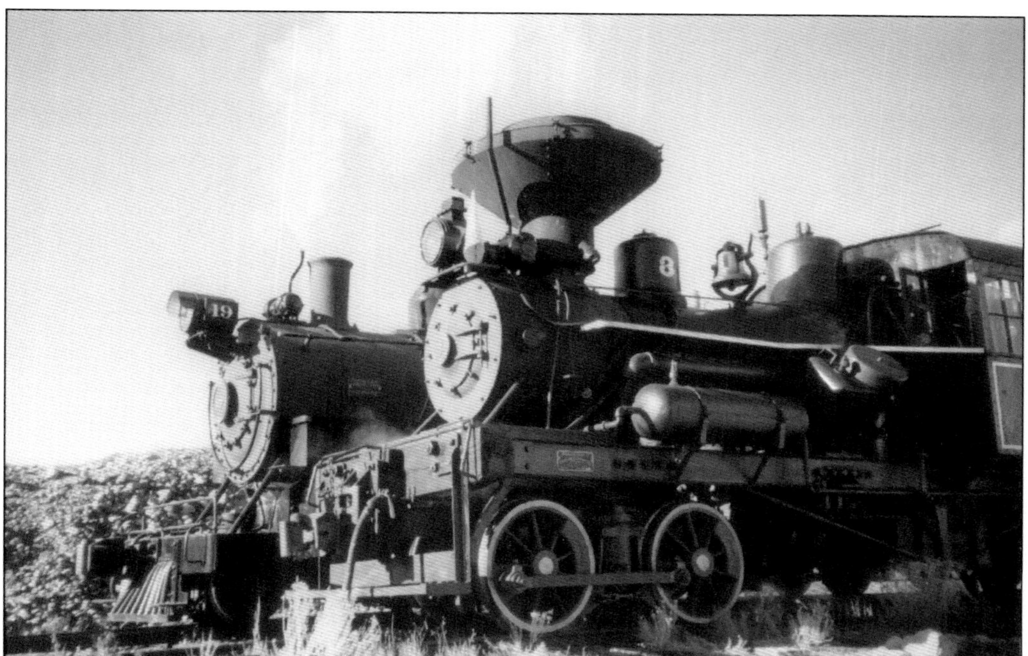

Two racehorses at the starting gate are steamed up and ready for the remainder of the day's work. Locomotive No. 19 and No. 3 rest at a ballast siding on a fall day in 2003. (Shekell Collection; Sumpter Valley Railroad Restoration, Inc.)

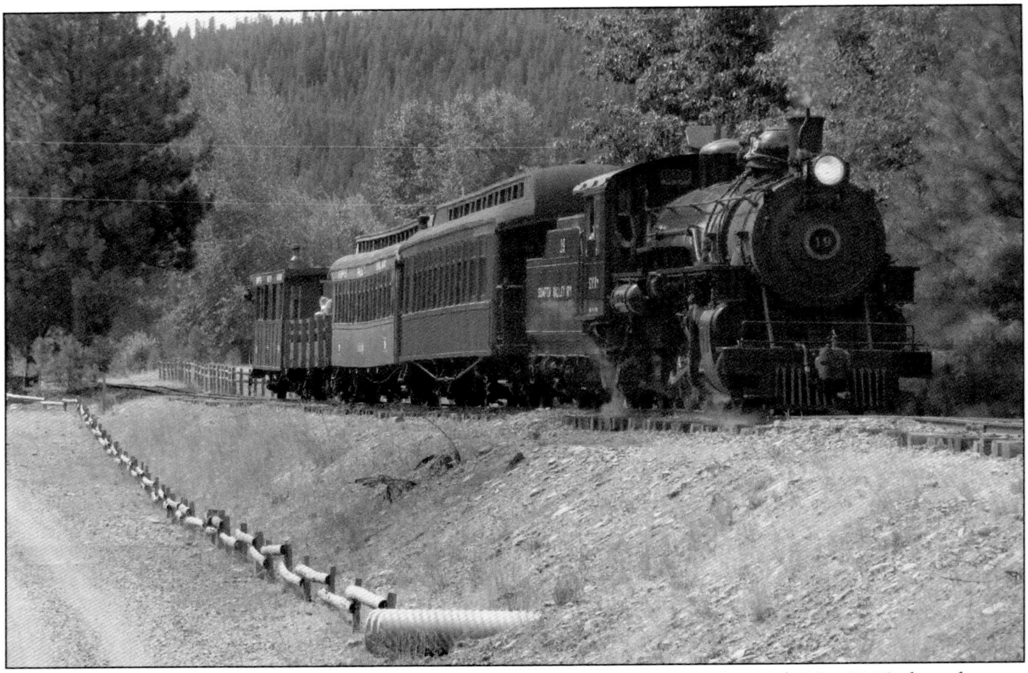

Mikado No. 19 with "Leviathan," coach No. 20, an excursion car, and coach No. 1110 thunders up the hill to the Sumpter Depot on a warm September day in 2008. (Alfred Mullett Collection.)

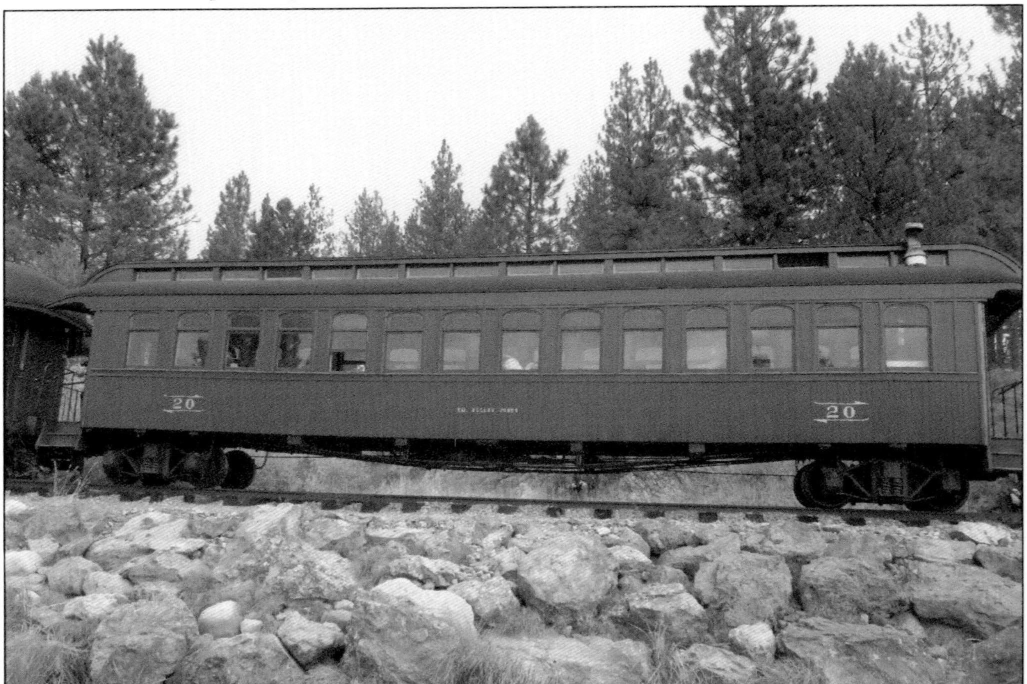

Coach No. 20, the "Emma Eccles Jones," is one of the original Utah and Northern passenger cars from 1890. (Taylor Rush Collection.)

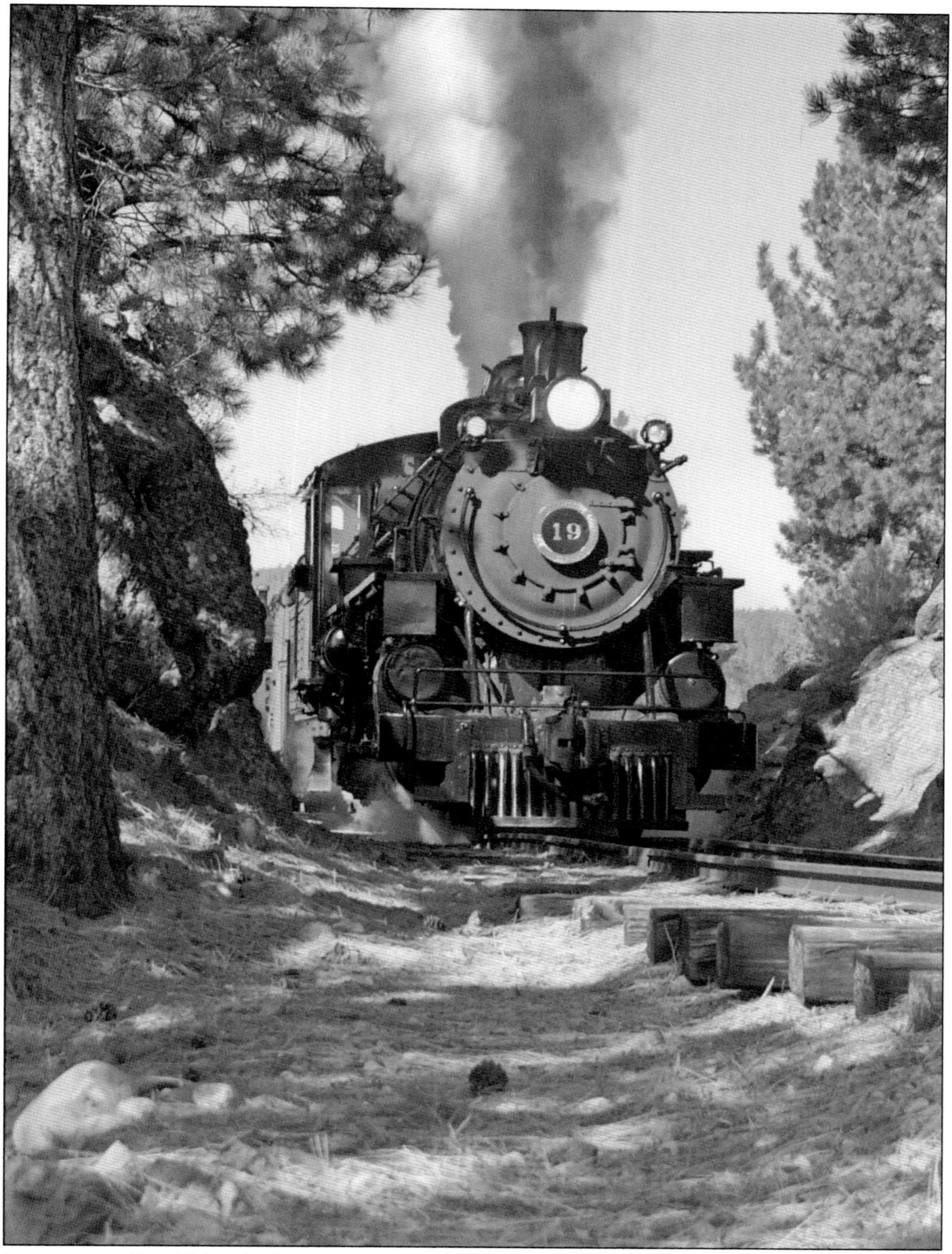

Locomotive No. 19 heads downgrade towards McEwen at Rock Cut, displaying a full head of steam as she leaves Sumpter in October 2008. (Mike Greenwood Collection.)

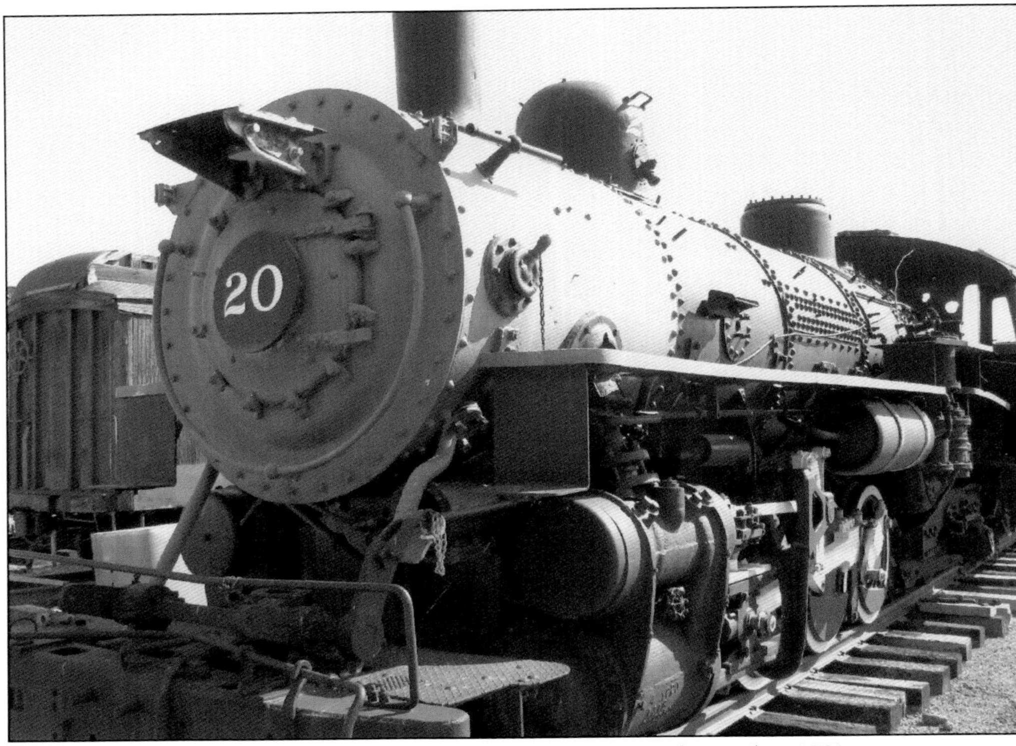

Locomotive No. 20 has been stabilized with plans to restore her to her 1921 appearance and function. Currently the railroad is collecting donations toward this and other projects. (Alfred Mullett Collection.)

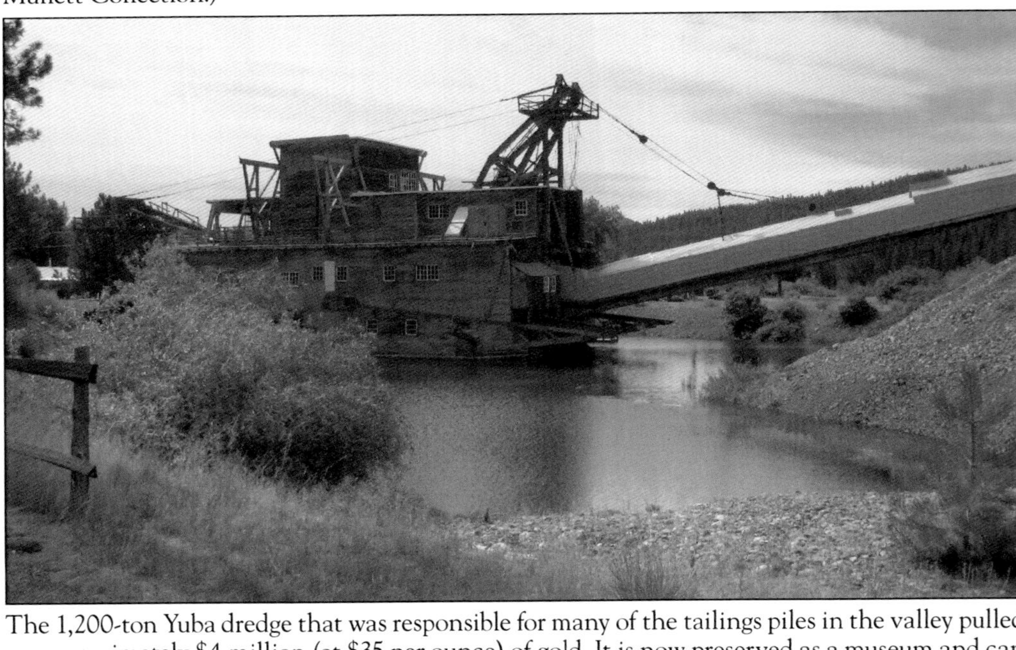

The 1,200-ton Yuba dredge that was responsible for many of the tailings piles in the valley pulled up approximately $4 million (at $35 per ounce) of gold. It is now preserved as a museum and can be toured during the layover at the Sumpter Depot. (Alfred Mullett Collection.)

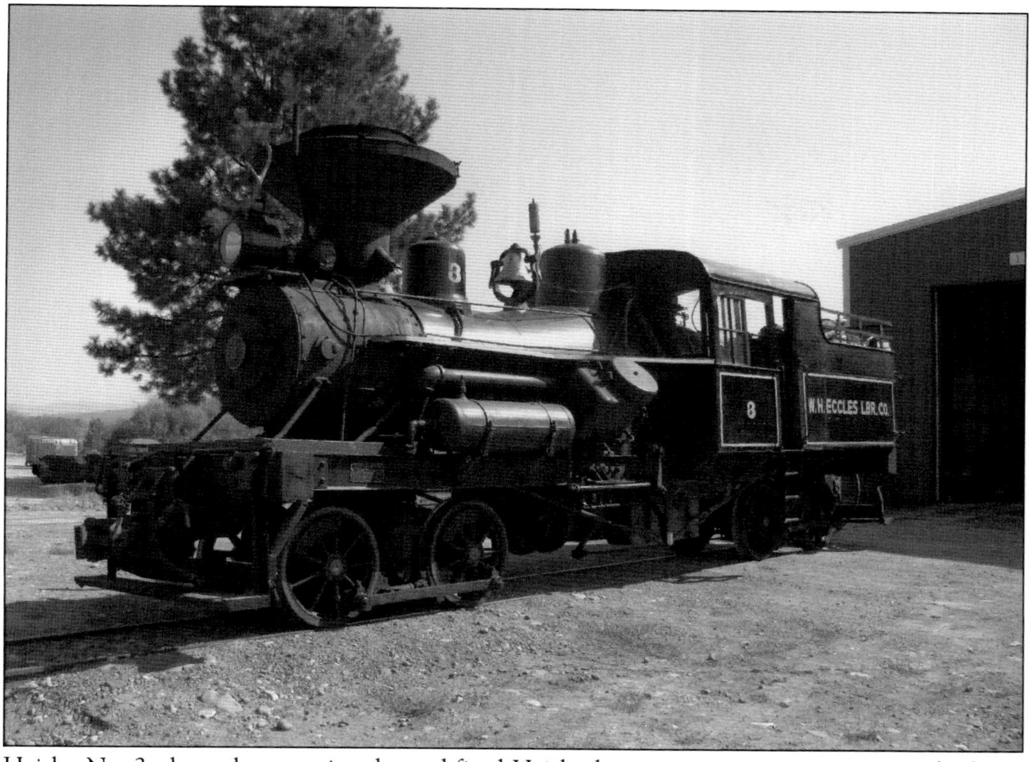

Heisler No. 3, the only operational wood-fired Heisler known to remain in existence, basks in the September afternoon sun. (Alfred Mullett Collection.)

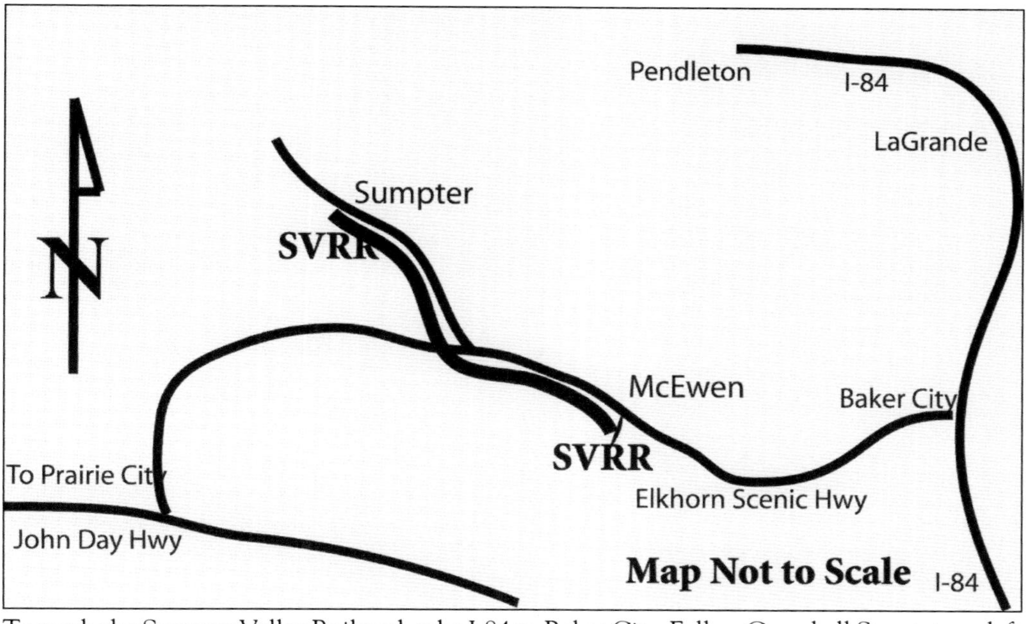

To reach the Sumpter Valley Railroad, take I-84 to Baker City. Follow Campbell Street; turn left on Main Street, which becomes the Elkhorn Scenic Highway. Follow the highway 23 miles to McEwen and turn left at the railroad.

BIBLIOGRAPHY

Barton, Joseph. Personal Diaries. Unpublished documents.
Culp, Edwin D. *Oregon the Way it Was*. Caldwell, ID: The Caxton Printers, Ltd., 1989.
Farrell, Mallory Hope. *Rail, Sagebrush and Pine*. San Marino, CA: Golden West Books, 1968.
Speroff, Leon. *The Deschutes River Railroad War*. Portland, OR: Arnica Publishing, 2007.
Sumpter Valley Railroad Restoration, Inc. *Steaming Toward Sumpter 1890–2002, A Brief History of the Sumpter Valley Railroad*. 2nd ed. Baker City, OR: privately printed, 2002.
———. *The Stump Dodger* (various issues). Baker City, OR: privately printed.
Tufford, Garrie. *Sumpter Valley Railway Locomotives 1890–1912*. Unpublished documents.
Winward, Ned and Marjorie. *The Pride of the Blue Mountains*. Prairie City, OR: Self-published, 1974.

Sumpter Valley Railroad Restoration, Inc.

Sumpter Valley Railroad Restoration, Inc., (SVRR) fought its way into existence in 1971 and in the ensuing years has become one of the West's premier narrow-gauge railroad museums. Through the perseverance of an all-volunteer organization, 6 miles of the railroad has been rebuilt on the original right-of-way, three steam locomotives have been returned to their old haunts (two currently operational), and a bevy of original rolling stock has been or is in the process of being rebuilt.

Part of what made the original Sumpter Valley Railway special was the varied and diverse equipment it used. Today's Sumpter Valley Railroad holds the same appeal; where else can one find equipment or parts from the Sumpter Valley Railway, White Pass and Yukon, Denver and Rio Grande Western, Westside Lumber Company, Nevada County Narrow Gauge, Southern Pacific Narrow Gauge, Utah and Northern, and the Union Pacific Narrow Gauge, just to name a few?

The SVRR also has the world's only known operating narrow-gauge, two-truck, wood-burning Heisler, as well as a very handsome and capable inside-frame 2-8-2.

The SVRR wends through scenery that is an attraction all to itself. The Elkhorn Mountains rise to nearly 9,000 feet and look down on McEwen, which sits at nearly half that altitude. Tailings left from gold dredges that churned the valley floor in the first half of the 20th century follow the mainline, now covered with trees and wildlife. One of the 1,200-ton Yuba dredges remains in Sumpter and can be toured during the train's layover in the small town that echoes its boom-time past.

Most of all, the SVRR is a living, working railroad museum. Every weekend and holiday during the summer months, steam-powered trains make the run up the line just as they did during the railroad's glory days.

For more information about the SVRR, please go to www.svry.com for schedules, ticket information, and more history.

—Casey S. Carlson
Sumpter Valley Railroad Restoration Director

This book is not complete without a ride on the Scenic Sumpter Valley Railroad. We are so sure you will enjoy your visit that we are offering one free coach pass per book. Present this book with this page at the depot and have your ticket stamp canceled. This offer is only good for regularly scheduled trains and is on a first-come, first-serve basis. This offer has no cash value and is not valid unless presented with an uncanceled page.

Ticket
Stamp
Here